THE REVELS PLAYS

General Editor: Clifford Leech

DOCTOR FAUSTUS

The Tragicall History
of the Life and Death
of Doctor FAVSTVS.

With new Additions.

Written by *Ch. Mar*.

Printed at London for *Iohn Wright*, and are to be fold at his
fhop without Newgate, 1624.

Title-page of the Quarto of 1624

Doctor Faustus

CHRISTOPHER MARLOWE

EDITED BY

JOHN D. JUMP

THE REVELS PLAYS

METHUEN & CO LTD
LONDON

This edition first published 1962
Reprinted 1965 and 1968
SBN 416 67060 1

First published as a University Paperback 1968
Reprinted 1969
Reprinted twice 1970
Reprinted 1971
SBN 416 29660 2

Introduction, Apparatus Criticus, etc.
© 1962 J. D. Jump
Type set by the Broadwater Press
Reprinted by lithography in Great Britain
by Latimer Trend Ltd, Whitstable

Distributed in the U.S.A.
by Barnes & Noble Inc.

General Editor's Preface

The Revels Plays began to appear in 1958, and in the General Editor's Preface included in the first few volumes the plan of the series was briefly sketched. All those concerned in the undertaking recognized that no rigid pattern could be proposed in advance: to some extent the collective experience of the editors would affect the series as it developed, and the textual situation was by no means uniform among the plays that we hoped to include. The need for flexibility is still recognized, and each editor indicates in his introduction the procedures that have seemed best in relation to his particular play.

Nevertheless, we were fairly convinced that in some matters our policy would remain constant, and no major change in any of these respects has been made. The introduction to each volume includes a discussion of the provenance of the text, the play's stage-history and reputation, its significance as a contribution to dramatic literature, and its place within the work of its author. The text is based on a fresh examination of the early editions. Modern spelling is used, archaic forms being preserved only when rhyme or metre demands them or when a modernized form would not give the required sense or would obscure a play upon words. The procedure adopted in punctuation varies to some extent according to the degree of authority which an editor can attribute to the punctuation of the copy-text, but in every instance it is intended that the punctuation used in a Revels volume should not obscure a dramatic or rhetorical suggestiveness which may be discerned in the copy. Editorial stage-directions are enclosed in square brackets. The collation aims at making clear the grounds for an editor's choice wherever the original or a frequently accepted modern reading has been departed from. Annotations attempt to explain difficult passages and to provide such comments and illustrations of usage as the editor considers desirable.

When the series was planned, it was intended that each volume should include a glossary. At an early stage, however, it was realized that this would mean either an arbitrary distribution of material between the glossary and the annotations or a duplication of material. It has therefore become our practice to dispense with a glossary but to include an index to the annotations, which avoids duplication and facilitates reference.

Act-divisions are employed if they appear in the copy-text or if the structure of the play clearly points to a five-act division. In other instances, only scene-numbers are inserted. All act- and scene-indications which do not derive from the copy-text are given unobtrusively in square brackets. In no instance is an editorial indication of locality introduced into a scene-heading. When an editor finds it necessary to comment on the location of a scene, this is done in the annotations.

The series continues to use the innovation in line-numbering that was introduced in the first volume. Stage-directions which occur on lines separate from the text are given the number of the immediately preceding line followed by a decimal point and 1, 2, 3, etc. Thus 163.5 indicates the fifth line of a stage-direction following line 163 of the scene. At the beginning of a scene the lines of a stage-direction are numbered 0.1, 0.2, etc.

The Revels Plays have begun with the re-editing of a number of the best-known tragedies and comedies of the later Elizabethan and Jacobean years, and there are many such plays to which the techniques of modern editing need to be applied. It is hoped, however, that the series will be able to include certain lesser-known plays which remain in general neglect despite the lively interest that an acquaintance with them can arouse.

It has always been in the forefront of attention that the plays included should be such as deserve and indeed demand performance. The editors have therefore given a record (necessarily incomplete) of modern productions; in the annotations there is, moreover, occasional conjecture on the way in which a scene or a piece of stage-business was done on the original stage. Perhaps, too, the absence of indications of locality and of editorial scene-headings will suggest the advantage of achieving in a modern theatre some approach to the characteristic fluidity of scene and the neutrality of acting-space that Shakespeare's fellows knew.

CLIFFORD LEECH

Durham, 1962

Contents

Illustrations

Preface

It has been my good fortune, in preparing this edition, to be authorized to base it upon that prepared by F. S. Boas and published in 1932. So extensive has been my use of his work that I should have wished his name to accompany mine on the title-page but for the fact that I have incurred an even greater debt, more especially in the textual field, to W. W. Greg. Had I sought permission to name both of these distinguished scholars on my title-page, it might have seemed that I was trying to use their authority to hide my deficiencies. So I have chosen to make my acknowledgement, with as much emphasis as possible, here in the opening lines of my preface. Having made it, I feel free to assume that the specialist reader who desires a detailed discussion of any matter on which I accept Greg's findings will, if necessary, turn for it to Greg's great parallel-text edition, and that my own introduction and commentary may legitimately be designed more specifically for the normal reader of a modern-spelling text. I am grateful to the Clarendon Press, Oxford, for permission to quote from Greg's work.

In this place, too, I can most appropriately admit my considerable dependence, in framing my explanatory comments, upon the *Oxford English Dictionary*. Acknowledgement of this indebtedness on every occasion on which I was aware of it would have resulted in a commentary too much cluttered by references; and a reader who wishes to know more about any word that I have explained will naturally start by consulting the *Oxford English Dictionary*, whether I have inserted the initials '*O.E.D.*' or not. So I have made particular reference to the *O.E.D.* only when there seemed to be special reason for doing so.

To friends and colleagues I owe too great a debt for adequate acknowledgement to be possible here. D. M. Leahy has been extraordinarily generous in placing his classical knowledge at my disposal. In the field of German studies S. S. Kerry has been equally ready to assist me. Frank Kermode has at all stages shown a most helpful interest in the work. Clifford Leech, as General Editor of the Revels Plays, subjected the whole edition to a close and penetrating scrutiny and made a large number of suggestions which I have been happy to adopt. To all of these, and to very many others, I am deeply grateful.

*   *   *

It is nearly three years since I wrote the preceding paragraphs for the first printing of this edition. Reprinting has now enabled me to revise my work slightly. The text and the collation are unaltered; but a few short passages in the 'Introduction' have been rewritten, and a number of changes have been made in the commentary, in order to incorporate information that has become available since 1962.

JOHN D. JUMP

Manchester, 1964

Abbreviations

The abbreviations used in referring to the early quartos of *Doctor Faustus* are explained in section 3 of the 'Introduction'.

Boas   *The Tragical History of Doctor Faustus*, edited by F. S. Boas, London, 1932.

Bullen   *The Works of Christopher Marlowe*, edited by A. H. Bullen, 3 vols., London, 1885.

Chambers, *E.S.*   E. K. Chambers, *The Elizabethan Stage*, 4 vols., Oxford, 1923.

Cunningham   *The Works of Christopher Marlowe*, edited by F. Cunningham, London, 1870.

Damnable Life   *The historie of the damnable life, and deserued death of Doctor Iohn Faustus*, translated by P. F., London, 1592.

Dilke   *Old English Plays*, [edited by C. W. Dilke,] 6 vols., London, 1814–15.

Dyce   *The Works of Christopher Marlowe*, edited by A. Dyce, 3 vols., London, 1850.

Dyce 2   *The Works of Christopher Marlowe*, edited by A. Dyce, London, 1858.

Ellis   *Christopher Marlowe*, edited by H. Ellis, London, 1887 (*Mermaid Series*).

Greg   *Marlowe's 'Doctor Faustus' 1604–1616: Parallel Texts*, edited by W. W. Greg, Oxford, 1950; and *The Tragical History of the Life and Death of Doctor Faustus by Christopher Marlowe: A Conjectural Reconstruction*, edited by W. W. Greg, Oxford, 1950.

Kirschbaum — *The Plays of Christopher Marlowe*, edited by L. Kirschbaum, Cleveland, 1962.

Kocher — *The Tragical History of Doctor Faustus*, edited by P. H. Kocher, New York, 1950.

Kocher, *C.M.* — P. H. Kocher, *Christopher Marlowe*, Chapel Hill, 1946.

McKerrow — R. B. McKerrow, *Printers' and Publishers' Devices in England and Scotland 1485–1640*, London, 1913.

O.E.D. — *Oxford English Dictionary*.

Oxberry — *The Tragicall Historie of the Life and Death of Doctor Faustus, with New Additions. Written by Ch. Mar.*, [edited by W. Oxberry,] London, 1818.

Robinson — *The Works of Christopher Marlowe*, [edited by G. Robinson,] 3 vols., London, 1826.

Root — R. K. Root, 'Two Notes on Marlowe's *Doctor Faustus*', *Englische Studien*, XLIII (1910–11), pp. 144–9.

Tilley — M. P. Tilley, *A Dictionary of the Proverbs in England in the Sixteenth and Seventeenth Centuries*, Ann Arbor, 1950.

Tucker Brooke — *The Works of Christopher Marlowe*, edited by C. F. Tucker Brooke, Oxford, 1910.

Wagner — *Christopher Marlowe's Tragedy of Doctor Faustus*, edited by W. Wagner, London, 1877.

Ward — *Marlowe, Tragical History of Dr. Faustus: Greene, Honourable History of Friar Bacon and Friar Bungay*, edited by A. W. Ward, Fourth Edition, Oxford, 1901.

PERIODICALS

E.L.H.	*English Literary History.*
E.S.	*Englische Studien.*
J.E.G.P.	*Journal of English and Germanic Philology.*
Libr.	*The Library.*
M.L.N.	*Modern Language Notes.*
M.L.Q.	*Modern Language Quarterly.*
M.L.R.	*Modern Language Review.*
M.P.	*Modern Philology.*
N. & Q.	*Notes and Queries.*
P.M.L.A.	*Publications of the Modern Language Association of America.*
P.Q.	*Philological Quarterly.*
R.E.S.	*Review of English Studies.*
T.L.S.	*Times Literary Supplement.*

Quotations and line-numbers for other works by Marlowe are taken from the six-volume edition published under the general direction of R. H. Case between 1930 and 1933; those for Shakespeare from the Oxford edition.

Introduction

Christopher Marlowe was born early in 1564, the son of a fairly prosperous Canterbury shoemaker.[1] Just before he reached the age of fifteen, he obtained a scholarship to the King's School, Canterbury; and slightly less than two years later he went up to Corpus Christi College, Cambridge, as the holder of a further scholarship to which he was regularly elected shortly afterwards. The terms of this second scholarship make it probable that by 1584 he was regarded as a candidate for holy orders.

His university career began towards the end of 1580. During his six-and-a-half years at Cambridge, he must have satisfied university requirements, for in 1584 he received the degree of B.A., and on 31 March 1587 it was officially acknowledged that he had earned that of M.A. But at the last moment the university authorities showed themselves reluctant to confer this second degree. No less a body than the Queen's Privy Council then intervened on Marlowe's behalf, passing the following resolution:

> Whereas it was reported that Christopher Morley was determined to haue gone beyond the seas to Reames [Rheims] and there to remaine Their Lordships thought good to certefie that he had no such intent, but that in all his accions he had behaued him selfe orderlie and discreetelie wherebie he had done her Majestie good service, and deserued to be rewarded for his faithfull dealinge: Their Lordships request was that the rumor thereof should be allaied by all possible meanes, and that he should be furthered in the degree he was to take this next Commencement: Because it was not her Majesties pleasure that anie one emploied as he had been in matters touching the benefitt of his Countrie should be

[1] Authorities for the facts of Marlowe's life include C. F. Tucker Brooke, *The Life of Marlowe and The Tragedy of Dido Queen of Carthage*, London, 1930, and F. S. Boas, *Christopher Marlowe*, Oxford, 1940.

defamed by those that are ignorant in th'affaires he went about.[1]

Understandably, the University yielded; and Marlowe took the degree a few days later.

It can be inferred from this document that the university authorities had suspected Marlowe of being a convert to Roman Catholicism and planning to transfer himself to the English seminary at Rheims. In scotching this rumour, the Privy Council allowed it to emerge that he had in fact been employed upon a confidential mission of some political importance. We cannot be sure what kind of mission this had been. But it would be rash to assume that Marlowe was a government spy. Would the Privy Council in that case have called for the allaying 'by all possible meanes' of a rumour which could have served his purposes very well?

When he left Cambridge in 1587, Marlowe had apparently no intention of entering holy orders. He achieved immediate success as a playwright. *Tamburlaine* brought a new kind of hero, a superman dominated by the thirst for rule, on to the English stage; and the power and music of its speeches guaranteed the triumph of blank verse as the standard literary vehicle for the English drama of the age of Shakespeare and after. The popularity of the first part of *Tamburlaine* led Marlowe at once to write a second. This shows Tamburlaine still trampling down all human opposition but able to do nothing to prevent the death of his wife, the cowardice of one of his sons, and finally his own death.

In 1589, Marlowe seems to have been living conveniently near to the London playhouses called the Theatre and the Curtain. In September of that year, he was involved in a sword-fight in Hog Lane, near Finsbury Fields, in the course of which his friend Thomas Watson, the poet, killed a man. The coroner's jury found that Watson had acted in self-defence. Less than three years later, a constable and under-constable of Shoreditch sought the protection of the law against Marlowe.[2] Such glimpses as these leave the impression that Marlowe was of a somewhat violent and unruly

---

[1] J. L. Hotson, *The Death of Christopher Marlowe* (London, 1925), pp. 58–9.

[2] For a full account of what is known about these two incidents, see M. Eccles, *Christopher Marlowe in London*, Cambridge, Mass., 1934.

nature; and this impression is reinforced by Thomas Kyd's allusion to his 'rashnes in attempting soden pryvie iniuries to men'.[1]

Nor was this Kyd's only allegation against the man who, he said, had shared a room with him during 1591. If Kyd is to be believed, Marlowe had not only refrained from entering holy orders but had gone so far as habitually 'to iest at the devine scriptures gybe at praiers, & stryve in argument to frustrate & confute what hath byn spoke or wrytt by prophets & such holie men'.[2] Admittedly, this charge was made shortly after Marlowe's death, at a time when Kyd was himself under suspicion and was perhaps trying to clear himself by the harmless expedient of blaming one who was already beyond the reach of the authorities. But Kyd was not alone in charging Marlowe with free-thinking, and free-speaking, on the subject of religion. A certain Richard Baines at about the same time was testifying to Marlowe's 'damnable Judgment of Religion, and scorn of Gods word'. If Baines is to be believed, Marlowe had argued, among other things, that the human race was older than the book of Genesis implied; that Moses was a juggler who imposed upon a primitive people; that 'Christ was a bastard and his mother dishonest'; that the twelve disciples were 'base fellowes neyther of wit nor worth'; and that 'the first beginning of Religioun was only to keep men in awe'.[3] It is regrettable that we have no means of assessing accurately the reliability of Kyd and Baines as reporters or the spirit in which Marlowe uttered such of these statements as may have been truly his. Nevertheless, there is no avoiding an impression of Marlowe as a bold and sceptical spirit, addicted to uninhibited iconoclastic talk.

Even in his plays, where a greater reticence was obligatory than in private conversation, Marlowe seems to have taken a special pleasure in portraying Christians disparagingly. In 2 *Tamburlaine* much is made of Christian perfidy. *The Jew of Malta*, written a year or two later, is an anti-Semitic play; its protagonist is presented as detestable and absurd, both as a Jew and as a 'Machiavellian'. But

[1] British Museum, Harleian MS. 6848, fol. 154. Tucker Brooke, *op. cit.*, pp. 107–8.

[2] *Ibid.*

[3] British Museum, Harleian MS. 6848, fol. 185–6. Tucker Brooke, *op. cit.*, pp. 98–100.

Marlowe places in his mouth some memorable criticism of his Christian enemies and shows these enemies to be hypocritical, treacherous, and predatory.

Evidently Marlowe enjoyed challenging conventional suscepti-bilities. Baines ascribed to him the aggressive statement that 'all they that loue not Tobacco & Boies were fooles'.[1] *Edward II*, com-pleted a year or two before his death, may reasonably be regarded as another expression, necessarily more discreet because more pub-lic, of a sympathy with homosexuality. Certainly this chronicle-history play differs markedly from those of Shakespeare in that its author is interested almost exclusively in the personal relations of his characters and hardly at all in the political aspects of his theme.

There is no reliable information regarding the source or the amount of Marlowe's income during this period of almost six years between his leaving Cambridge and his death. His earnings as a writer cannot have been large. Yet he appears to have lived in-dependently and to have associated with men of some means, Sir Walter Raleigh and Thomas Walsingham among others. Of his fellow-writers, Thomas Watson and Thomas Nashe were his friends.

In May 1593 he was at Thomas Walsingham's country house, the manor of Scadbury near Chislehurst in Kent, having perhaps taken refuge there from the plague which was raging in London. He may well have been busy on his narrative poem, *Hero and Lean-der*. Then, for the second time, the Privy Council interfered actively in his affairs.

The spring of 1593 had seen an outbreak of political disorder. On 12 May, Kyd was arrested on suspicion of having had a hand in fomenting this and was found to have heretical documents in his possession. He declared that these belonged to his former room-mate, Marlowe. It was a natural next step for the Privy Council on 18 May to issue a warrant for Marlowe's arrest. He was back in London on 20 May and was ordered to attend on their lordships daily until he was licensed to the contrary. But it seems possible that he was not questioned before his death ten days later.

This occurred at Deptford, where he may have been lodging

[1] *Ibid.*

while obliged to wait upon the Privy Council. Deptford was a short distance outside the plague-stricken city in the direction of Scadbury, to which he very likely hoped to return. On the morning of 30 May he went to the tavern of a widow named Eleanor Bull, apparently at the invitation of a certain Ingram Frizer. Frizer, an agent of Thomas Walsingham, was a distinctly unsavoury character. He ended his days as a churchwarden; but, if we believe a seemingly well-substantiated accusation of a few years after Marlowe's death, he and Nicholas Skeres, also a member of the party at Eleanor Bull's tavern, were swindlers as accomplished as Ben Jonson's Subtle and Face. The fourth member of the party, Robert Poley, perjurer and double-spy, was perhaps the most sinister of Marlowe's three shady companions.

The men lunched together, walked in the garden of the tavern, and supped together. After supper, Frizer and Marlowe quarrelled about the payment of the reckoning. Marlowe snatched Frizer's dagger and gave him two shallow wounds with it. Frizer struggled to defend himself; and in the course of this struggle the dagger was driven into Marlowe's head over his right eye to a depth of two inches. According to those who were present, he died immediately. If so, the wound described cannot in itself have been the cause of death. At the inquest, which was held on the next day but one, the coroner accepted the story summarized here and found that Frizer had killed Marlowe in self-defence. Accordingly, a month later, the Queen issued to Frizer her formal pardon.[1]

Three works of Marlowe's call for mention in addition to those named in the course of this biographical sketch. *Dido, Queen of Carthage*, in which Nashe had a hand, was probably an early work. *The Massacre at Paris*, which survives only in a badly mangled text, was probably a late one. Neither of them has the interest and importance of *Tamburlaine* or *The Jew of Malta* or *Edward II*. But none even of these has the interest and importance of *Doctor Faustus*.

---

[1] The documents supporting this account of Marlowe's last day are printed in J. L. Hotson, *op. cit.*, pp. 26–37.

2. THE DATE OF THE PLAY

In 1587, there was published in Frankfurt-on-Main a German prose book *Historia von D. Iohañ Fausten*, the work of an anonymous Lutheran. Within a few years, an English translation had appeared. The sole surviving copy of a 1592 edition of this is now in the British Museum (C.27.b.43). It has the following title-page:

THE / HISTORIE / of the damnable / life, and deserued death of / *Doctor Iohn Faustus,* / Newly imprinted, and in conueni- / *ent places imperfect matter amended:* / according to the true Copie printed / at Franckfort, *and translated into* / *English by* P.F. *Gent.* / Seene and allowed. / [Device] / *Imprinted at London by Thomas Orwin, and are to be* / solde by Edward White, dwelling at the little North / doore of Paules, at the signe of the Gun. 1592.

This translation, by an author whose initials have not sufficed to identify him for us, was the main source of the English play.

The words 'Newly imprinted' inform us that there had been an edition of the *Damnable Life* prior to that of 1592; apparently all copies of this have perished. Orwin's claim that he has amended '*imperfect matter*' resembles claims made by other publishers of the time when printing what they held to be more authoritative texts of works already issued by others. But the most definite information about the lost first edition has been deduced from an entry in the Court Book of the Stationers' Company. On 18 December 1592, the Court adjudicated between two claimants to the copyright in the *Damnable Life*, 'Abell Ieffes' and 'Tho. Orwin'. Orwin's claim was based on an alleged entrance of the book in the Stationers' Register by one 'Richard Oliff'. The Court ruled that, if the book had not in fact been entered 'before Abell Ieffes claymed the same wch was about May last', the copyright was the property of Jeffes. No one had entered the book, and Jeffes retained the copyright. Since his claim was not based upon an entrance, it was presumably based upon the publication, 'about May' 1592, of the lost first edition. Those who accept this deduction will find it easy to suppose that Orwin was glancing at the real or imagined deficiencies of Jeffes' edition when he spoke of having amended '*imperfect matter*' in the edition which he put out during the latter half of 1592.

This line of argument is W. W. Greg's; it receives its fullest and best expression in the 'Introduction' to his parallel-text edition of *Doctor Faustus*. His conclusion that the *Damnable Life* was first published about May 1592 is important in view of the fact that the English play was unquestionably based upon P.F.'s version of the Faustus story (see section 7 of this 'Introduction'). If Marlowe cannot have read this before the spring of 1592, the writing of *Doctor Faustus* must have begun during the last year of his life. It was generally held at one time that the play was written some three or four years earlier than this; and the view still has its supporters. But readers who find a remarkable emotional maturity in the best scenes of *Doctor Faustus* may reasonably hesitate to ascribe to it a date too close to that of *Tamburlaine*.

Those who favour the earlier date draw attention to the fact that *A ballad of the life and deathe of Doctor FFAUSTUS the great Cunngerer* was entered in the Stationers' Register on 28 February 1589. But it would be rash to assume that this ballad derives from either the *Damnable Life* or the play, when all that we know about it is contained in the thirteen-word title just quoted. They cite early allusions to the Faustus story. But, of those produced so far, some betray no knowledge of the *Damnable Life* or the play, and others cannot themselves be accurately dated. They allege that two early comedies, the anonymous *Taming of a Shrew* and Greene's *Friar Bacon and Friar Bungay*, implicitly refer to *Doctor Faustus*, the one by echoing it, the other by emulating it. But the earliest text of *A Shrew* belongs to as late a date as 1594; and Greene's play, far from emulating Marlowe's, may well have preceded it. They take T.M.'s reference in *The Black Book* (1604) to a certain performance of *Doctor Faustus* as implying that the play was acted at the Theatre in Shoreditch in 1590–1. But it is at least equally likely that what is implied is a performance in the same theatre in 1593–4. They seize upon allusions in the play to particular historical facts (see comments on i. 92, 95). But these allusions could belong as easily to 1592 as to 1588–9. Finally, they explain the parallel recorded in the comment on vi. 18 as a borrowing from *Doctor Faustus* in a play first performed on 10 June 1592. But Marlowe may have been the borrower; or the line may have been borrowed from *Doctor Faustus* at any time up to 1594, when the other play was first printed; or the repetition may even have been accidental.

So the case for the later date remains the stronger. Metrical tests reinforce it.[1] It is not conclusive, however, and our acceptance of it can only be provisional.

3. THE EARLY EDITIONS, 1604–31

Doctor Faustus is known to have been acted on many occasions between the autumn of 1594 and that of 1597. Five years later, there was a plan to revive it, and on 22 November 1602 Philip Henslowe, the theatrical manager, paid £4 to William Birde and Samuel Rowley 'for ther adicyones in doctor fostes'.[2] This was nearly two years after Thomas Bushell had staked his claim to print the play by entering it in the Stationers' Register. His entry is dated 7 January 1601. But the earliest edition of the play of which a copy has survived did not appear until 1604. This, a black-letter quarto, has the following title-page:

> THE / TRAGICALL / History of D. Faustus. / *As it hath bene Acted by the Right / Honorable the Earle of Nottingham his seruants.* / Written by Ch. Marl. / [Device: McKerrow, No. 142] / LONDON / Printed by V. S. [Valentine Simmes] for Thomas Bushell. 1604.

The only recorded copy is in the Bodleian Library (Malone 233 (3)).

Was this the first edition? It is unlikely that it was. Of the nine editions of *Doctor Faustus* known to have been published between 1604 and 1631, no fewer than five have perished except for single surviving copies. Such a casualty-rate authorizes us to conjecture that one edition or more may have disappeared entirely. It seems natural to suppose that Bushell, having laid claim to the book in the first week of 1601, would have wished to publish it much sooner than 1604. Moreover, the Earl of Nottingham's or Lord Admiral's Men, who became Prince Henry's Men probably during 1603, are given their obsolete name on the 1604 title-page. Presumably, this title-page simply echoed that of an earlier edition, now lost.

In the absence of any copies of this hypothetical first edition, the

---

[1] See K. Muir, 'The Chronology of Marlowe's Plays', *Proceedings of the Leeds Philosophical and Literary Society*, v (1938–43), pp. 345–56.

[2] *Henslowe's Diary*, fol. 108ᵛ.

1604 quarto is our earliest and most authoritative print of what is generally and conveniently known as the A-text of *Doctor Faustus*. Bushell before long transferred the copyright in this text to another publisher, John Wright, who re-issued it in 1609 with its title luridly expanded to *The Tragicall History of the horrible Life and death of Doctor Faustus*. Wright published it again in 1611. In what follows, these three editions are referred to as A1, A2, and A3.

Then, in 1616, this same publisher, John Wright, printed a radically different text of the play, so different that it is usually distinguished as the B-text; and he did this without claiming, as he might legitimately have done, to have made important additions and amended '*imperfect matter*'. This black-letter quarto, B1, has the following title-page:

> The Tragicall History / of the Life and Death / of *Doctor Faustus*. / Written by *Ch. Mar.* / [Woodcut of Faustus raising the devil] / *LONDON*, / Printed for *Iohn Wright*, and are to be sold at his shop / without Newgate, at the signe of the / Bible. 1616.

The only copy recorded is in the British Museum (C.34.d.26). This has been cropped and the woodcut on the title-page consequently damaged; so the title-page of a later edition of the B-text has been used for the frontispiece of the present volume.

Altogether, six early editions of the B-text are represented by extant copies. These appeared in 1616, 1619, 1620, 1624, 1628, and 1631. On the title-page of the second of them, B2 of 1619, Wright belatedly inserted the words 'With new Additions' between the title and the author's name; and this phrase duly prefaces each of the subsequent quartos. Otherwise, these six title-pages differ significantly only in their dates. The misprint 'Histoy' disfigures that of B3 of 1620.

'4. THE A-TEXT AND THE B-TEXT

Does the A-text or the B-text offer the more original version of *Doctor Faustus*? In trying to answer this question, we need concern ourselves only with A1 and B1, the earliest extant editions of the two texts. All but one of the other early quartos are mere reprints. Such changes as they introduce can claim no special authority. The one exception is B2, the 1619 quarto, which is in the main a reprint of B1 but occasionally departs from it in a fashion that implies some independent knowledge of the play. Greg suggests that these departures are due to a reviser who knew *Doctor Faustus* from current performances. He may be right; but the available evidence leaves us well short of certainty on the point.

As preserved in the quartos of 1604 and 1616, the texts differ widely from each other. The A-text is very much the shorter; it occupies only 1517 lines of print against the B-text's 2121. The greater elaboration of B is most evident after Faustus' arrival in Rome. The A-text knows nothing of Bruno the antipope either at the papal or at the imperial court; it knows nothing of the plan of revenge by the injured knight and his friends or of its frustration by Faustus; and it is equally ignorant of the conspiracy by the Horse-courser and his associates and of their humiliation at Vanholt. Without these B-scenes, the section of the play which shows Faustus exercising his dearly-bought power is scrappy and disconnected. In addition, the A-text omits from the last three scenes a number of incidents, mainly of a supernatural or spectacular kind.

Critics used to hold that the passages contained in B but not in A were chiefly those added, as recorded by Henslowe, late in 1602. But a Shakespearian allusion of 1600 or 1601 to the punishment which Faustus inflicts upon the injured knight and his friends (see comment on xiv. 4–5) suggests that the scenes concerned with the hostility of this knight, Benvolio, to Faustus must have been in existence before Birde and Rowley intruded.[1] If so, the passages concerned with Bruno the antipope were presumably also in existence by 1600 or 1601, since Benvolio and his friends in scene xi speak with constant awareness of Bruno's recent arrival from Rome. The remaining passages peculiar to B would hardly have sufficed to command £4 from Henslowe.

In any case, there is something extravagantly silly about the picture of Birde and Rowley, armed with scissors and paste, busily and meticulously dovetailing the disconnected episodes of A into more coherent 'adicyones' of their own. Surely it is clear that B is not an expansion of A at all; that, on the contrary, A is a curtailment of a

---

[1] The same inference may be drawn from the parallel recorded in the comment on xiii. 73–4.

more original text that has come down to us as B. This is Greg's
view. He supports it by pointing out that on three occasions scenes
which should be distinct from each other are run together in A
owing to the suppression of the matter which separates them in B;
by explaining the misplacement of scene vii, which in A appears
immediately before scene x, as meaning that A retained both scenes
only as alternatives; by showing that the Horse-courser's account
of his ducking in A derives not only from the corresponding passage
in scene xv of B but also from his second account of the calamity in
scene xvi of B, a scene which is not in A but which must already
have been in existence when A's conflated account was composed;
and by setting forth other evidence and arguments which it is impossible, if only for reasons of space, to reproduce here. But perhaps
this is the best place for an acknowledgement that the whole present
analysis of the two texts is substantially his.

Even if we reject the old belief that the 1602 expansion is what
chiefly differentiates B from A, we have not necessarily done with
Birde and Rowley. The possibility remains that their additions,
while not to be identified simply with the passages peculiar to B,
are nevertheless contained somewhere in B and that A is a curtailment of a text which already included them. But Bushell entered
the play for publication early in 1601 and is likely to have issued it
before the end of 1602, when the additions were composed; and it
is natural to think of the 1604 quarto as a reprint of its hypothetical
predecessor. Even if the 1604 quarto was the first, Bushell may well
have used then the manuscript which he had held in 1601. So we
may tentatively assume that A and B are two versions of the play
as it stood prior to the 1602 expansion and that the additions of
Birde and Rowley are lost.

A, then, is an abbreviated text. Confirmation that B is the more
original comes from the anonymous *Taming of a Shrew*, printed in
1594. Five passages in this echo passages in *Doctor Faustus* (see
comments on i. 82–3, iii. 1–4, iv. 1–4, vi. 28–9, and xiii. 73–4). The
second and third of them echo passages which differ in A and B;
and in each instance it is the B-text that *The Taming of a Shrew*
proves to have been current in 1594 or earlier. Conversely, the
A-text alone contains an allusion to Roderigo Lopez (xv. 41 in

Appendix I), which is unlikely to have been made before 1594.

This interpolation occurs in a scene of clownage. It is noteworthy that, despite the fact that A is a shortened text, those scenes of clownage which it preserves tend to be elaborated in a manner that would strengthen their appeal to unsophisticated audiences. It is also noteworthy that, whereas a performance of the B-text would call for the full resources of a normally-equipped Elizabethan theatre, the A-text is quite suitable for acting on a bare stage. There can be little doubt that A is a version designed for production in more primitive circumstances than those envisaged in the case of B. Nor does it seem to have reached its present state as the result of a single revision. It contains no fewer than three pairs of what appear to be alternative passages. One of these, already mentioned, consists of its versions of scenes vii and x; another is discussed in the comment on x. 29.1–44.1 in Appendix I. These presumably resulted from a revision subsequent to that which first produced the abridged text. It looks as if the adaptation to circumstances was progressive.

At the same time, it is possible to say something about how the A-text was originally compiled. A very large body of evidence assembled by Greg establishes that it was a reconstruction of the play made from memory by persons who included at least one actor associated with the original production. It has the usual characteristics of such memorial reconstructions. It offers many readings which impair sense, grammar, and metre; it inserts unnecessary connective phrases and passages; it introduces bits of actors' gag and echoes of other plays; it assimilates to one another phrases deliberately varied by the author—or authors, if the general critical opinion that Marlowe was not the sole author is correct; it allows speeches to be infected by recollections and anticipations of passages occurring elsewhere; and it loosens expression, it paraphrases, vulgarizes, and exaggerates.

Greg's concluding summary co-ordinates his findings. He believes that the play was written

> during the last year of Marlowe's life. It was performed, presumably on the London stage, by some unidentified company, no doubt before the plague of 1592–4 reached its height and put a stop to all

acting. But this was a time of great dislocation in the theatrical world, during which most companies were forced to travel and some came to grief. The text we have in A appears to be a version prepared for the less critical and exigent audiences of provincial towns, and prepared, not in an orderly manner by making cuts and alterations in the authorized prompt-book, but by memorial reconstruction from the London performance, and therefore either by the original company after they had lost or parted with their prompt-book, or by some other company that included actors, or at least one member, who had taken part in or been somehow intimately connected with the original production. This report or reconstruction served as a new prompt-book for provincial performance, and in the course of its use as such it suffered further degeneration, partly by the insertion of bits of gag, sometimes of a topical sometimes of an unseemly character, that had proved attractive to a vulgar audience, but also by provision for further shortening and simplification as time or the dwindling resources of the company demanded. Some insertions must have been made at least two years after the original production of the play.[1]

In short, as Leo Kirschbaum pointed out in 1946,[2] A1 is a 'bad' quarto in the broad sense in which the first quartos of, for example, *Romeo and Juliet*, *Hamlet*, *Henry V*, and *The Merry Wives of Windsor* are generally so described. But what of B1 ? It has already been shown that it is the fuller and more original text. Can the analysis of it be taken further ?

Much of it is evidently quite independent of the earlier quartos. But its indebtedness in places to the A-text can be amply demonstrated. One example must suffice. Between scenes vii and viii, B has a speech of twenty-four lines by the Chorus. A cuts this speech down to eleven lines and places it in Wagner's mouth. B uses precisely these eleven lines, still disfigured by A's corruption of the last of them, to plug a hole between scenes v and vi that was apparently left by the total disappearance of a scene from both texts. A sprinkling of errors common to the two quartos proves that B1's indebtedness was in fact to a copy of A3 (see textual notes to i. 12, 74, 93, 111, etc.). The juggling with the eleven-line speech and the equally conspicuous censoring of much that might be thought pro-

---

[1] *Marlowe's 'Doctor Faustus'* (Oxford, 1950), p. 60.
[2] 'The Good and Bad Quartos of *Doctor Faustus*', *Libr.*, Fourth Series, XXVI (1945-6), pp. 272-94.

fanity are unmistakable signs in B1 of the presence of an editor.

When preparing the copy used in printing B1, this editor drew both on a manuscript source and on A3. He employed A3 mainly in the more tragic scenes, which are well preserved in the A-text. From it, he took the Prologue; scene i; scene iii; v. 0.1–14, 95–116; the eleven-line chorus which he used as a stop-gap between scenes v and vi; viii. 0.1–24; xviii. 10.1–27.2; xix. 41–86, 132.1–190.1; and the Epilogue. This amounts to almost one-quarter of the whole play. For nearly one-third he had necessarily to depend upon the manuscript, since the passages in question do not occur in A at all. For the remainder, a little less than half of the whole, he relied again upon the manuscript; but he kept A3 in view and sometimes took over details from it, especially in the way of stage-directions.

When following A3, the editor sometimes went to considerable trouble to insert corrections from the manuscript. But such emendation is so intermittent as to drive us to the conclusion that in places the manuscript was damaged or illegible and so of no use to him. Can it be, then, that the manuscript was an old and dilapidated prompt-book—perhaps superseded fourteen years earlier, when the additions of Birde and Rowley may well have necessitated the preparation of a new one? Greg thinks not. He points out that in scene xviii the Scholars' speeches in praise of Helen differ considerably in the two texts. Both versions sound like Marlowe; and the version in A appears to represent a revision of that in B. A, being a memorial reconstruction, presumably reports the words used in the theatre. It seems, therefore, that Marlowe must have written the A-version of the Scholars' speeches in, or for, the prompt-book; and consequently that the play must have been finished and in process of production before his death. Nor is this by any means the only point at which we may infer revision in the original prompt-book. Greg goes so far as to suggest that those passages in scene xix which A omits, passages which stress the 'morality' element in the play, may have been dropped at that stage, and even that this revision may have given us Faustus' final soliloquy in the form in which it has come down to us. But he admits that in so doing he may be transgressing the bounds of legitimate speculation; and it would surely be easier to believe that the cutting of the 'morality' passages was done in the later, memorially reconstructed prompt-book which gave us the A-text. After all, this prompt-book was evidently designed to record an abridged and simplified version of the play. What is important for the moment, however, is that, since A does appear to report a number of revisions made in or for the original prompt-book, the manuscript used by the editor of B must have had a place prior to that of the prompt-book in the chain of transmission.

In fact, it looks as if that manuscript may well have been the authors' own draft of the play, the so-called 'foul papers', from which the original prompt-book itself would be prepared. There has been a little editorial tinkering with the text, tinkering which certainly went beyond the censoring of supposed profanity already mentioned. Moreover, the compositors have apparently left their mark upon more than the mere accidentals of spelling and punctuation; the preference of one of them for 'O' as against 'Ah', for example, results in the obliteration of some meaningful distinctions which are preserved even in the reported A-text. But in general we may say that when B1 is following manuscript it brings us very close indeed to what the authors wrote.

Greg again provides us with a useful summary of his findings:

> The text of 1616 I believe to have been prepared for publication by an editor on the basis of a manuscript containing the authors' drafts from which the prompt-book had in the first instance been transcribed. In the course, however, of preparing the prompt-book, the text underwent an appreciable amount of revision which, of course, found its way into the stage version that underlies the 1604 text. Moreover, the manuscript was incomplete and in parts damaged or illegible, so that the editor was sometimes forced to reproduce passages from the earlier version, either as they stood or with such corrections as could be deciphered in the manuscript. From the 1604 text he also took over some of the prompt-book revisions and even some of the interpolations of the report, besides some stage directions. Finally the editor made a number of cuts and alterations of his own, mostly on the score of profanity, but a few on literary grounds.[1]

Greg believes that the editor sent to the printer the actual 'foul papers' and a marked copy of A3. Against this, Fredson Bowers

[1] *Op. cit.*, pp. vii–viii.

has argued persuasively on bibliographical grounds that the editor provided a transcript.[1] This disagreement does not weaken Bowers' conviction that Greg is right in his main contentions. But the acceptance of Bowers' view does introduce into the picture yet another possible source of variant readings.

5. THE PRESENT EDITION

In accordance with this analysis, the present edition is based mainly upon the B-text, and upon that text in its earliest form, B1.

More than three-quarters of B1 derives from an authoritative manuscript, very likely the authors' 'foul papers'. It might seem that an editor could not do better than reprint this three-quarters with scrupulous fidelity; and admittedly he ought not to depart from it rashly. But he must remember that, if our analysis is correct, there are places where the A-text reports revisions made in the original prompt-book; and that such revisions may be authorial and therefore authoritative. He must remember that the B-text was prepared by an editor who took it upon himself to make alterations in it, most of them to eliminate supposed profanity but some of them, such as that recorded in the textual note to xix. 185, to satisfy his sense of literary fitness. He must also remember that this editor probably sent a transcript of the 'foul papers' to the printer and that the scribe responsible for this copy, perhaps the editor himself, would almost inevitably introduce errors into it. Nor will he be able to forget that what he has in front of him is not the transcript itself but a print of it, incorporating, no doubt, a number of compositorial slips and blunders. So he is justified in departing from B1 whenever he considers that A1 offers him an authorial revision and whenever he detects what he believes to be signs of editorial, scribal, or compositorial corruption in B1.

What of the parts of B1 that derive from A3? Since A3 is itself a reprint, A1 in general offers the most original text of these. But the editor of B1 corrected the text which he took from A3 by reference to the 'foul papers'; so any reading in B1 which can be plausibly regarded as a correction so sanctioned must be accepted in pre-

---

[1] 'The Text of Marlowe's *Faustus*', *M.P.*, XLIX (1951–2), pp. 195–204.

ference to the A1 alternative. On the other hand, some of the divergences between the two texts in these parts cannot be so regarded. Editorial, scribal, or compositorial corruption in B1 provides a more likely explanation of them; and it is occasionally possible to show that B1 simply took over from A3 a compositorial error or miscorrection which had originated there or in A2. In all such instances, A1 must clearly have preference.

The modern editor, then, will find himself relying mainly upon B1. At the same time, in view of what has been ascertained regarding the history and nature of the A and B texts, he will recognize that each version has authority within certain limits. His editorial policy will therefore be eclectic; but his eclecticism will be controlled by the available bibliographical and textual knowledge. This knowledge and the principles governing its application will not, however, provide an automatic solution for all his difficulties. He will repeatedly be thrown back upon such powers of discrimination and judgement as he may possess. It will not be surprising if he feels dismay when he reviews the qualifications required for tackling one of the most difficult textual problems in the field of Elizabethan drama; and he will have good reason to be grateful that scholars of the distinction of Boas and Greg have already devoted their energies to it and made their work available for his guidance.

Neither A1 nor B1 makes any attempt to divide the play into acts and scenes, so no such distribution is given prominence in the present edition. But for easy reference the scenes are numbered serially in square brackets on the left-hand side of the page. The following table relates these serial numbers to the act and scene numbers adopted by Boas and Greg:

Scenes i–iv correspond to Act I, Scenes i–iv.
Scenes v–vii correspond to Act II, Scenes i–iii.
Scenes viii–x correspond to Act III, Scenes i–iii.
Scenes xi–xvii correspond to Act IV, Scenes i–vii.
Scenes xviii–xx correspond to Act V, Scenes i–iii.

Throughout the present edition, spelling and punctuation have been modernized. No exception has been made in favour of those archaic forms which have sometimes been cherished even in modern-spelling texts: for example, 'clifts' for 'clefts', 'guesse' for 'guests', and 'vild' for 'vile'. Nor has Italian spelling been regarded as exempt from this kind of attention. Abbreviations have been silently expanded, obvious misprints silently corrected, and inconsistencies in the forms given to speech-prefixes—*Euill An.* for *Bad An.* being the extreme case—silently ironed out. Elisions have been used consistently in the verb-endings -ed and -est where the metre seemed to authorize them. Otherwise, elisions within words have been avoided.

The textual notes are designed primarily to display the sources of the present text and to give in a convenient form as much information as possible about A1 and B1. They provide a full list of the substantive variants between these two. While ignoring differences in the wording of speech-prefixes similar to those mentioned above, they record all other variations in wording, whether in the dialogue or in the stage-directions, and all differences in verse-lineation; they indicate certain differences in punctuation which appreciably affect the sense; and they ignore all other differences in punctuation and all differences in spelling, use of capitals, and typography. When the present text departs from both A1 and B1, the notes give the source of the reading adopted and record the rejected readings of A1 and B1; if these rejected readings are substantively the same, a single reading spelt and punctuated as in B1 is ascribed to both quartos, regardless of any possible difference in accidentals. Since, as already explained in section 4 of this 'Introduction', B2 may possess some kind of authority, a few readings from it have been recorded, in addition to those which have earned a place in the text.[1] The other seventeenth-century quartos have been treated on exactly the same footing as more modern editions: if their variants seem to be plausible conjectures, they are admitted to the notes, or even to the text, as such, but not as having any special authority. The only exception to this is that room has been found for a few readings of A2 and A3 which have no value in themselves but are evidential for the relationship of B1 to A1. If, however, one of these readings from another seventeenth-century quarto is noted as iden-

---

[1] Both the unique copy of B2 and the sets of photostats known to have been made from it are at present untraceable, so all these readings have been taken from Greg's textual notes.

tical with a reading from A1 or B1, it should be understood that what is alleged is identity in substance and not necessarily in accidents.

This last paragraph calls for immediate qualification. The A and B versions of scenes iv, vii, x, xii, and xv differ so completely in wording that it is impracticable to digest their variants into textual notes. So Appendix I accommodates the A-versions of these in their entirety, while the B-versions have undisputed possession in the play itself. The textual notes to each of these widely divergent scenes record only variants between the scene as printed and the appropriate copy-text, together with a few of the emendations made by previous editors.

6. OTHER EDITIONS, 1663–1964

A quick review of the chief editions of *Doctor Faustus* since 1631 will conveniently conclude this account of the textual problem and of its proposed editorial solution.

The last seventeenth-century quarto appeared in 1663. In this, a scene at the court of the Soldan in Babylon replaces the scenes at the Papal court, and a passage of some sixty lines is appended to scene xvi. Tucker Brooke and Boas print both of these in appendices to their editions of the play. The title-page of 1663 announces, with some exaggeration, 'several New Scenes'. It announces also the inclusion of a list of the characters, which is naturally based upon this quarto's quite unauthoritative version of the drama. What it does not announce is that this edition far outdoes B1 in the censoring of suspected profanity.

Over a century and a half later, in 1814, C. W. Dilke, the friend of Keats, placed *Doctor Faustus* at the beginning of a selection of old English plays. In 1818, William Oxberry, the actor, issued it separately without indication of editorship; and, nine years afterwards, his texts of all of Marlowe's plays were brought out in a single volume, this time with his name prefixed. In the previous year, 1826, *Doctor Faustus* had appeared in a three-volume collection of Marlowe's works published by Pickering and edited anonymously by George Robinson. All of these editors print the B-text of the play.

The collection of Marlowe's works which Alexander Dyce brought out in three volumes in 1850, and in one volume with some revision in 1858, contains the first scholarly edition of *Doctor Faustus*. Dyce differs from all except his remotest predecessors in taking his main text from A1; but he gives the whole of B1 in smaller type. Having perceived that the *Damnable Life* is the source of the play, he quotes from it in his footnotes. In 1870, his textual procedure was reversed in Francis Cunningham's one-volume edition of Marlowe's works. Cunningham grounds his main text upon B1 but makes the A-text also available to the reader. He then surprises us on p. xiv of his 'Introductory Notice' by expressing the belief that the A-version is the closer to Marlowe. Whereas Dyce, like Dilke, does not divide the play at all, Cunningham, like Oxberry and Robinson, apportions it into acts and scenes.

In 1877, Wilhelm Wagner, too, adopted such an apportionment in a separate edition of the tragedy. This is based upon A1, but B1's additional and variant passages are printed in the critical commentary. A. W. Ward similarly underestimated the B-text, regarding as unauthorized additions the passages which the A-text omits. His text of *Doctor Faustus* was printed with one of Greene's *Friar Bacon and Friar Bungay* in 1878. It is accompanied by a particularly valuable critical commentary. A. H. Bullen's three-volume collection of Marlowe's works, published in 1885, and Havelock Ellis' volume of 1887 in the Mermaid Series contain texts of *Doctor Faustus* which, again, are founded upon A1. But Bullen saw that there is work by Marlowe himself in the passages preserved only in B; these occupy an appendix to his text. In 1897, Israel Gollancz produced an eclectic text, the result mainly of inserting into the A-text such of the passages peculiar to the B-text as are additional and not alternative to what the A-text gives.

He was helped in preparing this by the prior appearance of the earliest edition that was the product of really thoroughgoing textual scholarship. This was Hermann Breymann's parallel-text edition of 1889, which preserves the original spelling and punctuation—it was the first to do so—and records variants in all early quartos rediscovered by that date. Breymann follows Ward, Bullen, and Havelock Ellis in dividing the A-text into scenes only.

In 1910, in his old-spelling edition of Marlowe's works, C. F. Tucker Brooke in his turn adhered to the general opinion that A1 represented Marlowe's original version. He gives B1's additions and lengthier variations in an appendix. John S. Farmer brought out a facsimile of A1 in 1920.

The twentieth century has seen the amassing of a great deal of systematic knowledge about Elizabethan theatrical documents and about the printed books which normally contain our earliest extant texts of the plays. In the light of this growing information, F. S. Boas and W. W. Greg were able to advance considerably the analysis of the two basic texts of *Doctor Faustus* and to demonstrate the superiority of B. Boas maintained that B1 incorporated the additions of 1602 but that nevertheless it was on the whole the more original and the better text. His modern-spelling edition, which appeared in 1932, was the first really scholarly edition to rely chiefly upon it. Greg, who had himself made a prodigious contribution to the growing knowledge of dramatic manuscripts and prints, produced a much more detailed analysis and came out even more strongly in favour of B1. He rejected the theory that the 1602 additions had survived in it. But it is unnecessary to say more about an analysis which has already been outlined in section 4 of the present 'Introduction' and which is basic to the present text. Greg states his case very fully in the 'Introduction' and notes to his old-spelling parallel-text edition of *Doctor Faustus*; and in his 'conjectural reconstruction' published in the same year, 1950, he applies his principles to the task of editing a modern-spelling version. Both Boas and Greg follow the example of the earlier nineteenth-century editors in dividing the play into acts and scenes (see section 5 of this 'Introduction').

The conservatism which has made P. H. Kocher the staunchest of living defenders of the early date for *Doctor Faustus* presumably accounts for his basing a text of the play upon A1 eighteen years after the publication of Boas' work. He uses modern spelling and divides the play into scenes only. Leo Kirschbaum, in another edition designed for college use, prefers B1 and is more faithful to it than is Greg. His text of Marlowe's principal plays appeared in 1962.

7. THE LITERARY SOURCES OF THE PLAY

The historical Georgius or Johannes Faustus seems to have been a strolling scholar and reputed magician whose public career extended from about 1510 to about 1540.[1] Wonderful stories, some of which had been current for centuries, began to be associated with his name; and this was increasingly the case after his death, which itself became the subject of one of them. His fame spread. He was mentioned in England as early as 1572: 'There are also coniurers founde euen at this day, who bragge of themselues that they can so by inchauntments saddle an horse, that in a fewe houres they will dispatch a very long iourney. God at the last wil chasten these men with deserued punishment. What straunge things are reported of one *Faustus* a German, which he did in these our dayes by inchauntments ?'[2]

In the spiritual climate of the time, the legend acquired a strongly anti-papal colouring; and it was evidently a Lutheran who compiled the German *Historia von D. Iohañ Fausten* in 1587. His moral tale achieved immediate popularity.

As we have already seen, an English version by one P.F. followed within five years. Like other Elizabethan translators, P.F. takes appreciable liberties with his original. Thus, he adds considerably to the record of Faustus' travels in chapter xxii of the *Damnable Life*, corresponding with chapter xxvi of the German. The original contains no mention of Virgil's tomb, but P.F. says: 'there saw he the Tombe of Virgil; & the high way that hee cutte through that mighty hill of stone in one night, the whole length of an English mile'. Having referred to the famous Piazza in Venice, P.F. on his own responsibility tells of 'the sumptuous Church standing therein called Saint *Markes*; how all the pauement was set with coloured stones, and all the Roode or loft of the Church double gilded ouer'. In the same way, he amplifies the account of Rome by introducing the four bridges over the Tiber, upon one of which 'is the Castle of

---

[1] Ward's 'Introduction' contains a useful summary of what is known about the historical Faustus.

[2] *Of ghostes and spirites walking by nyght... Written by Lewes Lauaterus... And translated into Englyshe by R.H.* (London, 1572), p. 170.

S. *Angelo*, wherein are so many great cast peeces as there are dayes in a yeare'.

These particular interpolations have been cited here because each of them is unmistakably the source of a passage found in both early versions of the play. Reviewing his travels, Faustus says in viii. 13–20:

> There saw we learned Maro's golden tomb,
> The way he cut, an English mile in length,
> Thorough a rock of stone in one night's space.
> From thence to Venice, Padua, and the rest,
> In midst of which a sumptuous temple stands,
> That threats the stars with her aspiring top,
> Whose frame is pav'd with sundry colour'd stones
> And roof'd aloft with curious work in gold.

Describing Rome, where they now are, Mephostophilis speaks of the Tiber in viii. 37–44:

> Over the which four stately bridges lean,
> That make safe passage to each part of Rome.
> Upon the bridge call'd Ponte Angelo
> Erected is a castle passing strong,
> Where thou shalt see such store of ordinance
> As that the double cannons forg'd of brass
> Do match the number of the days contain'd
> Within the compass of one complete year.

This perfunctory versifying does not represent Marlowe at his best; but it is of importance here because his close adherence to the wording of the *Damnable Life* proves that he used P.F.'s English translation in writing *Doctor Faustus*. Nor is further evidence hard to find. The articles of Faustus' compact with Lucifer as given in scene v of the play agree with P.F.'s version in that the fourth of them is a conflation of the fourth and fifth articles of the German original; whereas the German author makes Faustus blow in the Pope's face, the playwright in scene ix follows P.F. in making him smite the Pope on the face; and in the same scene the playwright takes over from P.F. the addition to the Pope's curse of 'Bel, Booke, and Candle'. On the other side, not one significant instance has been found of the play's agreeing with the German version when the English translation disagrees with it. Admittedly, it has been suggested[1] that Marlowe borrowed not from the German version itself but from a hypothetical Latin version which preceded it and which differed widely from it. There is nothing in his play, however, that requires us to assume any such indebtedness; and there seems to be little point in discussing Marlowe's imperceptible obligations to an unproducible original.

So *Doctor Faustus* derives from the *Damnable Life*, and only through that does it owe anything to the *Historia von D. Iohañ Fausten*. In Appendix II are assembled the chief passages of the *Damnable Life* employed in the composition of the play. It will be seen that the use made of these passages varied widely: sometimes a few words sufficed to suggest a whole episode, such as Faustus' conference with Valdes and Cornelius in scene i; at other times, as when Faustus meets the Duke and Duchess of Vanholt in scene xvii, the playwrights echoed the very phrases of P.F. Only a few scenes of clownage, and the passages concerning the rivalry of Pope Adrian and the antipope, Bruno, appear to owe nothing to this source.

It is interesting to observe that the reporter responsible for AI knew the *Damnable Life*, too. He evidently pieced out his imperfect recollections of scene xii by reference to it. His version of this scene, here printed in Appendix I, reproduces its wording very closely indeed.

What may not appear from the extracts which are all that can be offered in Appendix II is the extent to which certain of P.F.'s departures from his original involve the ascription to Faustus of a genuine intellectual ardour. P.F. had no German authority, for example, for allowing Faustus in chapter xxii to describe himself as 'the vnsatiable Speculator'. By touches of this kind, he was already beginning to modify Faustus in one of the ways in which Marlowe was completely to transform him.

Marlowe's presentation of Faustus is the outcome partly of what he found in the *Damnable Life* and even more of what he himself wished or needed to express by means of it. But P. H. Kocher[2] has

---

[1] H. Jantz, 'An Elizabethan Statement on the Origin of the German Faust Book', *J.E.G.P.*, LI (1952), pp. 137–53.

[2] Kocher, *C.M.*, pp. 138–72.

shown that a third factor contributed to the final achievement. He holds that Marlowe had some knowledge of the European literature of witchcraft and from this source enriched the portrait of Faustus which he found in the *Damnable Life*. Marlowe attributed to Faustus motives such as were said to have animated other witches; in scenes i and iii, he made him promise himself certain specific powers which magic was traditionally supposed to confer; and he showed him, in scene v, employing a conjuring procedure and re-citing a Latin incantation which conformed in many details with authoritative pronouncements on the subject. Moreover, his whole treatment of the relationship between Faustus and the evil spirits is in keeping with orthodox witch theory. On the one hand, Faustus cannot control them, though he can attract them; on the other, they cannot control him, though they can terrify him, delight him, and tempt him. To the last, it is possible for him to repent; but the spirits can place obstacles in his way by binding his tongue, his hands, and his tears when he strives to do so, and by rending his heart for naming of his Christ. We may legitimately ask whether it was necessary for Marlowe to turn to witch lore for all of these ideas. Those concerning the relationship between Faustus and the spirits cannot have been strange to any thoughtful man of Christian edu-cation; and the motives of such persons as resorted to witchcraft must have been fairly obvious to anyone who had ever reflected upon human nature. Nevertheless, Kocher has unquestionably identified the general source of some of the materials used, as already indicated, in scenes i, iii, and v.

A third and last literary source remains for mention. This is John Foxe's *Acts and Monuments*, better known as Foxe's Book of Mar-tyrs. From this came some of the material used in the short passages in scene viii concerning Pope Adrian's recent victory over the im-perial forces and his humiliation of the captured Bruno, the rival pope chosen by the Emperor. The relevant quotations from Foxe are given in the comment on viii. 90–6.

8. THE AUTHORSHIP OF THE PLAY

Very few students of *Doctor Faustus* are prepared to ascribe it en-tirely to Marlowe. Its characteristic subject leaves us in little doubt

that it was he who conceived the play; and the verse style of its
most important scenes, together with the occasional echoes of his
other works found in them, makes it clear that these scenes came
from his pen. But they show us a tragic Faustus oscillating between
arrogance and remorse, a very different Faustus from the cheerful
anti-papist wonder-worker of the scenes at Rome, at the imperial
court, and at Vanholt. This second Faustus is the creation, surely,
of another author.

Nor is this the play's only major inconsistency. In the Marlowan
scene iii, Mephostophilis explains that Faustus' charms have no
coercive power over him. But in scene x we find him complaining
that the charms recited by a couple of clowns have dragged him all
the way from Constantinople (see comment on x. 32–4). It seems
to follow that at least this one of the farcical prose scenes was not
written by Marlowe himself. Indeed, there is general agreement
among editors and critics that few, if any, of them are his.

His hand is most evident in the Prologue; scenes i, iii, and v; the
earlier part of scene vi; Chorus 1; the first four or five speeches of
scene viii; Chorus 2; scenes xviii, xix, and xx; and the Epilogue.
Greg may well be right in adding scene ii to this list. But his minute
subdivision of some of these scenes between Marlowe and a collaborator is less easy to accept. The evidence is usually too scanty
to authorize such meticulous apportionment.

Nearly all those parts of the play which we have not ascribed
principally to Marlowe fall into one or other of two stylistic categories. In the first place, there is the mainly prose farce of scene iv;
of the latter part of scene vi; and of scenes vii, x, xv, xvi, and xvii.
This is undistinguished, run-of-the-mill stuff, though less undis-
ciplined than the writing with which the reporter of A1 replaced
much of it (see Appendix I). Kocher[1] ascribes it to Nashe; but this
seems unduly hard on a prose-writer who, whatever his faults, did
not lack liveliness.

The greater part of scene viii and the whole of scenes ix, xi, xii,
xiii, and xiv are written in a blank verse differing markedly from
that of Marlowe. It has a prim, earnest formality, which is empha-

---

[1] 'Nashe's Authorship of the Prose Scenes in *Faustus*', *M.L.Q.*, III
(1942), pp. 17–40.

sized by its author's taste for antitheses, for rhymes, and for proverbs and other stereotyped expressions. It completely lacks the impetus and the splendour of Marlowe's verse.

Who was the author, or who were the authors, who contributed to the play the parts falling into these two categories? If a candidate must be named, the likeliest seems to be Samuel Rowley. He was an actor and dramatist for the Admiral's Men who survived Marlowe by more than thirty years. His only extant play is *When You See Me You Know Me, or The Famous Chronicle History of King Henry VIII*. This play, like the scenes at the papal court in *Doctor Faustus*, incorporates material taken from Foxe's Book of Martyrs and is evidently the work of a fervent Protestant. Its verse, moreover, bears some resemblance to the un-Marlowan verse in *Doctor Faustus*. In particular, Rowley likes to place polysyllabic adjectives ending in 'al' after the nouns that they describe. Greg records five instances in *When You See Me;* and there is a sixth instance, duplicating one of his five, in l. 2312.[1] There are six instances in the parts of *Doctor Faustus* which are now in question, namely in viii. 92, 105, 144, 182, 194, and xii. 30; and there is a seventh in another part, in i. 149. It is worth noting that both in *When You See Me* and in *Doctor Faustus* the combination is usually placed at the end of the verse line. Greg also draws attention to Rowley's use in l. 2879 of his play of the word 'situation'; the sense which it seems to have both there and in *Doctor Faustus*, viii. 51, is one that is rare enough to be unknown to the *Oxford English Dictionary*.

Even so, the case for Rowley cannot be regarded as overwhelmingly strong. We know nothing about him before 1597. We have only one play by him, and that a play written eleven or twelve years after the first draft of *Doctor Faustus*. Nor was a fondness for combinations such as 'demonstrations magical' by any means peculiar to him. This very example of it occurs in the Marlowan scene i. Admittedly, Greg suggests that Marlowe's collaborator inserted ll. 149–51, which contain this example, into a scene which was otherwise Marlowe's own. But the suggestion smacks of special pleading; and in any case we find 'science metaphysical' at the end of the verse line in 2 *Tamburlaine*, IV. ii. 63.

Ed. F. P. Wilson, Oxford, 1952.

Nevertheless, Rowley was obviously fond of this kind of combination; and so was the author of the un-Marlowan verse scenes in *Doctor Faustus*. For this reason, and for the other reasons mentioned earlier, Rowley would seem to be the least unlikely candidate so far proposed as the author of these scenes. His strongest rival is Dekker.

H. Dugdale Sykes[1] would give Rowley the farcical prose scenes, too. The evidence for his authorship of these is even slighter than that for his authorship of the un-Marlowan verse scenes. It is merely that he was fond of certain words and phrases which are used in them. But 'zounds', 'I warrant you', 'as passeth', 'O brave', and 'much ado' were surely the commonest of common property. Their use in two different texts proves little or nothing. The most we can say is that the suggestion that Rowley wrote the farcical prose scenes in *Doctor Faustus* is not demonstrably unplausible.

At one time, editors and critics used to believe that the passages first printed in the 1616 quarto of *Doctor Faustus*, passages which are predominantly un-Marlowan, were those added in 1602 by Birde and Rowley. But from the recognition that A1 gives a reported text of later date than the more original one provided by B1 it follows that these additions are embodied either in both of the early versions or in neither of them. Reasons have already been given, in section 4 of this 'Introduction', for supposing them lost; and this supposition has received support from the subsequent indication that B1 may well have been printed from the authors' 'foul papers'.

So the un-Marlowan parts of *Doctor Faustus* would appear to have been written in collaboration with Marlowe during the original period of composition in 1592–3. The collaborator may have been Samuel Rowley, who later made additions to the play which seem to have perished. Greg admits the possibility of Rowley's participation. He is also ready to acknowledge as a less strong possibility that there may have been two collaborators. Nothing is gained by thinking of the other author of the 1602 additions, William Birde, in this connection; as a writer, he is a completely unknown quantity, no piece bearing his name having survived. Marlowe's

[1] *Sidelights on Elizabethan Drama* (Oxford, 1924), pp. 49–78.

collaborator, whoever he was, or his collaborators, whoever they were, evidently worked in subordination to him. Marlowe had presumably conceived the play; and, writing its crucial scenes himself, he made it essentially his own. For this reason, we do no great wrong to anybody in commonly speaking of it as his work.

9. DOCTOR FAUSTUS

The early nineteenth-century editors and critics of *Doctor Faustus* deserve our gratitude for having secured the play's admission to the canon of English Literature. Not that they hesitate to condemn what they believe to be its weaknesses. Dilke, for example, considers it 'by no means a favourable specimen of the plays' in his charge; but he praises its poetry and its representation of Faustus himself.[1] Writing in *Blackwood's Magazine*, Henry Maitland describes it as 'exceedingly imperfect and disproportioned'; but he too admires the portrayal of the protagonist.[2] William Hazlitt has fewer reservations. In his *Lectures on the Age of Elizabeth*, he follows Oxberry in claiming that this is Marlowe's best play and, like Oxberry and Maitland, gives special praise to the apostrophe to Helen and the last soliloquy of Faustus. He writes:

> Faustus himself is a rude sketch, but it is a gigantic one. This character may be considered as a personification of the pride of will and eagerness of curiosity, sublimed beyond the reach of fear and remorse. He is hurried away, and, as it were, devoured by a tormenting desire to enlarge his knowledge to the utmost bounds of nature and art, and to extend his power with his knowledge. He would realise all the fictions of a lawless imagination, would solve the most subtle speculations of abstract reason; and for this purpose, sets at defiance all mortal consequences, and leagues himself with demoniacal power, with 'fate and metaphysical aid.'[3]

In conclusion, Hazlitt observes that he 'cannot find, in Marlowe's play, any proofs of the atheism or impiety attributed to him'.[4]

[1] Pp. 8–9.
[2] 'Marlow's Tragical History of the Life and Death of Doctor Faustus', *Blackwood's Magazine*, I (1817), pp. 388–94.
[3] *Complete Works* (ed. P. P. Howe, 21 vols., London, 1930–4), vi. 202–3.
[4] *Ibid.*, vi. 207.

Those who have claimed to find something of the sort have usually argued that Marlowe presents Faustus in such a way as to enlist our sympathy and admiration for him in his revolt. Even Maitland, who acknowledges that Faustus is a sinner, goes so far as to say that he does not seem 'to deserve the fearful punishment finally inflicted on him'. Later in the century, however, this liberal view is expressed more frequently and more forcibly. For Cunningham, 'the last scene of *Faustus* fills the soul with love and admiration as for a departed hero';[1] Wagner regrets that Marlowe was not liberal enough to allow Faustus finally to escape damnation;[2] and Havelock Ellis sees Faustus not as a sinner but as 'a hero, a Tamburlaine, . . . who at the thought of vaster delights has ceased to care for the finite splendours of an earthly crown'.[3] What some of these critics seem to want is Goethe as part-author of Marlowe's play.

Similar interpretations have found able exponents in the present century. According to U. M. Ellis-Fermor, 'The sin for which punishment is meted out to Faustus is more often alluded to than explained. . . . Faustus, as far as we have been able to follow him, has been foolish and frivolous, but never criminal.'[4] Philip Henderson sees the play as 'simply a parable of the fight for intellectual freedom', with the Bad Angel externalizing Faustus' 'progressive and adventurous impulses'.[5] F. S. Boas wonders what occasion for repentance there was in a life passed so largely in academic debate with Mephostophilis.[6] Harry Levin, finally, gives vigorous and subtle expression to a view which requires very much the same orientation of our sympathies.[7]

But many voices have been raised in opposition during recent decades. These agree in suggesting that Marlowe takes, and intends us to take, a more critical view of his protagonist. In James Smith's opinion, the play is an allegory embodying an orthodox Christian attitude towards Faustus' career.[8] Lily B. Campbell sees it as dramatizing a case of conscience such as fascinated Protestant theo-

[1] P. xvi.   [2] Pp. xxxiii–xxxiv.   [3] P. xxxviii.
[4] *Christopher Marlowe* (London, 1927), p. 78.
[5] *And Morning in his Eyes* (London, 1937), pp. 310, 312.
[6] *Christopher Marlowe* (Oxford, 1940), p. 211.
[7] *The Overreacher* (London, 1954), pp. 129–59.
[8] 'Marlowe's *Dr. Faustus*', *Scrutiny*, VIII (1939–40), pp. 36–55.

logians during the sixteenth century; she gives an account of one such case which instructively parallels that of Faustus.[1] Greg's reminder that Faustus, in becoming the lover of Helen of Troy, is guilty of the sin of demoniality[2] must also be counted on this side in the debate. So must a fair amount of censorious moralizing which others have chosen to offer as literary criticism of the play. Their excesses balance those of such sentimentalists as Cunningham on the other side.

We need not commit ourselves wholly to either party. Indeed, the wiser of the critics already named would have had no difficulty in accepting J. B. Steane's discovery of division and uncertainty in the play.[3] If we contend both that Marlowe felt a profound sympathy for his hero and that he acquiesced in that hero's fall, we are merely arguing that he conceived his play as a genuine tragedy.

The opening speech of the Chorus announces his purpose. Faustus, a man of humble origin, has acquired great learning; but his arrogance will cause him to overreach and ruin himself. We are to witness a tragedy of presumption.

This motive held a strong attraction for the poet whose most-favoured character had declared that Nature

> Doth teach us all to have aspiring minds.
> (I *Tamburlaine*, II. vii. 20)

The attraction makes itself felt from the beginning of the play. In the first scene, Faustus dismisses the traditional subjects of study and turns instead to magic. With impatient scorn, he rejects philosophy, medicine, law, and divinity; and with almost breathless eagerness he contemplates the

> world of profit and delight,
> Of power, of honour, of omnipotence
> (i. 52–3)

which he expects to enjoy as a magician. The whole earth, and the

---

[1] '*Doctor Faustus:* A Case of Conscience', *P.M.L.A.*, LXVII (1952), pp. 219–39. The case which she parallels with that of Faustus is dramatized in N. Woodes, *The Conflict of Conscience* (1581). The protagonist's expression of despair in this play bears a general resemblance to that in *Doctor Faustus*, xix. See Hazlitt's Dodsley, vi. 119.

[2] 'The Damnation of Faustus', *M.L.R.*, XLI (1946), pp. 97–107.

[3] *Marlowe: A Critical Study* (Cambridge, 1964), pp. 117–65.

winds and clouds above it, will be subject to his control. While waiting for his friends Valdes and Cornelius, who are to instruct him in 'concealed arts' (i. 101), he swiftly reviews some of the widely varied uses to which he intends to put the skill he seeks. These testify to his ardent curiosity, his desire for wealth and luxury, and his nationalism, as well as to the longing for power which he has already voiced. Such qualities mark him unmistakably as a man of the Renaissance; and a whole series of allusions maintains throughout the scene our sense of the extended horizons of that age of discovery. Faustus craves for gold from the East Indies, for pearl from the depths of the ocean, and for 'pleasant fruits and princely delicates' (i. 84) from America; Valdes refers to the Indians in the Spanish colonies, to Lapland giants, to the argosies of Venice, and to the annual plate-fleet which supplied the Spanish treasury from the New World. There was much here to fire the imaginations of English theatregoers; and they would heartily approve of Faustus' determination to chase the Prince of Parma from the Netherlands. After all, only the defeat of the Spanish Armada had prevented Parma from invading England in 1588. Nor were Englishmen ignorant of 'the fiery keel at Antwerp's bridge' (i. 95). Its Italian inventor had been in the English service in 1588; and the Spaniards had recalled his 'hell-burner' when the fireships were loosed against them off Calais.[1]

So Faustus' dream of power includes much that must have appealed strongly to the people for whom Marlowe wrote; and the liveliness and zest with which it is expressed show that much in it must likewise have appealed strongly to the poet himself. At the same time, Faustus' declaration,

> A sound magician is a demi-god,
>
> (i. 61)

forces us to recognize the presumptuous nature of his ambition. He evidently aspires to be something more than a man. Without surprise, we learn that his conscience is uneasy. Not that he admits as much at this stage; but the internal conflict is externalized for us in the admonitions of his Good and Bad Angels. The first sentence of

[1] Garrett Mattingly, *The Defeat of the Spanish Armada* (London, 1959), pp. 276–7.

the Good Angel, a warning against incurring 'God's heavy wrath' (i. 71), crystallizes our fears for one who has much of our sympathy; and these fears are augmented when, in the following scene, the two Scholars perceive the 'danger of his soul' (ii. 31).

Faustus, however, persists in his chosen course. In scene iii, he succeeds in calling up Mephostophilis and proposes his bargain with Lucifer; in scene v, he signs his soul away to Lucifer and questions Mephostophilis about hell; in scene vi, he questions Mephostophilis about astronomy and is later entertained by an infernal show of the Seven Deadly Sins which is designed to distract him from thoughts of repentance.

But matters go less smoothly than this summary suggests. During these three scenes, Faustus suffers a number of rebuffs. Having performed the ritual by which, he believes, 'the spirits are enforc'd to rise' (iii. 13), he naturally regards the appearance of Mephostophilis as a proof that he can order him about. He proceeds to do so with a quite absurd arrogance. Mephostophilis disillusions him. Faustus' charms, he explains, did not compel him to come; they merely drew his attention to Faustus' attractively sinful frame of mind, and he came of his own accord, 'in hope to get his glorious soul' (iii. 51). In scene v, after the signature of the bond, Faustus asks for a wife. Marriage is a sacrament, however; so Mephostophilis cannot give him one. Moreover, it may well be that Faustus' presumptuous isolation of himself from his fellow-men is making him incapable of marriage. Mephostophilis' reply takes the form of a crude practical joke, followed by a promise of concubines galore. In scene vi, when Faustus questions him about astronomy, Mephostophilis tells him nothing Wagner could not have told him; and, when Faustus asks who made the world, Mephostophilis, reluctant to acknowledge the Creator, refuses to say. His refusal provokes a crisis in their relations.

Anyone less infatuated than Faustus might have inferred from these rebuffs that the power he was acquiring so presumptuously fell far short of the 'omnipotence' of which he had dreamed. Faustus, however, brings himself to disregard not only these checks but also several quite explicit warnings. Of these, the most obvious is provided by the congealing of his blood, and its forming the words 'Homo fuge' (v. 77), when he is busy signing the bond with it. Even Lucifer's grotesque show of the Seven Deadly Sins, with Pride appropriately at their head, can be seen as potentially admonitory in effect, whatever may have been the impresario's intention and Faustus' actual response to the performance. But the most eloquent warnings come from that melancholy, sombre, tortured, and surprisingly truthful fiend, Mephostophilis himself. Within fifty lines of their first meeting, Faustus asks him what caused the fall of Lucifer. Mephostophilis ascribes it correctly to 'aspiring pride and insolence' (iii. 70), that is, to factors such as are visible in Faustus himself. 'And what are you', inquires Faustus, 'that live with Lucifer?'

> *Meph.* Unhappy spirits that fell with Lucifer,
> Conspir'd against our God with Lucifer,
> And are for ever damn'd with Lucifer.
> *Fau.* Where are you damn'd?
> *Meph.*   In hell.
> *Fau.* How comes it then that thou art out of hell?
> *Meph.* Why, this is hell, nor am I out of it.
> Think'st thou that I, who saw the face of God
> And tasted the eternal joys of heaven,
> Am not tormented with ten thousand hells
> In being depriv'd of everlasting bliss?   (iii. 72–82)

Mephostophilis, no doubt, means only to voice his own anguish. But his words would have conveyed a warning if Faustus had been capable of receiving one. It is the same after the signing of the bond in scene v. Faustus asks where hell is. Mephostophilis first locates it in the centre of the sublunary, elemental part of the universe, then goes on to speak of it, as he did in scene iii, as the spiritual condition of those who are entirely separated from God:

> Hell hath no limits, nor is circumscrib'd
> In one self place, but where we are is hell,
> And where hell is, there must we ever be;
> And, to be short, when all the world dissolves
> And every creature shall be purify'd,
> All places shall be hell that is not heaven.
> *Fau.* I think hell's a fable.
> *Meph.* Ay, think so still, till experience change thy mind.
> (v. 122–9)

Faustus does not merely neglect these warnings. He sweeps them aside with impatient, flippant arrogance. When his blood congeals to prevent his signing away his soul, he asks himself indignantly: 'is not thy soul thine own?' (v. 68). Admittedly, the injunction '*Homo fuge*' shakes his complacency for a moment. But he receives the Seven Deadly Sins with unreflecting jocularity; and in his glib and insensitive retorts to Mephostophilis' sombre speeches about hell he boastfully asserts his human self-sufficiency. To the first, he replies:

> What, is great Mephostophilis so passionate
> For being deprived of the joys of heaven?
> Learn thou of Faustus manly fortitude
> And scorn those joys thou never shalt possess.
>
> (iii. 85–8)

In response to the second, he denies the existence of hell.

> *Meph.* But I am an instance to prove the contrary,
>   For I tell thee I am damn'd and now in hell.
> *Fau.* Nay, and this be hell, I'll willingly be damn'd:
>   What, sleeping, eating, walking, and disputing!
>
> (v. 137–40)

Faustus, then, concludes an infamous bargain in order to enjoy the knowledge, the pleasure, and above all the power for which he craves. In scene i, we felt a certain degree of sympathy, and even of admiration, for him. This becomes more and more severely qualified as the play proceeds and his swallowing-down of rebuffs and refusals, together with his frivolous dismissal of one warning after another, exposes the inordinate appetite which dominates him. He is wilful, headstrong, and blind.

His bargain requires him to abjure God. As early as in the original evocation of Mephostophilis, he is fully prepared to do this. At the beginning, he feels few misgivings. Indeed, scene iii ends with a further expression of the kind of elation which characterized him in scene i. But shortly before signing the bond he wavers. Again the Good and Bad Angels appear and externalize his internal struggle with his conscience. 'Contrition, prayer, repentance', which could reconcile him with God, are denounced by the Bad Angel as 'illusions, fruits of lunacy' (v. 17–19). Such doctrine helps Faustus to

silence the voice of conscience. Once more he achieves the heady
elation of scene i,

> Why, the signory of Emden shall be mine,　　(v. 24)

but not before he has glimpsed a further temptation—to 'despair'
(v. 4).

This temptation recurs momentarily when he first sees the words
'*Homo fuge*'. It confronts him in full strength, however, at the beginning of scene vi. The Bad Angel then assures the man who has
abjured God that he is beyond the reach of the divine mercy.
Faustus confesses that his heart is hardened, that his conviction of
his own damnation prevents him from repenting, and that he has
thought of suicide:

> And long ere this I should have done the deed
> Had not sweet pleasure conquer'd deep despair.
> > (vi. 24–5)

But fifty lines later, after Mephostophilis' refusal to say who made
the world, Faustus comes near to achieving repentance. For once,
he seems to be listening to the Good Angel, and words of prayer
begin to pass his lips. At this crisis, Mephostophilis invokes the aid
of Lucifer and Beelzebub. They intimidate Faustus and, as soon as
he again abjures God, 'gratify' (vi. 103) him with the show of the
Seven Deadly Sins.

It is clear from this scene that the legalistic deed of gift which
Lucifer required Faustus to sign is not really binding—in other
words, that his initial sin has not damned him once and for all. The
utterances of the Good and Bad Angels on their two appearances
would be pointless if it were not still possible for Faustus to repent
and by so doing to cancel the bond; and the emergency measures
taken by Mephostophilis show that he certainly recognizes the possibility. 'For although . . . [Faustus] had made . . . [Satan] a promise,
yet hee might haue remembred throughe true repentance sinners
come again into the fauour of God' (*Damnable Life*, xiii). In fact,
the deed is validated from minute to minute only by Faustus' per-
sistent refusal to relinquish such power as he has acquired by his
presumption.

So Faustus, abjuring God in the hope of becoming something

more than a man, succeeds in fact in separating himself from God, isolating himself in large measure from his fellows, and consigning himself to the hell so powerfully suggested by Mephostophilis in scenes iii and v. Repentance remains possible; he represses yet another spontaneous impulse towards it as late as in scene xv. But it is unlikely to develop in one so lacking in humility and so greedy for the satisfactions, incomplete though they tend to be, which his sin brings him.

Incomplete they are indeed in comparison with what he felt able to promise himself in scene i. From scene viii to scene xvii, we watch him exploit his dearly-bought power. He goes on the rampage in the Vatican; he intervenes, effectively but inconclusively, in the strife between the Pope and the Emperor; he conjures for Charles V and revenges himself on a heckler; when the heckler retaliates, he takes a second revenge; he conjures for the Duke and Duchess of Vanholt; he tricks a horse-dealer; and, when the horse-dealer retaliates, he takes his revenge on him, too. For the 'world of profit and delight' which these escapades represent, Faustus voluntarily barters his soul.

Admittedly, these passages seem to be mainly the work of Marlowe's collaborator; and the change of authorship no doubt accounts for the temporary transformation of Faustus from an ambitious but sometimes fearful sinner into a jaunty pope-baiter and practical joker. But we are entitled to assume that the authors were writing to an agreed scenario, drafted perhaps by Marlowe himself. If they were, they presumably wished us to see that Faustus had made an even worse bargain than had at first appeared; and they presumably meant the rebuffs and refusals which Faustus endures, as already described, in scenes iii, v, and vi to prepare us for this perception. The collaborator had little talent, however, and produced a Faustus who is a poor substitute for Marlowe's. Nevertheless, the purpose embodied in the agreed scenario is still traceable in the text of the play.

We have observed several crises of conscience on Faustus' part. One more of these occurs towards the end of the twenty-four years allowed him in the deed of gift. In scene xviii, an Old Man exhorts him to repent before it is too late:

> Though thou hast now offended like a man,
> Do not persever in it like a devil.
> Yet, yet, thou hast an amiable soul,
> If sin by custom grow not into nature:
> Then, Faustus, will repentance come too late,
> Then thou art banish'd from the sight of heaven;
> No mortal can express the pains of hell.
>
>   (xviii. 41–7)

As Greg remarks, this Old Man might almost be the personified abstraction Good Counsel from a morality play. Equally reminiscent of the same older form of drama are Marlowe's use throughout of the two Angels, and of the diabolical characters, and his taking as his theme the struggle between the forces of good and evil for the soul of a representative man.

The good counsel has an immediate effect upon Faustus. But, since he lacks faith in God's mercy, this effect is merely to drive him towards despair.

> Damn'd art thou, Faustus, damn'd; despair and die!
>   (xviii. 56)

Mephostophilis hands him a dagger, and only the Old Man's intervention and his assurance that God's mercy is still available prevent Faustus from stabbing himself. As he struggles to repent and fights against despair, Mephostophilis repeats the treatment which proved so successful in scene vi. First he terrorizes Faustus:

> Revolt, or I'll in piecemeal tear thy flesh;   (xviii. 76)

then, when Faustus has submitted and has offered to renew the bond, he gratifies him with the 'sweet embraces' (xviii. 94) of Helen of Troy. Naturally, this is not Helen herself. Just as 'the royal shapes / Of Alexander and his paramour' (xii. 45–6) were presented by spirits, so Helen, too, is impersonated by a spirit; and Faustus in embracing her commits the sin of demoniality, or bodily intercourse with demons. The Old Man, learning this, concludes that he can now do nothing for Faustus; and by the next scene, his last, Faustus has finally added to his original presumption and abjuring of God the further mortal sin of despair.

Before he surrenders himself to Helen, Faustus utters his famous apostrophe, beginning:

> Was this the face that launch'd a thousand ships
> And burnt the topless towers of Ilium?
>
> (xviii. 99–100)

Frequent allusions in Marlowe's works show that he had fed his imagination on classical poetry and classical legend; and here, as already in ll. 23–32, he re-creates in highly evocative romantic terms the world of the *Iliad*. For this purpose he employs, perhaps for the last time, that formal, lyrical blank verse which he had developed in *Tamburlaine*. He shapes the latter part of the speech into two stanzas, each consisting of three rhymeless couplets, and then adds a concluding unpaired line to take the full weight of the vow with which Faustus finally commits himself:

> I will be Paris, and for love of thee
> Instead of Troy shall Wittenberg be sack'd,
> And I will combat with weak Menelaus
> And wear thy colours on my plumed crest,
> Yea, I will wound Achilles in the heel
> And then return to Helen for a kiss.
> O, thou art fairer than the evening's air
> Clad in the beauty of a thousand stars,
> Brighter art thou than flaming Jupiter
> When he appear'd to hapless Semele,
> More lovely than the monarch of the sky
> In wanton Arethusa's azur'd arms,
> And none but thou shalt be my paramour.
>
> (xviii. 106–18)

Throughout this rhapsody we hear once more the note of elation which was so strong in the earlier scenes of the play; and the long-continued popularity of the speech apart from its context shows that readers have been able without misgiving to take it as expressing a simple, eager aspiration. But the speech is actually addressed to a fiend, who will indeed suck forth Faustus' soul; it is the immediate prelude to the sin which plunges him into irremediable despair; and its significance is underlined by the presence during most of it of the Old Man, whose comment becomes vocal at its close. Arousing these conflicting responses, the incident may reasonably be regarded as epitomizing the basic theme of the whole play.

By scene xix, then, Faustus has entirely lost hope. In a prose

passage which must be one of the very few we have by Marlowe,
he takes a moving farewell of the Scholars. Mephostophilis assures
him that it is now too late to repent; and when the Angels enter
immediately afterwards they merely moralize upon the fact of his
damnation. There follows the great soliloquy which expresses
Faustus' states of mind and feeling during his last hour.

There is general agreement that this is Marlowe's most mature
passage of dramatic verse. It contrasts sharply not merely with the
set speeches in *Tamburlaine* but even with the apostrophe to Helen.
Whereas they are passages of more or less formal eloquence, this
develops flexibly, unpredictably, even disconcertingly. Shrinking
in terror, Faustus first addresses himself in a long series of mono-
syllables terminated emphatically by the polysyllable which focuses
his dread:

> Now hast thou but one bare hour to live,
> And then thou must be damn'd perpetually.
>
> (xix. 134–5)

He appeals for time, for

> A year, a month, a week, a natural day,   (xix. 140)

in which to repent, thus implicitly admitting that his deed of gift
did not make repentance impossible; and this appeal culminates in
his poignant quotation of a line of Latin verse. Ovid, whom he
quotes, wished to lengthen out the pleasure of the night; Faustus
wishes simply to postpone the anguish of the morrow. The useless-
ness of the appeal is conveyed in a two-line sentence which, starting
with an almost stately slowness, accelerates sharply to allude again
to his imminent damnation:

> The stars move still, time runs, the clock will strike,
> The devil will come, and Faustus must be damn'd.
>
> (xix. 143–4)

Even as late as this, he has an intimation of the divine mercy, though
it is now unattainable by him:

> See, see where Christ's blood streams in the firmament!
>
> (xix. 146)

and he seems to strain upwards in the broken alexandrine which
immediately follows. Again he quails when tormented by the

fiends; and by calling desperately upon Lucifer to spare him he surrenders himself afresh.

Enough has been said, perhaps, to display something of the dramatic urgency and widely varied expressiveness of this great monologue, in which Faustus shows himself agonizingly aware of 'the heavy wrath of God' (xix. 153) against which his Good Angel warned him in scene i. Towards its close, he forswears his humanism. Having prided himself on his self-reliance, and having even striven to be more than a man, he now longs to be less than a man; he wishes he could be 'a creature wanting soul' (xix. 172), 'some brutish beast' (xix. 176), which at death would face mere extinction and not eternal damnation. He curses his parents for engendering him. No doubt the 'books' (xix. 190) which he offers to burn are primarily his books of magic. But the word reminds us of his exclamation to the Scholars earlier in the scene: 'O, would I had never seen Wittenberg, never read book!' (xix. 45–6); and we retain the impression that Faustus is ascribing his downfall in part to his learning. Hearing or reading these concluding lines, and relating them to all that has preceded them, we can surely have no hesitation in thinking of Faustus as embodying the new inquiring and aspiring spirit of the age of the Renaissance, and of Marlowe as expressing in this play both his fervent sympathy with that new spirit and, ultimately, his awed and pitiful recognition of the peril into which it could lead those whom it dominated. Perhaps this is not quite the Faustus we should have expected from the Marlowe described in section I of this 'Introduction'. But we must beware of assuming too simple a relationship between any artist and his work; and, even if the relationship was in this instance a simple one, *Doctor Faustus* apparently belongs to the last year of Marlowe's life and therefore to the latest stage of whatever development he was undergoing.

The farcical prose scenes call for little attention. Naturally, topics which are important in the more serious scenes tend to be echoed in them. Wagner, for example, asserts that Robin 'would give his soul to the devil for a shoulder of mutton' (iv. 9–10); and in scene x Robin conjures up an irate Mephostophilis. No doubt there is a touch of crude burlesque in such places. But the current critical fashion ordains that we should go further and discern in them a profound, subtle, and sustained irony. We shall do well to remember that there is a limit to the violence that we are entitled to do to common sense in the name of literary criticism. Most of the resemblances which have been traced between these unfunny scenes and the more serious action of the play are quite remarkably slight. One instance will suffice. In scene ix, Faustus snatches away the Pope's food and drink; in scene x, the two clowns enter with a cup they have stolen from an inn. What kind of resemblance is this? As Captain Fluellen might have said, 'There is drinking-vessels (of one sort or another) in both!'

10. THE STAGE-HISTORY OF THE PLAY

The earliest stage-history of *Doctor Faustus* is conjectural. Greg suggests that the play belonged originally to the Earl of Pembroke's Men and that they acted it both at court in the winter of 1592–3 and at the Theatre, during a brief intermission of the plague, in January 1593. But the playhouses were closed again early in 1593 by one of the century's worst outbreaks of the plague. Pembroke's Men, like others, went on tour in the provinces. Even so, they were in financial difficulties by the autumn. Greg conjectures that they then sold their prompt-copy of *Doctor Faustus* to Philip Henslowe but afterwards reconstructed the text from memory to make up a new book for themselves.[1]

At all events, *Doctor Faustus* was in Henslowe's hands by 30 September 1594 when the Lord Admiral's Men at the Rose staged the earliest performance of it of which we have a record. Though the play was not new, the takings amounted to as much as £3 12s.[2] Edward Alleyn appears to have played Faustus at this period, and an informant writing fifteen years later describes him, somewhat surprisingly, as wearing for this purpose

a surplis,
With a crosse vpon his breast.[3]

Henslowe in his *Diary* records ten more performances during the following four-and-a-half months and a further twelve during the

---

[1] Pp. 60–2.   [2] *Henslowe's Diary*, fol. 10ʳ.
[3] S. Rowlands, *The Knave of Clubs* (London, 1609), p. 29.

subsequent period of nearly two years ending 5 January 1596/7. On this last occasion, the takings amounted to a mere 5s.[1] But, as soon as Pembroke's Men joined forces with the Admiral's at the Rose in October 1597, *Doctor Faustus* was staged once more. It is regrettable that Henslowe has left no record of the receipts on this occasion.[2]

During this same month the Lord Admiral became the Earl of Nottingham. The title-page of the 1604 quarto of *Doctor Faustus* describes the actors as the Earl of Nottingham's servants. If they performed the play while bearing that name, they must have done so during the six years starting October 1597, since they became Prince Henry's Men shortly after the accession of James I in 1603. It is reasonable to assume that a revival followed Henslowe's payment of £4 on 22 November 1602 for the additions by Birde and Rowley. But there is no saying which version of the play had a place in the repertory of the company of English actors which was at Graz in Styria in 1608.[3] The publication of as many as nine quarto editions between 1604 and 1631 may be regarded as evidence that *Doctor Faustus* maintained its popularity in England during the early Stuart period. G. E. Bentley has shown[4] that it was still being performed at the Fortune by Prince Charles' Men a year or so before the theatres were closed on the outbreak of war in 1642.

In a work published in 1620, John Melton tells something of how *Doctor Faustus* was produced at 'the *Fortune* in *Golding-Lane*' by the Palsgrave's Men, formerly Prince Henry's Men. 'There indeede', he writes, 'a man may behold shagge-hayr'd Deuills runne roaring ouer the Stage with Squibs in their mouthes, while Drummers make Thunder in the Tyring-house, and the twelue-penny Hirelings make artificiall Lightning in their Heauens.'[5] Such representations offended the Puritans, who put into circulation stories such as that of 'the *visible apparition of the Devill on the Stage at the Belsavage Play-house, in Queene* Elizabeths *dayes, (to the great amazement both of the Actors and Spectators) whiles they were there*

---

[1] *Henslowe's Diary*, fol. 25ᵛ.   [2] *Ibid.*, fol. 27ᵛ.
[3] Chambers, *E.S.*, ii. 281.
[4] *The Jacobean and Caroline Stage* (5 vols., Oxford, 1941–56), i. 318–19.
[5] *Astrologaster* (London, 1620), p. 31.

prophanely playing the History of Faustus (the truth of which I have
heard from many now alive, who well remember it,) *there being some
distracted with that fearefull sight*.[1] Similar to this is the account of
'Certaine Players at Exeter, acting upon the stage the tragical storie
of Dr. Faustus the Conjurer', who were overcome by the conviction
that 'there was one devell too many amongst them; and so after a
little pause desired the people to pardon them, they could go no
further with this matter; the people also understanding the thing
as it was, every man hastened to be first out of dores. The players
(as I heard it) contrarye to their custome spending the night in reading and in prayer got them out of the town the next morning.'[2] John
Aubrey, too, has a version of this story, which bears a curious resemblance to one that the Roman Catholics told about a play which
had offended them in 1586.[3]

During the Commonwealth period, all theatres were closed. But
after the Restoration Samuel Pepys took his wife to see *Doctor
Faustus* at the Red Bull on 26 May 1662. It was 'so wretchedly and
poorly done, that we were sick of it.'[4] Dr Edward Browne apparently saw it at the end of the same year.[5] They must have seen the
version 'as it is now Acted With several New Scenes' that was
printed in 1663. Very likely this version served for the performance
by the Duke of York's Company before royalty on 28 September
1675.[6] In the same year, Edward Phillips, the nephew of John
Milton, declared that, of all Marlowe's plays, *Doctor Faustus* had
created the greatest stir.[7]

It then disappeared from the English stage for two centuries.
Certain of its episodes were preserved in a mutilated form, and
diversified by the introduction of Harlequin and Scaramouche, in

---

[1] W. Prynne, *Histrio-Mastix* (London, 1633), fol. 556.
[2] Chambers, *E.S.*, iii. 424.
[3] Winifred Smith, 'Anti-Catholic Propaganda in Elizabethan London',
M.P., xxviii (1930–1), pp. 208–12.
[4] *Diary* (ed. H. B. Wheatley, 10 vols., London, 1893–9), ii. 244.
[5] L. Hotson, *The Commonwealth and Restoration Stage* (Cambridge,
1928), pp. 178–9.
[6] Allardyce Nicoll, *A History of English Drama 1660–1900* (6 vols., Cambridge, 1952–9), i. 348.
[7] *Theatrum Poetarum* (ed. Egerton Brydges, Geneva, 1824), pp. xvii–
xviii.

a farce which William Mountfort produced in the autumn of 1688.[1] But not even as tenuous a relationship as this existed between Marlowe's play and the two rival pantomimes which were performed in London in 1723: *Harlequin Doctor Faustus* by John Thurmond at Drury Lane, and *The Necromancer, or Harlequin Doctor Faustus* at Lincoln's Inn Fields.[2] Pope derides these and other similarly spectacular productions in *The Dunciad*, iii. 233–40. *Harlequin and Faustus*, acted at Covent Garden in 1793, was another pantomime.[3] Except in such pieces, and in puppet-plays, Faustus made no entry upon the eighteenth-century English stage.

When he returned in the nineteenth century it was for a long time only in various operatic and other more or less free adaptations of Goethe's *Faust*. Theatrically, these culminated in the production of W. G. Wills' version at the Lyceum in December 1885, with Henry Irving as Mephistopheles and with a Brocken scene that was especially admired.[4] At last, at the end of the century, on 2 and 4 July 1896, the Elizabethan Stage Society, under the direction of William Poel, revived Marlowe's play in St George's Hall on a stage reproducing that of the old Fortune playhouse which had once resounded to the roaring of the 'shagge-hayr'd Deuills'. The same society gave performances at the Court Theatre and at Terry's Theatre in October and December 1904 and also in various English and Scottish towns during a six-week tour.[5] The first German production, apart from those of the visiting companies of English actors in the seventeenth century, was at Heidelberg in 1903;[6] the earliest American production was at Princeton University, under the supervision of R. K. Root, in the spring of 1907.[7]

Since then the play has been acted many times in all of these countries. In England, the Phoenix Society revived it at the New

[1] L. Hughes, 'The Date of Mountfort's *Faustus*', *N. & Q.*, CXCII (1947), pp. 358–9.

[2] Allardyce Nicoll, *op. cit.*, ii. 360, 379.   [3] *Ibid.*, iii. 330.

[4] Austin Brereton, *The Life of Henry Irving* (2 vols., London, 1908), ii. 85–96.

[5] There is a good account of this production in R. Speaight, *William Poel and the Elizabethan Revival* (London, 1954), pp. 113–19.

[6] H. M. Flasdieck, 'Zur Datierung von Marlowes Faust', *E.S.*, LXIV (1929), p. 321, n. 4.

[7] Root, reviewing three studies of *Faustus*, *E.S.*, XLIII (1910–11), p. 130.

Oxford Theatre on 25 October 1925. On the previous 24 July, William Poel had directed a rendering of selected scenes by Marlowe, including episodes from *Doctor Faustus*, at the Haymarket Theatre in aid of the fund for the completion of the Marlowe Memorial at Canterbury. Henry Ainley was one of the actors. The 1929 Festival of Music and Drama at Canterbury included three performances of the tragedy on 20, 22, and 24 August by the Norwich Maddermarket Theatre players under the direction of Nugent Monck.[1] There was a further revival at the Rudolf Steiner Hall, London, on 12 March 1940.

In 1942, the directors of the Liverpool repertory theatre, the Playhouse, let their premises to the Old Vic for the duration of the war and a year beyond; and in this theatre the Old Vic company staged a successful production of *Doctor Faustus* on 16 May 1944. D. A. Clarke-Smith played Faustus, Noel Willman played Mephostophilis, and John Moody produced the play. Two more revivals followed soon afterwards. As part of the Stratford Festivals of 1946 and 1947, the play was put on at the Shakespeare Memorial Theatre. Walter Hudd produced it. His Faustus was Robert Harris; his Mephostophilis was Hugh Griffith in 1946, Paul Scofield in 1947. In the following year, on 7 October 1948, the Old Vic company presented the play at the New Theatre, London. Cedric Hardwicke played Faustus, Robert Eddison Mephostophilis; the direction was in the hands of John Burrell. This production evidently disappointed the critics.[2] They thought it less imaginative than that at Stratford, and they found its Faustus too sober. They were more favourable to the same company's staging of the play at the Edinburgh Festival of 1961. Michael Benthall's production made impressive use of an open stage, and the performances of Paul Daneman as Faustus and Michael Goodliffe as Mephostophilis were highly praised, as was also Robert Atkins' playing of the Old Man.[3]

In 1950, the Compass Players included a severely cut but still

[1] These British performances from 1896 to 1929 are recorded by H. Child, 'Revivals of English Dramatic Works', *R.E.S.*, II (1926), pp. 177–88, and III (1927), pp. 169–85; and by Boas.

[2] See Audrey Williamson, *Old Vic Drama* 2 (London, 1957), pp. 15–17.

[3] See *Guardian*, 23 August 1961, and *Times*, 24 August 1961.

effective version of *Doctor Faustus* in their touring repertory. Their producer was John Crockett. On 6 April 1956, the Tavistock Repertory Company presented the play, under the direction of Eva Halterman, at the Tower, Canonbury. There have also been a number of relatively unpublicized provincial revivals, including some by student and other amateur dramatic societies.

One of these, by the O.U.D.S., was broadcast on 13 April 1934. The British Broadcasting Corporation has sponsored nine other presentations of the play on sound radio since early in 1929. Listeners have heard, among others, Ion Swinley, William Devlin, Robert Donat, Ralph Richardson, Alec Guinness, Robert Harris, and Stephen Murray as Faustus, and Robert Farquharson, Marius Goring, Ernest Milton, Laidman Browne, Peter Ustinov, and Esmé Percy as Mephostophilis. Stephen Harrison produced the play on B.B.C. television on 22 June 1947 with David King-Wood as Faustus and Hugh Griffith as Mephostophilis. On 21 February 1958, in a B.B.C. television programme for schools, William Squire and James Maxwell played these two parts under the direction of Ronald Eyre. Eyre produced the play again in a programme for schools, with the same Mephostophilis but with Alan Dobie as Faustus, on 7 and 14 November 1961.[1]

An outstanding American staging of *Doctor Faustus* was sponsored by the Works Progress Administration in 1937. The producer was Orson Welles, who played Faustus. Jack Carter played Mephostophilis, and Joseph Cotten was also in the cast. It was a great triumph and ran at the Maxine Elliott Theatre, New York, for six months. Welles himself considers this to have been the most satisfying of all his stage productions, and it is now generally regarded as a landmark of the twentieth-century American theatre. Welles also played Faustus in Paris in 1950 in his own version of the play, with Eartha Kitt as Helen and with music by Duke Ellington.[2]

---

[1] This paragraph is based upon information supplied by the B.B.C.
[2] Peter Noble, *The Fabulous Orson Welles* (London, 1956), pp. 80–2, 222–4.

THE TRAGICAL HISTORY OF
THE LIFE AND DEATH OF
DOCTOR FAUSTUS

[DRAMATIS PERSONAE

CHORUS.

DOCTOR JOHN FAUSTUS.
WAGNER, *a student, his servant.*
VALDES, } *friends to Faustus.*
CORNELIUS,   5
THREE SCHOLARS, *students under Faustus.*
AN OLD MAN.

POPE ADRIAN.
RAYMOND, *King of Hungary.*
BRUNO, *the rival Pope.*   10
THE CARDINALS OF FRANCE AND PADUA.
THE ARCHBISHOP OF RHEIMS.
CHARLES V, *Emperor of Germany.*
MARTINO,
FREDERICK, } *gentlemen at his court.*   15
BENVOLIO,
THE DUKE OF SAXONY.
THE DUKE OF VANHOLT.
THE DUCHESS OF VANHOLT.
BISHOPS, MONKS, FRIARS, SOLDIERS, *and* ATTENDANTS.   20

ROBIN, *called the Clown.*
DICK.

Dramatis Personae] *not in A1, B1.*

Dramatis Personae] There is no such list in any quarto before that of 1663, which contains an inaccurate one. Dyce provides one for each version of the play. The present list derives to some extent from those of Boas and Greg.

   8. *Pope Adrian*] See comment on viii. 90–6.

   9–10.] Raymond and Bruno seem to have had no historical originals.

   18–19.] Boas alters this name to 'Anholt' on the authority of the *Damnable Life.* But both A1 and B1 consistently print 'Vanholt'.

   22. *Dick*] known in A1 as 'Ralph'. See Appendix I.

A VINTNER.
A HORSE-COURSER.
A CARTER.   25
A HOSTESS.

GOOD ANGEL.
BAD ANGEL.
MEPHOSTOPHILIS.
LUCIFER.   30
BEELZEBUB.
PRIDE,
COVETOUSNESS,
ENVY,
WRATH,   } the Seven Deadly Sins.   35
GLUTTONY,
SLOTH,
LECHERY,
ALEXANDER THE GREAT,
HIS PARAMOUR,   40
DARIUS, *King of Persia,*   } *spirits.*
HELEN,
TWO CUPIDS,
DEVILS *and* A PIPER.]

---

29. *Mephostophilis*] This is B1's usual spelling of the name. Greg retains it in his modern-spelling edition. See also Appendix II.

The Tragical History of the Life and Death of Doctor Faustus

[Prologue]

Enter Chorus.

Cho. Not marching in the fields of Trasimene
    Where Mars did mate the warlike Carthagens,
    Nor sporting in the dalliance of love
    In courts of kings where state is overturn'd,
    Nor in the pomp of proud audacious deeds   5
    Intends our muse to vaunt his heavenly verse:
    Only this, gentles—we must now perform
    The form of Faustus' fortunes, good or bad:
    And now to patient judgements we appeal,
    And speak for Faustus in his infancy.   10
    Now is he born, of parents base of stock,

Heading. The . . . Faustus] *B1 (title-page); THE TRAGEDIE OF Doctor Faustus. B1 (heading); The tragicall Historie of Doctor Faustus. A1 (heading).*
Prologue. 1. *Cho.] Oxberry; not in A1, B1.*   in the] *B1;* now in *A1.*
2. warlike Carthagens] *B1;* Carthaginians *A1.*   6. vaunt] *B1;* daunt *A1.*
7. gentles] *B1;* Gentlemen *A1.*   now] *B1; not in A1.*   9. And now] *B1; not in A1;* And so *Greg.*   appeal] *B1;* appeale our plaude *A1.*   11. of parents] *B1;* his parents *A1.*

    1–2. *marching . . . Carthagens*] There is no other trace of this play on Hannibal in Italy. Since its author must surely have known, and shown, that the Carthaginians were victorious in the battle of Lake Trasimene (217 B.C.), 'mate' should be understood not as 'defeat' but as 'ally himself with'.

    3–5.] If the references here are to extant plays by Marlowe, that in ll. 3–4 is presumably to *Edward II* and that in l. 5 to *Tamburlaine*.

    4. *state*] government.

    6. *our muse*] our poet.

    vaunt] display proudly.

    7–8. *perform The form*] Marlowe was fond of jingles of this sort: see Prologue, 16–17, and vi. 42.

4

In Germany, within a town call'd Rhode;
At riper years to Wittenberg he went,
Whereas his kinsmen chiefly brought him up.
So much he profits in divinity,   15
The fruitful plot of scholarism grac'd,
That shortly he was grac'd with doctor's name,
Excelling all, and sweetly can dispute
In th' heavenly matters of theology;
Till, swollen with cunning of a self-conceit,   20
His waxen wings did mount above his reach,
And, melting, heavens conspir'd his overthrow;
For, falling to a devilish exercise,
And glutted now with learning's golden gifts,
He surfeits upon cursed necromancy;   25
Nothing so sweet as magic is to him,
Which he prefers before his chiefest bliss:
And this the man that in his study sits.   *Exit.*

12. Rhode] *Boas; Rhodes A1, B1.*   13. At] *B1;* Of *A1.*   15. much]
B1; soone *A1.*   16. The . . . grac'd,] *A1; not in B1.*   18. and . . .
dispute] *B1;* whose sweete delight disputes *A1.*   19. th'] *B1; not in A1.*
20. of] *A1, B1;* and *B2.*   24. now] *B1;* more *A1.*   28. *Exit.*] *A1;
not in B1.*

12. *Rhode*] Roda (since 1922, Stadtroda) in central Germany.
14. *Whereas*] where.
16.] 'the fruitful garden of scholarship being adorned by him' (Ward).
17. *grac'd with doctor's name*] Boas points out that Marlowe evidently
had in mind the Cambridge official 'grace' permitting a candidate to pro-
ceed to his degree.
18. *and sweetly can dispute*] Greg rejects this as a piece of rewriting by
the editor of B1, who disregarded 'the fact that sweetness, while appropriate to delight, is an unusual quality in theological controversy'. But
'sweetly' here means 'persuasively'. See *O.E.D., sweet, adj.,* 5c.
20. *cunning of a self-conceit*] 'intellectual pride engendered by arrogance'
(Greg).
22. *melting*] i.e. the wings melting. Marlowe refers to the death of Icarus,
who flew too close to the sun, with the result that it melted the wax attach-
ing his wings to his body and he fell into the sea. Compare *Dido, Queen of
Carthage,* v. i. 243–5.
   heavens conspir'd his overthrow] Compare 1 *Tamburlaine,* IV. ii. 8–11:
'God . . . / Will sooner burn the glorious frame of heaven / Than it should
so conspire my overthrow.'
27. *before his chiefest bliss*] to his hopes of salvation.

[Scene i]

FAUSTUS *in his study.*

Fau. Settle thy studies, Faustus, and begin
        To sound the depth of that thou wilt profess;
        Having commenc'd, be a divine in show,
        Yet level at the end of every art,
        And live and die in Aristotle's works.   5
        Sweet Analytics, 'tis thou hast ravish'd me!
        Bene disserere est finis logices.
        Is to dispute well logic's chiefest end?
        Affords this art no greater miracle?
        Then read no more, thou hast attain'd that end;   10
        A greater subject fitteth Faustus' wit.

i. 0.1. FAUSTUS] *B1; Enter Faustus A1.*   7. *logices*] *B4; Logicis A1, B1.*
10. that] *B1;* the *A1.*

---

i. 0.1. *Faustus* in his study] The Chorus, before leaving, draws aside a
curtain and reveals Faustus.

1–37.] In this earlier part of Faustus' soliloquy, Marlowe seems to owe
something to Lyly's *Euphues* (ed. Bond, i. 241): 'Philosophie, Phisicke,
Diuinitie, shal be my studie. O yᵉ hidden secrets of Nature, the expresse
image of morall vertues, the equall ballaunce of Iustice, the medicines to
heale all diseases, how they beginne to delyght me. The *Axiomaes* of *Aristotle*, the *Maxims* of *Iustinian*, the *Aphorismes* of *Galen*, haue sodaynelye
made such a breache into my minde that I seeme onely to desire them which
did onely earst detest them.'

2. *profess*] claim proficiency in and teach.

3. *commenc'd*] taken a degree, here the doctorate in divinity. Like 'grac'd'
in Prologue, 17, 'commenc'd' is a technical Cambridge term.

4. *level*] aim.

5–7.] At this date, Aristotle still dominated the university curriculum,
but his supremacy had recently been challenged by the intellectual re-
former and opponent of scholasticism Petrus Ramus (Pierre de la Ramée,
1515–72). While Marlowe was at Cambridge, William Temple was success-
fully defending Ramism against the attacks of Everard Digby. *The Massacre
at Paris*, vi, testifies to Marlowe's knowledge of Ramus' theories and of
their author's violent death; and it is interesting to note that the Latin defi-
nition of the purpose of logic in the present passage, 'To argue well is the
end of logic', derives, as Ward discovered, not from Aristotle but from
Ramus.

6. *Analytics*] the name given to two works by Aristotle on the nature of
proof in argument.

11. *wit*] understanding.

Bid *on kai me on* farewell, Galen come,
Seeing *ubi desinit philosophus, ibi incipit medicus.*
Be a physician, Faustus, heap up gold,
And be eterniz'd for some wondrous cure.   15
Summum bonum medicinae sanitas,
The end of physic is our body's health.
Why, Faustus, hast thou not attain'd that end ?
Is not thy common talk sound aphorisms ?
Are not thy bills hung up as monuments,   20
Whereby whole cities have escap'd the plague
And thousand desperate maladies been cur'd ?
Yet art thou still but Faustus, and a man.
Couldst thou make men to live eternally
Or being dead raise them to life again,   25
Then this profession were to be esteem'd.
Physic, farewell! Where is Justinian ?

---

12. *on kai me on*] Bullen; Oncaymæon *A1;* Oeconomy *A2, A3, B1.*   Galen]
A1; and Galen *B1.*   13. Seeing . . . *medicus.*] *A1; not in B1.*   19. Is . . .
aphorisms ?] *A1; not in B1.*   22. thousand] *A1, B1;* diuers *B2.*   cur'd]
B1; easde *A1.*   24. Couldst] *B1;* wouldst *A1.*   men] *B1;* man *A1.*

---

12. on kai me on] As Bullen saw, this is Marlowe's transliteration of the
Greek phrase meaning 'being and not being'. But Bullen, Ward, Boas,
Kocher, and Greg are surely mistaken in describing the formula as Aris-
totelian. Its earliest appearance seems to be in Gorgias, cited by Sextus
Empiricus, *Adversus Mathematicos,* vii. 66.

Galen] This second-century Greek physician and prolific author was
accepted throughout the Middle Ages as the leading authority on medical
science.

13. ubi . . . medicus] Where the philosopher leaves off, there the physician
begins. The sentence is freely adapted from Aristotle, *De Sensu,* 436a.

15. *eterniz'd*] immortalized.

16.] The greatest good of medicine is health. Latinized from Aristotle,
Nicomachean Ethics, 1094a.

19. *sound aphorisms*] reliable medical precepts. The term 'aphorisms' in
this sense comes from the title of a work by Hippocrates, the 'Father of
Medicine'.

20. *bills . . . monuments*] prescriptions displayed as enduring examples of
medical art.

22. *thousand desperate maladies*] Greg, taking 'maladies' to mean 'diseases' or 'epidemics', feels 'thousand' to be excessive and imports B2's
'diuers' in its place. But 'thousand' ceases to be excessive if 'maladies' is
taken to mean 'individual cases of sickness'.

Si una eademque res legatur duobus, alter rem, alter valorem rei, etc.

A petty case of paltry legacies!   30

Exhereditare filium non potest pater, nisi—
Such is the subject of the Institute
And universal body of the law.
This study fits a mercenary drudge
Who aims at nothing but external trash,   35
Too servile and illiberal for me.
When all is done, divinity is best.
Jerome's Bible, Faustus, view it well.

Stipendium peccati mors est. Ha! *Stipendium, etc.* The reward of sin is death: that's hard. *Si peccasse negamus,* 40 *fallimur, et nulla est in nobis veritas.* If we say that we have no sin, we deceive ourselves, and there's no truth in us. Why, then, belike we must sin, and so consequently die.

Ay, we must die an everlasting death.   45

28. *legatur*] *Dilke; legatus A1, B1.*   30. petty] *B1;* pretty *A1.*   31. *Exhereditare*] *Dyce; Exhereditari A1, B1.*   33. law] *B1;* Church *A1.* 34. This] *B1;* His *A1.*   36. Too servile] *B1;* The deuill *A1.*   39–44.] *Prose as here Dyce; verse divided after etc.,* hard, veritas, no sin, us, must sin, die *A1, B1.*   42. there's] *A1;* there is *B1.*

28–9.] If one and the same thing is bequeathed to two persons, one of them shall have the thing, the other the value of the thing, etc. As Ward shows, this derives in part from a passage in book II, title xx, of the *Institutes* of Justinian, the sixth-century emperor who codified the Roman law.

31.] A father cannot disinherit his son, except—. This expresses incompletely the sense of a passage in book II, title xiii, of the *Institutes.*

35. *trash*] contemptuously applied to money.

37. *When all is done*] after all.

38. *Jerome's Bible*] the Vulgate, the edition of the Latin Bible prepared mainly by St Jerome. The sentences which Faustus quotes and translates in ll. 39–43 are from Rom. vi. 23 and 1 John i. 8.

39–45.] There is nothing subversive of Christian doctrine in a syllogism which shows that man is condemned by the letter of the law. What is unorthodox is Faustus' refusal to see that man, thus condemned, may be redeemed by the sacrifice of Christ. There is a refutation on these lines of the identical syllogism in the opening pages of *The Dialogue Between the Christian Knight and Satan* by Thomas Becon (1512–67). See Kocher, *C.M.,* pp. 106–7.

What doctrine call you this ? *Che sarà, sarà*:
What will be, shall be! Divinity, adieu!
These metaphysics of magicians
And necromantic books are heavenly;
Lines, circles, letters, and characters: 50
Ay, these are those that Faustus most desires.
O, what a world of profit and delight,
Of power, of honour, of omnipotence,
Is promis'd to the studious artisan!
All things that move between the quiet poles   55
Shall be at my command: emperors and kings
Are but obey'd in their several provinces,
Nor can they raise the wind or rend the clouds;
But his dominion that exceeds in this
Stretcheth as far as doth the mind of man: 60
A sound magician is a demi-god;
Here tire, my brains, to get a deity!

50. letters] *B1;* sceanes, letters *A1;* signs, letters *Greg.*   and] *A1; not in*
B1.   53. of omnipotence] *A1;* and omnipotence *B1.*   58. Nor . . .
clouds;] *A1; not in B1.*   59. exceeds] *A1, B1;* excels *Greg.*   61. demi-
god] *B1;* mighty god *A1.*   62. tire, my] *B1; Faustus* trie thy *A1.*   get]
B1; gaine *A1, B2.*

46-7. Che . . . *adieu*] The Italian proverb, without Faustus' translation
of it, and the farewell to divinity are quoted verbatim with an ascription
to Faustus among certain marginalia in a copy of a book by John Leland
published in 1589. These marginalia are almost certainly in the hand of
Thomas Nashe. See P. H. Kocher, 'Some Nashe Marginalia Concerning
Marlowe', *M.L.N.*, LVII (1942), pp. 45-9. Marlowe has 'that shall be, shall
be' in *Edward II*, IV. vi. 94.
   48. *metaphysics*] supernatural arts.
   50.] Ward explains that magicians drew 'lines' and 'circles' around themselves for protection against evil spirits; that they made use of magical
combinations of 'letters' taken from the several forms of the divine name;
and that they employed as charms the 'characters' or signs appropriated
to good spirits of various kinds.
   54. *artisan*] artist.
   55. *quiet*] because motionless.
   57. *several*] respective.
   59. *his . . . this*] the dominion of him who excels in this art.
   62. *tire*] exhaust yourselves.
   get] beget.

Enter WAGNER.

Wagner, commend me to my dearest friends,
The German Valdes and Cornelius;
Request them earnestly to visit me.   65
Wag. I will, sir.   *Exit.*
Fau. Their conference will be a greater help to me
Than all my labours, plod I ne'er so fast.

Enter the Angel *and* Spirit.

Good Ang. O Faustus, lay that damned book aside
And gaze not on it lest it tempt thy soul   70
And heap God's heavy wrath upon thy head.
Read, read the scriptures; that is blasphemy.
Bad Ang. Go forward, Faustus, in that famous art
Wherein all nature's treasury is contain'd:
Be thou on earth as Jove is in the sky,   75
Lord and commander of these elements.   *Exeunt* Angels.
Fau. How am I glutted with conceit of this!
Shall I make spirits fetch me what I please,
Resolve me of all ambiguities,
Perform what desperate enterprise I will?   80
I'll have them fly to India for gold,

68.1. *Enter* ... Spirit.] *B1; Enter the good Angell and the euill Angell. A1.*
74. treasury] *A1;* treasure *A2, A3, B1.*   76. Angels] *B1; not in A1.*

---

67. *conference*] conversation.

68.1. Enter the *Angel* and *Spirit*] It is reasonable to assume that these
enter by separate doors and that each of them uses the same door throughout the play. But the only stage-direction to speak of their entering by
separate doors is at xix. 98.1. 'Spirit' is used throughout to mean specifically an evil spirit or devil.

72. *that*] i.e. the book of magic.

75. *Jove*] The application of this pagan name to the God of Christianity
was not rare during the Renaissance period. Marlowe so applies it twice
more in this play: in iii. 91, and in Cho. 1. 3.

76. *these elements*] used to mean 'the elements', both here and in v. 120.

77. *conceit of this*] the notion of obtaining such power.

79. *Resolve me of*] free me from doubt concerning.

81. *India*] The name was given at this time to 'both the'India's of spice
and Myne' (Donne, 'The Sunne Rising'). It is probable that the East Indies

Ransack the ocean for orient pearl,
And search all corners of the new-found world
For pleasant fruits and princely delicates;
I'll have them read me strange philosophy   85
And tell the secrets of all foreign kings;
I'll have them wall all Germany with brass
And make swift Rhine circle fair Wittenberg;
I'll have them fill the public schools with silk
Wherewith the students shall be bravely clad;   90
I'll levy soldiers with the coin they bring
And chase the Prince of Parma from our land
And reign sole king of all our provinces;
Yea, stranger engines for the brunt of war
Than was the fiery keel at Antwerp's bridge   95
I'll make my servile spirits to invent.

88. make] *A1, B1*; with *B2*.   89. silk] *Dyce;* skill *A1, B1*.   93. our]
A1; the *A2, A3, B1*.   95. Antwerp's] *A1; Anwerpe B1*.

---

are meant here in contrast to the 'new-found' America two lines later.

82–3.] These lines seem to be echoed in the anonymous *Taming of a
Shrew* (ed. Boas), II. i. 79–80: 'To seeke for strange and new-found pretious
stones, / And dive into the sea to gather pearle'.

82. *orient*] lustrous; strictly, from the eastern seas.

84. *delicates*] delicacies.

87. *wall . . . brass*] Friar Bacon planned to wall England with brass. See
Greene, *Friar Bacon and Friar Bungay* (ed. Greg), ll. 204, 351.

89. *the public schools*] the university lecture-rooms.

silk] Dyce's emendation receives some support from the fact that the
Nashe marginalia mentioned in the note on ll. 46–7 above include the jot-
ting, 'Faustus: studie in indian silke.' Whatever Nashe may have meant by
this, his words seem to derive from ll. 81 and 89–90 of the present speech.
Since the play was not printed until after his death, he was presumably
recollecting what he had heard in the theatre.

90. *bravely*] splendidly. The universities required students to dress
plainly.

92. *the Prince of Parma*] Spanish governor-general of the Netherlands,
then nominally part of the Empire, from 1579 until his death in 1592. He
was the foremost soldier of his time. In 1588 the Spanish Armada was to
have enabled him to invade England.

94. *brunt*] assault, onset.

95. *the fiery . . . bridge*] On 4 April 1585, a fire-ship dispatched by the
Netherlanders shattered the bridge which Parma had built over the Scheldt
to complete the blockade of Antwerp.

Enter VALDES *and* CORNELIUS.

Come, German Valdes and Cornelius,
And make me blest with your sage conference.
Valdes, sweet Valdes, and Cornelius,
Know that your words have won me at the last   100
To practise magic and concealed arts;
Yet not your words only, but mine own fantasy,
That will receive no object, for my head
But ruminates on necromantic skill.

Philosophy is odious and obscure,   105
Both law and physic are for petty wits,
Divinity is basest of the three,
Unpleasant, harsh, contemptible, and vile;
'Tis magic, magic, that hath ravish'd me.

Then, gentle friends, aid me in this attempt,   110
And I, that have with concise syllogisms
Gravell'd the pastors of the German church,
And made the flowering pride of Wittenberg
Swarm to my problems as the infernal spirits

96.1.] *Stage-direction placed as here Dilke; after 99 A1; in right-hand margin, 98–9, B1.*   98. blest] *A1, B1;* wise *B2.*   102–4. Yet . . . skill.] *A1; not in B1.*   107–8. Divinity . . . vile;] *A1; not in B1.*   111. concise syllogisms] *Dyce;* Consissylogismes *A1, A2;* subtle Sillogismes *A3, B1.*   114. Swarm] *A1;* Sworne *B1.*   the] *A1;* th' *B1.*

---

102. *fantasy*] imagination.

103. *will receive no object*] Ward thinks that Faustus' 'fantasy' is rejecting the four 'objective' disciplines, as philosophy, medicine, jurisprudence, and theology were sometimes called; he paraphrases, 'will not receive anything offered in the ordinary (academic) way'. Other suggestions are: 'will brook no objection (to the pursuit of magic)' (Logeman); 'will admit no obstacle' (Greg); and 'will not be impressed by solid realities' (Boas). Perhaps the passage is corrupt.

107–8.] the first of the passages deleted on grounds of suspected profanity by the editor of B1.

107. *basest of the three*] 'even baser than the other three' (Greg).

112. *Gravell'd*] brought to a stop, nonplussed.

114. *problems*] questions proposed for scholastic disputation.

114–15. *as . . . hell*] Musaeus, the legendary pre-Homeric Greek poet and pupil of Orpheus, is glimpsed standing head and shoulders above the spirits who throng around him in the underworld in the *Aeneid*, vi. 666–7.

On sweet Musaeus when he came to hell,   115
Will be as cunning as Agrippa was,
Whose shadows made all Europe honour him.
Val. Faustus, these books, thy wit, and our experience
Shall make all nations to canonize us.
As Indian Moors obey their Spanish lords,   120
So shall the spirits of every element
Be always serviceable to us three:
Like lions shall they guard us when we please,
Like Almain rutters with their horsemen's staves
Or Lapland giants trotting by our sides;   125
Sometimes like women or unwedded maids,
Shadowing more beauty in their airy brows
Than in the white breasts of the queen of love.
From Venice shall they drag huge argosies,
And from America the golden fleece   130
That yearly stuffs old Philip's treasury,

117. shadows] *A1;* shadow *B1.*   121. spirits] *B1;* subiects *A1.*   128. in the] *Greg;* in their *A1;* has the *B1;* haue the *B2.*   129. From] *B1;* For *A1.* drag] *B1;* dregge *A1.*   huge] *A1, B1;* whole *B2.*   131. stuffs] *A1;* stuff'd *B1.*

Marlowe may have had this passage in mind; or he may simply have confused Musaeus with Orpheus.

116. *cunning*] skilful.

116–17. *Agrippa . . . him*] Henry Cornelius Agrippa von Nettesheim (1486–1535), humanist and reputed magician, was credited with the power of calling up the 'shadows' of the dead.

119. *canonize*] accented on the second syllable.

120. *Moors*] used at this time of any dark-skinned people. Here, the natives of the American continent.

124.] like German cavalrymen with their lances.

125. *Lapland giants*] Marlowe has an earlier allusion to Arctic giants in 2 *Tamburlaine,* I. i. 26–8.

127. *Shadowing*] harbouring. Marlowe uses the phrase 'shadowing in her brows' in I *Tamburlaine,* v. ii. 450.

airy] ethereal, heavenly.

130–1.] Marlowe refers to the annual plate-fleet which supplied the treasury of Philip II of Spain. Perhaps the word 'argosies', often wrongly supposed to be derived from the name of Jason's ship, the *Argo,* suggested to Marlowe the use of the image of the golden fleece. In any case, it is highly characteristic of him.

If learned Faustus will be resolute.

Fau. Valdes, as resolute am I in this
    As thou to live; therefore object it not.

Corn. The miracles that magic will perform   135
    Will make thee vow to study nothing else.
    He that is grounded in astrology,
    Enrich'd with tongues, well seen in minerals,
    Hath all the principles magic doth require;
    Then doubt not, Faustus, but to be renown'd   140
    And more frequented for this mystery
    Than heretofore the Delphian oracle.
    The spirits tell me they can dry the sea
    And fetch the treasure of all foreign wrecks,
    Ay, all the wealth that our forefathers hid   145
    Within the massy entrails of the earth.
    Then tell me, Faustus, what shall we three want?

Fau. Nothing, Cornelius. O, this cheers my soul!
    Come, show me some demonstrations magical,
    That I may conjure in some lusty grove   150
    And have these joys in full possession.

Val. Then haste thee to some solitary grove,
    And bear wise Bacon's and Abanus' works,

138. in] *B1; not in A1.*   145. Ay] *A1;* Yea *B1.*   150. lusty] *A1;* bushy
B1.   153. Abanus] *Greg, conj. Düntzer; Albanus A1, B1; Albertus Dyce,
conj. Mitford.*

---

134. *object it not*] do not bring it forward as a condition that I should be
resolute.

138. *Enrich'd with tongues*] especially Latin, the language in which it was
believed spirits had to be addressed; also Greek and Hebrew.

well seen in minerals] well-versed in the properties of minerals.

141. *frequented*] resorted to.

mystery] skill, art.

146. *massy*] massive.

150. *lusty*] pleasant.

153. *Bacon's and Abanus'*] Pietro d'Abano (1250?–1316?) was an Italian
physician and philosopher and a suspected sorcerer. But some of the editors
substitute 'Albertus' for the '*Albanus*' found in A1 and B1. Albertus Magnus (1193–1280) was a German Dominican philosopher. His love of experi-
mental science links him with the early Franciscan philosophers of Oxford
among whom Roger Bacon (1214?–94) was important. Albertus and Bacon

The Hebrew Psalter, and New Testament;
And whatsoever else is requisite   155
We will inform thee ere our conference cease.

Corn. Valdes, first let him know the words of art,
And then, all other ceremonies learn'd,
Faustus may try his cunning by himself.

Val. First I'll instruct thee in the rudiments,   160
And then wilt thou be perfecter than I.

Fau. Then come and dine with me, and after meat
We'll canvass every quiddity thereof,
For ere I sleep I'll try what I can do:
This night I'll conjure though I die therefor.   *Exeunt omnes.*

[Scene ii]

Enter two Scholars.

1 Sch. I wonder what's become of Faustus, that was wont to
make our schools ring with *sic probo*.

Enter WAGNER.

2 Sch. That shall we presently know; here comes his boy.
1 Sch. How now, sirrah, where's thy master?
Wag. God in heaven knows.   5
2 Sch. Why, dost not thou know then?
Wag. Yes, I know; but that follows not.

165. omnes] *B1; not in A1.*

ii. 1. wont to] *A1;* wont / To *B1.*   2.1.] *Stage-direction placed as here B1;
after 3 A1.*   3. presently know;] *B1;* know, for see *A1.*   6. then] *B1;
not in A1.*

---

are linked further by the fact that each was popularly supposed to have
constructed a brazen head capable of speech.

154.] Ward explains that the Psalms and the opening verses of the Gospel
of St John were regularly used in conjurations.

159. *cunning*] skill.

163. *canvass every quiddity*] discuss every essential particular. 'Quiddity'
is a scholastic term.

ii. 2. sic probo] I prove it thus. Used in scholastic disputations.
3. *presently*] directly, at once.

1 Sch. Go to, sirrah, leave your jesting and tell us where he is.

Wag. That follows not by force of argument, which you, being
 licentiates, should stand upon; therefore acknowledge 10
 your error and be attentive.

2 Sch. Then you will not tell us?

Wag. You are deceived, for I will tell you. Yet, if you were not
 dunces, you would never ask me such a question. For is he
 not *corpus naturale*? and is not that *mobile*? Then where- 15
 fore should you ask me such a question? But that I am by
 nature phlegmatic, slow to wrath, and prone to lechery (to
 love, I would say), it were not for you to come within forty
 foot of the place of execution—although I do not doubt
 but to see you both hanged the next sessions. Thus having 20
 triumphed over you, I will set my countenance like a precisian and begin to speak thus: Truly, my dear brethren,
 my master is within at dinner with Valdes and Cornelius,
 as this wine, if it could speak, would inform your wor-

9. by] *B1;* necessary by *A1.* which] *B1;* that *A1.* 10. licentiates] *B1;*
licentiate *A1.* upon] *B1;* vpon't *A1.* 11–12.] *Between these lines A1
inserts:* 2. Why, didst thou not say thou knewst? / *Wag.* Haue you any
witnesse on't? / 1. Yes sirra, I heard you. / *Wag.* Aske my fellow if I be
a thiefe. 12. Then] *B1;* Well *A1.* 13. You are deceived, for] *B1;*
Yes sir *A1.* 14–15. he not] *B1;* not he *A1.* 20. but] *B1; not in A1.*
24. would] *B1;* it would *A1.*

---

 10. *licentiates*] holders of a degree permitting you to ascend to a master's
or doctor's degree.

 stand upon] rely upon.

 11–12.] In *A1*'s addition at this point, 'Aske my fellow if I be a thiefe'
is a popular proverbial saying. See Tilley, F177.

 14. *dunces*] Greg holds that this word probably retains here something
of its original sense, i.e. hair-splitting reasoners. But Wagner himself is the
hair-splitter, and as such he is scornful of the scholars as dunces in the
modern sense, i.e. blockheads.

 15. corpus naturale . . . mobile] Ward explains that 'corpus naturale seu
mobile', i.e. a body that is natural or liable to change, was the current
scholastic expression for the subject-matter of physics. It is an adaptation
of an expression of Aristotle's.

 19. *the place of execution*] i.e. the dining-room. But Wagner immediately
exploits the phrase in its more usual sense by saying that he expects to see
his hearers hanged.

 21–2. *a precisian*] a puritan.

 24. *this wine*] carried by Wagner.

ships: and so the Lord bless you, preserve you, and keep   25
you, my dear brethren.   *Exit.*

1 Sch. O Faustus, then I fear that which I have long suspected,
        That thou art fallen into that damned art
        For which they two are infamous through the world.

2 Sch. Were he a stranger, not ally'd to me,   30
        The danger of his soul would make me mourn.
        But come, let us go and inform the Rector:
        It may be his grave counsel may reclaim him.

1 Sch. I fear me, nothing will reclaim him now.

2 Sch. Yet let us see what we can do.   *Exeunt.* 35

[Scene iii]

> *Thunder. Enter* LUCIFER *and four* Devils [*above*]:
> FAUSTUS *to them with this speech.*

Fau. Now that the gloomy shadow of the night,
        Longing to view Orion's drizzling look,

26. my dear brethren] *B1;* my deare brethren, my deare brethren *A1.*
27–35.] *Verse as here B1; prose A1.*   27–8. O Faustus . . . fallen] *B1;*
Nay then I feare he is falne *A1.*   30. not] *B1;* and not *A1.*   31. The
. . . mourn] *B1;* yet should I grieue for him *A1.*   33. It may be] *B1;* and
see if hee by *A1.*   may] *B1;* can *A1.*   34. I] *B1;* O but I *A1.*   will]
B1; can *A1.*   now] *B1; not in A1.*   35. see] *B1;* trie *A1.*

iii. 0.1–2. Thunder . . . speech.] *B1; Enter Faustus to coniure. A1.*   0.1.
above] *Greg; not in A1, B1.*   1. night] *B1;* earth *A1.*   2. look] *A1, B1;*
looks *Greg.*

---

30. *ally'd to me*] in friendship.
32. *the Rector*] the head of the university.

iii. 0.1. Enter . . . above] These infernal characters are witnesses of what
Faustus does but are unseen by him.

1–4.] These lines are repeated in the anonymous *Taming of a Shrew* (ed.
Boas), Induction, i. 9–12: 'Now that the gloomie shaddow of the night /
Longing to view Orions drisling lookes, / Leapes from th'antarticke world
unto the skie / And dims the welkin with her pitchie breath'. This confirms
B1's reading 'night' as against A1's 'earth'. But it seems hardly sufficient
to justify Greg's rejection of A1's, and B1's, 'looke' in favour of *A Shrew's*
'lookes'. See additional note on p. 105.

2. *Orion's drizzling look*] This phrase appears to echo Virgil's 'nimbosus
Orion' (*Aeneid*, i. 535), i.e. the rainy constellation of Orion. Virgil has also
'aquosus Orion' (*Aeneid*, iv. 52), with a similar meaning.

Leaps from th' antarctic world unto the sky
And dims the welkin with her pitchy breath,
Faustus, begin thine incantations,   5
And try if devils will obey thy hest,
Seeing thou hast pray'd and sacrific'd to them.
Within this circle is Jehovah's name
Forward and backward anagrammatiz'd,
The breviated names of holy saints,   10
Figures of every adjunct to the heavens,
And characters of signs and erring stars,
By which the spirits are enforc'd to rise:
Then fear not, Faustus, to be resolute
And try the uttermost magic can perform.   *Thunder.* 15
Sint mihi dei Acherontis propitii! Valeat numen triplex
Iehovae! Ignei, aerii, aquatici, terreni spiritus salvete! Ori-
entis princeps Lucifer, Beelzebub inferni ardentis monarcha,

9. anagrammatiz'd] *B1;* and Agramithist *A1.*   10. The breviated] *A1;*
Th'abreuiated *B1.*   12. erring] *A1;* euening *B1.*   14. to] *B1;* but *A1.*
15. uttermost] *A1;* vtmost *B1.*   *Thunder.*] *B1; not in A1.*   17. aquatici]
Tucker Brooke; Aquatani A1, B1.   terreni] *Greg; not in A1, B1.*
18. *Lucifer*] *Greg; not in A1, B1.*

---

3. *from th' antarctic world*] Marlowe must have supposed, at least while
writing these lines, that the night advanced from the southern hemisphere!
10. *breviated*] abbreviated.
11. *adjunct to*] heavenly body fixed to.
12. *characters*] It was believed that heavenly bodies impressed their
characters or seals upon earthly things through stellar rays and that magicians who reproduced these characters were able by so doing to utilize the
peculiar virtues of particular heavenly bodies. See Johnstone Parr, *Tamburlaine's Malady* (Alabama, 1953), pp. 32–7.
signs and erring stars] signs of the Zodiac and planets.
14. *to be resolute*] as urged by Valdes in i. 132.
16–24.] May the gods of Acheron be favourable to me! Away with the
threefold spirit of Jehovah! Hail, spirits of fire, air, water, and earth!
Lucifer prince of the east, Beelzebub monarch of burning hell, and Demogorgon, we ask your favour that Mephostophilis may appear and rise! . . .
Why do you delay? By Jehovah, hell, and the holy water which I now
sprinkle, and by the sign of the cross which I now make, and by our
prayers, may Mephostophilis himself now rise, compelled to our service!
16–17. numen triplex Iehovae] the Trinity. In the lines that follow,
Faustus turns to the infernal trinity of Lucifer, Beelzebub, and Demogorgon.

et Demogorgon, propitiamus vos ut appareat et surgat Me-
phostophilis!   20

> Dragon [*appears briefly above*].

Quid tu moraris? Per Iehovam, Gehennam, et consecratam
aquam quam nunc spargo, signumque crucis quod nunc facio,
et per vota nostra, ipse nunc surgat nobis dicatus Mephosto-
philis!

> Enter a Devil.

I charge thee to return and change thy shape;   25
Thou art too ugly to attend on me.
Go, and return an old Franciscan friar,
That holy shape becomes a devil best.   *Exit* Devil.
I see there's virtue in my heavenly words.
Who would not be proficient in this art?   30
How pliant is this Mephostophilis,
Full of obedience and humility!
Such is the force of magic and my spells.
Now, Faustus, thou art conjuror laureate,
That canst command great Mephostophilis.   35
Quin redis, Mephostophilis, fratris imagine!

> Enter MEPHOSTOPHILIS.

20.1. Dragon . . . *above*.] *Boas* (subs.), *conj. Root; Dragon B1; not in A1.*
21. *Quid tu moraris?*] *Ellis, conj. Bullen; quod tumeraris A1, B1.*   23.
dicatus] *B3; dicatis A1, B1.*   34–6. Now . . . *imagine!*] *A1; not in B1.*   34.
Now] *Wagner, conj. Albers; No A1.*   36. redis] *Boas, conj. Root; regis A1.*

20.1. *Dragon* . . . above] This stage-direction is based on Root's explanation of the English word '*Dragon*' which appears disconcertingly in the
middle of the Latin invocation in B1 but not A1. The correctness of the
emendation is confirmed by a passage in the *Damnable Life*, ii (see Appendix II), and by the inclusion among the goods belonging to the Admiral's
Men in 1598 of 'j dragon in fostes' (*Henslowe Papers*, ed. Greg, p. 118).

21. Quid tu moraris?] Believing that the spirits would be reluctant to
appear, magicians commonly inserted such phrases as this into their spells.
See Kocher, *C.M.*, pp. 157–8.

24.1. a *Devil*] Mephostophilis.

29. *heavenly words*] 'scriptural phrases used for conjuration' (Boas).

34. *conjuror laureate*] a conjuror worthy of special distinction.

36.] Why don't you return, Mephostophilis, in the likeness of a friar!

Meph. Now, Faustus, what wouldst thou have me do?

Fau. I charge thee wait upon me whilst I live,
 To do whatever Faustus shall command,
 Be it to make the moon drop from her sphere   40
 Or the ocean to overwhelm the world.

Meph. I am a servant to great Lucifer
 And may not follow thee without his leave;
 No more than he commands must we perform.

Fau. Did not he charge thee to appear to me?   45

Meph. No, I came hither of mine own accord.

Fau. Did not my conjuring speeches raise thee? Speak.

Meph. That was the cause, but yet *per accidens*:
 For when we hear one rack the name of God,
 Abjure the scriptures and his saviour Christ,   50
 We fly, in hope to get his glorious soul;
 Nor will we come unless he use such means
 Whereby he is in danger to be damn'd.
 Therefore the shortest cut for conjuring
 Is stoutly to abjure the Trinity   55
 And pray devoutly to the prince of hell.

Fau. So Faustus hath
 Already done, and holds this principle,
 There is no chief but only Beelzebub,
 To whom Faustus doth dedicate himself.   60
 This word 'damnation' terrifies not him,

46. hither] *B2;* now hether *A1, B1.* 47. speeches] *A1; not in B1.*
48. *accidens*] *B4; accident A1, B1.* 55. the Trinity] *A1;* all godlinesse
B1. 57-8. Faustus hath / Already done, and holds] *Dyce 2; Faustus*
hath already done, and holds *A1, B1;* I have done, and hold *Greg.* 61.
him] *A1;* me *B1.*

48.] Your conjuring was the cause, not because of what it was in itself,
but because of something it happened to include. 'Per accidens' is another
scholastic expression.

49. *rack*] torment by anagrammatizing.

51. *glorious*] splendid in beauty. Greg mentions the possibility that the
meaning may be 'boastful', hence 'presumptuous'.

55. *the Trinity*] The bowdlerizing editor of B1 thought it more prudent
to print 'all godlinesse'.

For he confounds hell in Elysium:
His ghost be with the old philosophers!
But, leaving these vain trifles of men's souls,
Tell me, what is that Lucifer thy lord?   65
Meph. Arch-regent and commander of all spirits.
Fau. Was not that Lucifer an angel once?
Meph. Yes, Faustus, and most dearly lov'd of God.
Fau. How comes it then that he is prince of devils?
Meph. O, by aspiring pride and insolence,   70
For which God threw him from the face of heaven.
Fau. And what are you that live with Lucifer?
Meph. Unhappy spirits that fell with Lucifer,
Conspir'd against our God with Lucifer,
And are for ever damn'd with Lucifer.   75
Fau. Where are you damn'd?
Meph.   In hell.
Fau. How comes it then that thou art out of hell?
Meph. Why, this is hell, nor am I out of it.
Think'st thou that I, who saw the face of God
And tasted the eternal joys of heaven,   80
Am not tormented with ten thousand hells

62. he confounds] *A1;* I confound *B1.*   63. His] *A1;* My *B1.*   73. fell]
A1; liue *A2, A3, B1.*   79. who] *A1;* that *A2, A3, B1.*

---

62. *confounds hell in Elysium*] does not distinguish between hell and
Elysium. In his preface to Greene's *Menaphon* (1589), Nashe speaks of
writers 'that thrust *Elisium* into hell' (ed. McKerrow, iii. 316); but Marlowe had already bracketed the two names in I *Tamburlaine,* v. ii. 403.

63. *the old philosophers*] who share his disbelief in an eternity of punishment or reward. This line is the quotation of a saying attributed to Averroes
(1126–98), the Arab medical writer and commentator upon Aristotle. See
J. C. Maxwell, 'Two Notes on Marlowe's *Faustus*', *N. & Q.,* cxciv (1949),
pp. 334–5.

70. *aspiring*] Marlowe uses this word in several other key passages, most
notably in I *Tamburlaine,* II. vii. 20; it refers to one of the dominant themes
in his work.

78.] Milton's Satan testifies similarly, 'Which way I flie is Hell; my self
am Hell' (*Paradise Lost,* iv. 75).

81–2.] St John Chrysostom, the fourth-century Greek Father, states that
ten thousand hells are as nothing in comparison with the loss of celestial
bliss. See *Hom. in St Matt.,* xxiii. 9 (reference supplied privately by F. N.

In being depriv'd of everlasting bliss?
O Faustus, leave these frivolous demands,
Which strike a terror to my fainting soul.

Fau. What, is great Mephostophilis so passionate   85
For being deprived of the joys of heaven?
Learn thou of Faustus manly fortitude
And scorn those joys thou never shalt possess.
Go bear these tidings to great Lucifer:
Seeing Faustus hath incurr'd eternal death   90
By desperate thoughts against Jove's deity,
Say he surrenders up to him his soul
So he will spare him four-and-twenty years,
Letting him live in all voluptuousness,
Having thee ever to attend on me,   95
To give me whatsoever I shall ask,
To tell me whatsoever I demand,
To slay mine enemies and aid my friends,
And always be obedient to my will.
Go, and return to mighty Lucifer,   100
And meet me in my study at midnight,
And then resolve me of thy master's mind.

Meph. I will, Faustus.   *Exit.*

Fau. Had I as many souls as there be stars,
I'd give them all for Mephostophilis.   105
By him I'll be great emperor of the world,
And make a bridge thorough the moving air

---

84. strike] *A1*; strikes *A2, A3, B1*.   89. these] *B1*; those *A1*.   98. aid]
A1; to aid *A2, A3, B1*.   107. thorough] *B5*; through *A1, B1*.

Lees, following a hint in J. Searle's letter in *T.L.S.*, 15 February 1936).
        85. *passionate*] stirred by strong feeling.
        87. *manly*] expresses Faustus' buoyant humanism at this stage.
        93. *So*] on condition that.
        104–16.] As Greg points out, Faustus' eagerness in this soliloquy is
balanced by Mephostophilis' eagerness in his asides at v. 73 and 82.
        104–5.] This sentence is echoed in ll. 12–15 of the fifth addition to *The
Spanish Tragedy* (ed. Edwards): 'Had I as many lives as there be stars, /
As many heavens to go to as those lives, / I'd give them all, ay, and my soul
to boot, / But I would see thee ride in this red pool.'

To pass the ocean with a band of men;
I'll join the hills that bind the Afric shore
And make that country continent to Spain,   110
And both contributory to my crown;
The Emperor shall not live but by my leave,
Nor any potentate of Germany.
Now that I have obtain'd what I desire,
I'll live in speculation of this art   115
Till Mephostophilis return again.   *Exit.*
                            [*Exeunt* LUCIFER *and* Devils.]

[Scene iv]

                    Enter WAGNER *and the* Clown [ROBIN].

Wag. Come hither, sirrah boy.
Rob. Boy! O, disgrace to my person! Zounds, boy in your face!
    You have seen many boys with such pickedevants, I am
    sure.

108. ocean] *A1;* Ocean: (*without punctuation at end of line*) *B1.*   110.
country] *B1;* land *A1.*   114. desire] *A1;* desir'd *B1.*   116.1. *Exeunt* ...
Devils.] *This ed.; not in A1, B1.*

Scene iv.] *The A-version of this scene is given in Appendix I* (*see section 5 of
the 'Introduction'*).   0.1. ROBIN] *Greg; not in B1.*   2, 6, 11, etc. Rob.]
This ed.; Clo. or Clow. throughout this scene B1.   3. such pickedevants]
A1; beards *B1.*

___

109. *bind*] enclose.
110. *continent to*] continuous with. Marlowe had already used the word
in this sense in 1 *Tamburlaine*, I. i. 128.
115. *speculation*] contemplation, profound study.

iv. 1–4.] B1's version of these lines is repeated, with a few slight changes,
in the anonymous *Taming of a Shrew* (ed. Boas), II. ii. 1–4: '*Boy.* Come
hither, sirha, boy. / *San.* Boy, oh disgrace to my person, souns, boy / Of
your face, you have many boies with such / Pickadevantes I am sure'. A1
differs widely from both B1 and *A Shrew*; but it agrees with *A Shrew*
against B1 in reading 'such pickadevaunts'. Presumably these words appeared in the original version but were altered to 'beards' by the editor of
B1. A less close echo of part of Robin's speech occurs in the anonymous
comedy *Wily Beguiled* (ed. Greg), ll. 1095–7: 'Sounds, foole in your face:
foole? O monstrous intitulation: Foole? O disgrace to my person'.
3. *pickedevants*] fashionable pointed beards.

Wag. Sirrah, hast thou no comings in?   5

Rob. Yes, and goings out too, you may see, sir.

Wag. Alas, poor slave! see how poverty jests in his nakedness.
    I know the villain's out of service, and so hungry that I
    know he would give his soul to the devil for a shoulder of
    mutton, though it were blood-raw.   10

Rob. Not so, neither. I had need to have it well roasted, and
    good sauce to it, if I pay so dear, I can tell you.

Wag. Sirrah, wilt thou be my man and wait on me? and I will
    make thee go like *Qui mihi discipulus.*

Rob. What, in verse?   15

Wag. No, slave, in beaten silk and stavesacre.

Rob. Stavesacre! that's good to kill vermin. Then, belike, if I
    serve you, I shall be lousy.

Wag. Why, so thou shalt be, whether thou dost it or no; for,
    sirrah, if thou dost not presently bind thyself to me for   20
    seven years, I'll turn all the lice about thee into familiars
    and make them tear thee in pieces.

Rob. Nay, sir, you may save yourself a labour, for they are as
    familiar with me as if they paid for their meat and drink,
    I can tell you.   25

Wag. Well, sirrah, leave your jesting and take these guilders.

Rob. Yes, marry, sir, and I thank you too.

8. I know] *B1; not in Greg.*

---

5. *comings in*] i.e. earnings. This, as Greg remarks, gives Robin an oppor-
tunity of punning on 'goings out' (l. 6), i.e. expenses, by which he means
that he is coming through his tattered clothes, as is evident from Wagner's
allusion to his 'nakedness' (l. 7).

14. *Qui mihi discipulus*] you who are my pupil. These are the opening
words of a didactic poem, *Carmen de Moribus*, by William Lily (1466?–
1522) the schoolmaster, which was much read in Elizabethan grammar-
schools.

16. *beaten silk*] embroidered silk. But Wagner is punning and means also
that he will give Robin a thrashing.

stavesacre] the seeds of a kind of delphinium used to destroy vermin.

21. *familiars*] attendant demons.

23–4. *they are . . . drink*] 'they treat me with as little ceremony as if they
were guests who had paid for their dinner and I the waiter whose business
it was to serve them (with my own flesh and blood)' (Greg).

26. *take these guilders*] take these Dutch florins as hiring-money.

Wag. So, now thou art to be at an hour's warning, whensoever
and wheresoever the devil shall fetch thee.

Rob. Here, take your guilders again, I'll none of 'em.   30

Wag. Not I, thou art pressed, prepare thyself, for I will
presently raise up two devils to carry thee away. Banio!
Belcher!

Rob. Belcher! And Belcher come here, I'll belch him. I am not
afraid of a devil.   35

Enter two Devils, *and the* Clown *runs up and down crying.*

Wag. How now, sir, will you serve me now?

Rob. Ay, good Wagner, take away the devil then.

Wag. Spirits, away!   *Exeunt* [Devils].
Now, sirrah, follow me.

Rob. I will, sir. But hark you, master, will you teach me this   40
conjuring occupation?

Wag. Ay, sirrah, I'll teach thee to turn thyself to a dog, or a
cat, or a mouse, or a rat, or anything.

Rob. A dog, or a cat, or a mouse, or a rat! O brave, Wagner!

Wag. Villain, call me Master Wagner, and see that you walk   45
attentively, and let your right eye be always diametrally
fixed upon my left heel, that thou mayest *quasi vestigiis
nostris insistere.*

Rob. Well, sir, I warrant you.   *Exeunt.*

---

30. again] *A1, B2; not in B1.*   31. for] *B1;* or *Dyce 2.*   35.1. *and the
... crying*] *A1; not in B1.*   38. *Exeunt* Devils.] *Oxberry; Exeunt. A1;
not in B1.*   47–8. *vestigiis nostris*] *Dyce 2; vestigias nostras A1, B1.*

---

30. *Here ... again*] The scene of *The Taming of a Shrew* which begins
by repeating the opening lines of the present scene continues with what
could be some fainter echoes of it. Thus, Sander, like Robin, is twice
addressed as 'slave' and has occasion to protest, 'Here, here, take your two
shillings again' (*A Shrew*, II. ii. 32, 39, and 46). These are not very impressive parallels. But, for what they are worth, they support the view that
A1 and B2 were correct in including 'againe' in the present line.

31. *pressed*] hired, engaged.

34. *And*] if.

46. *diametrally*] directly, in a straight line.

47–8. quasi vestigiis nostris insistere] tread as it were in our footsteps.

[Scene v]

Enter FAUSTUS *in his study.*

Fau. Now, Faustus, must
    Thou needs be damn'd, and canst thou not be sav'd.
    What boots it then to think of God or heaven ?
    Away with such vain fancies, and despair;
    Despair in God, and trust in Beelzebub.   5
    Now go not backward; no, Faustus, be resolute:
    Why waver'st thou ? O, something soundeth in mine ears,
    'Abjure this magic, turn to God again!'
    Ay, and Faustus will turn to God again.
    To God ? He loves thee not;   10
    The god thou serv'st is thine own appetite,
    Wherein is fix'd the love of Beelzebub:
    To him I'll build an altar and a church
    And offer lukewarm blood of new-born babes.

Enter the two Angels.

Bad Ang. Go forward, Faustus, in that famous art.   15
Good Ang. Sweet Faustus, leave that execrable art.
Fau. Contrition, prayer, repentance, what of these ?
Good Ang. O, they are means to bring thee unto heaven.
Bad Ang. Rather illusions, fruits of lunacy,
    That make men foolish that do use them most.   20
Good Ang. Sweet Faustus, think of heaven and heavenly things.
Bad Ang. No, Faustus, think of honour and of wealth.

Exeunt Angels.

v. 1–2. must / Thou . . . sav'd.] *Dyce;* must . . . damnd, / And canst . . .
saued ? *A1;* must . . . damn'd ? / Canst . . . sau'd ? *B1.*   3. of] *A1;* on *B1.*
6. no] *A1; not in B1.*   Faustus] *A1, B1; not in Wagner.*   7. thou ? O]
A1, B1; not in Greg.   ears] *A1;* eare *B1.*   9. Ay . . . again.] *A1; not in
B1.*   10. To God ?] *A1;* Why *B1.*   10–11.] *Verse as here A1; one line
B1.*   14.1. *the two* Angels] *B1;* good Angell, and Euill *A1.*   15. Bad . . .
art.] *B1 (subs.); not in A1.*   17. these] *B1;* them *A1.*   20. make] *B1;*
makes *A1.*   men] *A1, B2;* them *B1.*   use] *B1;* trust *A1.*   22. and of]
B1; and *A1.*   22.1. Angels] *B1; not in A1.*

v.15.] This line, which is not found at this point in A1, exactly repeats i.73.
17. *what of these ?*] i.e. how can these help me now ?

Fau. Wealth!

    Why, the signory of Emden shall be mine.

    When Mephostophilis shall stand by me,   25

    What power can hurt me ? Faustus, thou art safe:

    Cast no more doubts! Mephostophilis, come,

    And bring glad tidings from great Lucifer.

    Is't not midnight ? Come, Mephostophilis,

    Veni, veni, Mephostophilis !   30

Enter MEPHOSTOPHILIS.

    Now tell me what saith Lucifer thy lord ?

Meph. That I shall wait on Faustus whilst he lives,

    So he will buy my service with his soul.

Fau. Already Faustus hath hazarded that for thee.

Meph. But now thou must bequeath it solemnly   35

    And write a deed of gift with thine own blood,

    For that security craves Lucifer.

    If thou deny it, I must back to hell.

Fau. Stay, Mephostophilis, and tell me what good

    Will my soul do thy lord ?

Meph.   Enlarge his kingdom.   40

Fau. Is that the reason why he tempts us thus ?

Meph. Solamen miseris socios habuisse doloris.

23–4. Wealth! / Why] *Dilke;* Wealth? Why *B1;* Of wealth, / Why *A1.*
26. power] *B1;* God *A1.*   me] *B1;* thee *A1.*   27. Mephostophilis,
come] *B1;* come *Mephastophilus A1.*   30. *Mephostophilis*] *B2; Mepho-*
stophile A1, B1.   31. me] *B1; not in A1.*   saith] *B1;* sayes *A1.*
32. *Meph.*] *A1; not in B1.*   he lives] *B1;* I liue *A1.*   35. now] *B1;*
Faustus, *A1.*   37. Lucifer] *B1;* great *Lucifer A1.*   38. must] *B1;* wil
A1.   39. and] *A1, B1; not in Boas.*   39–40. me what good / Will]
Wagner; me, / What good will *B1; prose A1.*   41. why] *B1; not in A1.*

---

24. *signory*] lordship.

Emden] This port in north-west Germany was in the sixteenth century
the headquarters of Europe's largest merchant fleet. It had trade relations
with England.

27. *Cast*] consider, ponder.

42.] To the unhappy, it is a comfort to have had companions in misfor-
tune. This line of Latin verse seems not to be of classical origin. It occurs
also in Greene's *Menaphon* (ed. Grosart, vi. 45) and other works of the

Fau. Why, have you any pain that torture other?

Meph. As great as have the human souls of men.
    But tell me, Faustus, shall I have thy soul?   45
    And I will be thy slave and wait on thee
    And give thee more than thou hast wit to ask.

Fau. Ay, Mephostophilis, I'll give it him.

Meph. Then, Faustus, stab thy arm courageously,
    And bind thy soul, that at some certain day   50
    Great Lucifer may claim it as his own;
    And then be thou as great as Lucifer.

Fau. Lo, Mephostophilis, for love of thee
    Faustus hath cut his arm, and with his proper blood
    Assures his soul to be great Lucifer's,   55
    Chief lord and regent of perpetual night.
    View here this blood that trickles from mine arm,
    And let it be propitious for my wish.

Meph. But, Faustus,
    Write it in manner of a deed of gift.   60

Fau. Ay, so I do. But, Mephostophilis,
    My blood congeals, and I can write no more.

Meph. I'll fetch thee fire to dissolve it straight.   *Exit.*

Fau. What might the staying of my blood portend?
    Is it unwilling I should write this bill?   65

---

43. Why] *B1; not in A1.*   torture] *B1;* tortures *A1.*   other] *B1;* others
A1.   48. I'll] *B1;* I *A1.*   him] *B1;* thee *A1.*   49. Faustus] *B1; not in
A1.*   thy] *B1;* thine *A1.*   53–5.] *Verse as here A1; two lines divided
after* arm *B1.*   54. Faustus hath cut his] *B1;* I cut mine *A1.*   his] *B1;*
my *A1.*   55. Assures his] *B1;* Assure my *A1.*   57. this] *B1;* the *A1.*
59–60.] *Verse as here B1; prose A1.*   60. Write] *B1;* thou must write *A1.*
61. do] *B1;* will *A1.*   61–2.] *Verse as here B1; prose A1.*

---

period. Previous editors have found the same idea expressed by mediaeval
authors, though not in hexameter form, and have traced it back as far as
Seneca, *De Consolatione ad Polybium*, xii. 2.

    43. *other*] others.
    48. *him*] i.e. Lucifer. Mephostophilis is merely his agent.
    50. *bind*] give a bond for.
    54. *proper*] own.
    55. *Assures*] conveys by deed.
    63, 70. *fire*] a disyllable.
    65. *bill*] deed.

Why streams it not, that I may write afresh?
'Faustus gives to thee his soul': O, there it stay'd.
Why shouldst thou not? is not thy soul thine own?
Then write again: 'Faustus gives to thee his soul'.

Enter MEPHOSTOPHILIS *with the chafer of fire.*

Meph. See, Faustus, here is fire; set it on.   70
Fau. So, now the blood begins to clear again:
      Now will I make an end immediately.
Meph. [*Aside*] What will not I do to obtain his soul!
Fau. *Consummatum est*: this bill is ended,
      And Faustus hath bequeath'd his soul to Lucifer.   75
      But what is this inscription on mine arm?
      Homo fuge! Whither should I fly?
      If unto God, he'll throw me down to hell.—
      My senses are deceiv'd, here's nothing writ.—
      O yes, I see it plain; even here is writ,   80
      Homo fuge! Yet shall not Faustus fly.
Meph. [*Aside*] I'll fetch him somewhat to delight his mind.   *Exit.*

Enter Devils, *giving crowns and rich apparel*
to FAUSTUS. *They dance and then depart.*
Enter MEPHOSTOPHILIS.

Fau. What means this show? Speak, Mephostophilis.

67. O] *B1;* ah *A1.*   69.1. *the*] *B1;* a *A1.*   fire] *B1;* coles *A1.*   70. See,
Faustus, here is fire] *B1;* Heres fier, come Faustus *A1.*   73. *Aside*] *Dyce;*
not in *A1, B1.*   What] *B1;* O what *A1.*   78. God] *A1;* heauen *B1.*
me] *B1;* thee *A1.*   80. O . . . here] *B1;* I see it plaine, here in this place
A1.   82. *Aside*] *Dyce; not in A1, B1.*   82.1. Devils] *B1; with diuels A1.*
82.2. *They*] *B1; and A1.*   82.3. *Enter* MEPHOSTOPHILIS.] *B1; not in A1.*
83. What . . . Mephostophilis.] *B1;* Speake Mephastophilis, what meanes
this shewe? *A1.*

69.1. chafer] portable grate. The *Damnable Life* says nothing about the
congealing of Faustus' blood and the bringing of fire.

70. *set it on*] i.e. put the saucer of blood on the chafer.

73, 82.] See comment on iii. 104–16.

74. Consummatum est] It is finished. See John xix. 30. Marlowe daringly
places in Faustus' mouth the last words of Christ on the cross.

77, 81. Homo fuge!] Fly, O man!

Meph. Nothing, Faustus, but to delight thy mind
  And let thee see what magic can perform.   85
Fau. But may I raise such spirits when I please?
Meph. Ay, Faustus, and do greater things than these.
Fau. Then, Mephostophilis, receive this scroll,
  A deed of gift of body and of soul:
  But yet conditionally that thou perform   90
  All covenants and articles between us both.
Meph. Faustus, I swear by hell and Lucifer
  To effect all promises between us made.
Fau. Then hear me read it, Mephostophilis.
  On these conditions following: 95
   First, that Faustus may be a spirit in form and substance;
   *Secondly, that Mephostophilis shall be his servant and at
his command;*
   *Thirdly, that Mephostophilis shall do for him and bring
him whatsoever;*   100
   *Fourthly, that he shall be in his chamber or house invis-
ible;*
   *Lastly, that he shall appear to the said John Faustus at all
times in what form or shape soever he please;*
   I, John Faustus of Wittenberg, doctor, by these presents do 105
  *give both body and soul to Lucifer, prince of the east, and his
minister Mephostophilis, and furthermore grant unto them
that, four-and-twenty years being expired, the articles above
written inviolate, full power to fetch or carry the said John*

---

84. mind] *B1;* minde withall *A1.* 85. let thee see] *B1;* to shewe thee *A1.*
86. such] *B1;* vp *A1.* 87–8.] *Between these lines, A1 inserts: Fau.* Then
theres inough for a thousand soules, 88. *Fau.* Then] *B1;* Here *A1.*
91. covenants and articles] *B1;* articles prescrib'd *A1;* covenant-articles
Greg. 93. made] *A1;* both *B1.* 94–5. it, Mephostophilis. / On] *B1;*
them: on *A1.* 97–8. *at his command*] *A1;* be by him commanded *B1.*
104. *form or shape*] *A1;* forme and shape *A2, A3;* shape and forme *B1.*
108. the] *A1;* and these *B1.* 109. inviolate] *A1;* being inviolate *B1.*

---

 91. *covenants and articles*] Greg normalizes the metre by altering this
phrase to 'covenant-articles', i.e. agreed conditions. But alexandrines are
by no means rare in *Doctor Faustus:* see, for example, xix. 147, 164.
 109. inviolate] not having been violated.

Faustus, body and soul, flesh, blood, or goods, into their habi- 110
tation wheresoever.

> *By me John Faustus.*

Meph. Speak, Faustus, do you deliver this as your deed?

Fau. Ay, take it, and the devil give thee good on't!

Meph. Now, Faustus, ask what thou wilt.   115

Fau. First will I question with thee about hell.
Tell me, where is the place that men call hell?

Meph. Under the heavens.

Fau. Ay, so are all things else; but whereabouts?

Meph. Within the bowels of these elements,   120
Where we are tortur'd and remain for ever.
Hell hath no limits, nor is circumscrib'd
In one self place, but where we are is hell,
And where hell is, there must we ever be;
And, to be short, when all the world dissolves   125
And every creature shall be purify'd,
All places shall be hell that is not heaven.

Fau. I think hell's a fable.

Meph. Ay, think so still, till experience change thy mind.

Fau. Why, dost thou think that Faustus shall be damn'd?   130

Meph. Ay, of necessity, for here's the scroll
In which thou hast given thy soul to Lucifer.

---

110. *or goods*] *A1; not in B1.*   114. on't] *A1;* of it *B1.*   115. Now] *A1;*
So, now *B1.*   what] *A1;* me what *B1.*   116. will I]*A1;* I will *B1.*
with] *A1; not in A2, A3, B1.*   119. so ... whereabouts] *B1;* but where
about *A1.*   123. but] *B1;* for *A1.*   124. there] *B1; not in A1.*   125.
be short] *B1;* conclude *A1.*   128. I] *B1;* Come, I *A1.*   fable] *A1, B1;*
meere fable *B2.*   130. dost thou think] *B1;* thinkst thou then *A1.*
132. In which] *B1;* Wherein *A1.*

120.] See comment on i. 76. In this line, Mephostophilis declares that
hell exists at the centre of the sublunary, elemental part of the universe.
In the remainder of his speech, he goes on to explain that hell is not merely
a particular place but a condition: 'where we are is hell' (l. 123). He has
already spoken to this effect in iii. 78, 'Why, this is hell, nor am I out of it.'
There is nothing like this in the *Damnable Life*.

123. *one self place*] one and the same place.

126. *every ... purify'd*] every created thing 'will be no longer mixed, but
of one essence, either wholly good or wholly evil' (Greg).

Fau. Ay, and body too; but what of that?
    Think'st thou that Faustus is so fond to imagine
    That after this life there is any pain?   135
    No, these are trifles and mere old wives' tales.

Meph. But I am an instance to prove the contrary,
    For I tell thee I am damn'd and now in hell.

Fau. Nay, and this be hell, I'll willingly be damn'd:
    What, sleeping, eating, walking, and disputing!   140
    But, leaving this, let me have a wife, the fairest maid in
    Germany, for I am wanton and lascivious and cannot live
    without a wife.

Meph. How, a wife! I prithee, Faustus, talk not of a wife.

Fau. Nay, sweet Mephostophilis, fetch me one, for I will have 145
    one.

Meph. Well, thou wilt have one. Sit there till I come; I'll fetch
    thee a wife in the devil's name.   [*Exit.*]

Enter with a Devil *dressed like a woman,*
with fireworks.

    Tell me, Faustus, how dost thou like thy wife?
Fau. Here's a hot whore indeed! No, I'll no wife.   150
Meph. Marriage is but a ceremonial toy;
    And if thou lov'st me, think no more of it.

134-5. fond to imagine / That] *B1;* fond, / To imagine, that *A1.*   136.
No] *B1;* Tush *A1.*   137. I] *B1;* Faustus I *A1.*   138. I tell thee] *B1;*
not in *A1.*   now] *B1;* am now *A1.*   139-40.] *Verse as here B1;* How?
now in hell? nay and this be hell, Ile willingly be damnd here: what walking, disputing, &c. *A1.*   141-3.] *Prose as here A1, B1; verse divided after*
wife, I, lascivious, wife *Boas.*   141. this] *B1;* off this *A1.*   144-9.
Meph. How . . . thy wife?] *A1; Meph.* Well *Faustus,* thou shalt haue a wife. /
He fetches in a woman deuill. / *Faust.* What sight is this? / *Meph.* Now
Faustus wilt thou haue a wife? *B1.*   148. *Exit.*] *Dyce; not in A1, B1.*
149. Tell me] *Dyce;* Tel *A1;* Now *B1.*   150. Here's . . . wife.] *B1;* A
plague on her for a hote whore. *A1.*   151-2.] *Verse as here B1; prose A1.*
151. Marriage] *B1;* Tut Faustus, marriage *A1.*   152. And] *B1; not in A1.*
no] *B1; not in A1.*

134. *fond*] foolish.
152. *And if*] if. Tautological, but more emphatic than 'and' (e.g.,
iv. 34).

I'll cull thee out the fairest courtesans
And bring them every morning to thy bed;
She whom thine eye shall like, thy heart shall have,   155
Were she as chaste as was Penelope,
As wise as Saba, or as beautiful
As was bright Lucifer before his fall.
Hold; take this book, peruse it thoroughly:
The iterating of these lines brings gold;   160
The framing of this circle on the ground
Brings thunder, whirlwinds, storm, and lightning;
Pronounce this thrice devoutly to thyself
And men in harness shall appear to thee,
Ready to execute what thou command'st.   165

Fau. Thanks, Mephostophilis; yet fain would I have a book
    wherein I might behold all spells and incantations, that I
    might raise up spirits when I please.

Meph. Here they are in this book.   *There turn to them.*

Fau. Now would I have a book where I might see all charac- 170
    ters of planets of the heavens, that I might know their
    motions and dispositions.

Meph. Here they are, too.   *Turn to them.*

---

156. Were] *B1;* Be *A1.*   159. Hold] *A1;* Here *B1.*   peruse it
thoroughly] *A1;* and peruse it well *B1.*   162. thunder, whirlwinds,
storm] *B1;* whirlewindes, tempests, thunder *A1.*   164. harness] *B1;*
armour *A1.*   165. command'st] *B1;* desirst *A1.*   166–79. *Fau.* Thanks
. . . thee. *Turn to them.*] *A1; Faust.* Thankes *Mephostophilis* for this sweete
booke. / This will I keepe, as chary as my life. *Exeunt. B1.*   171. of
planets] *Greg;* and planets *A1.*

---

153. *cull*] choose.
156. *Penelope*] the faithful wife of Ulysses.
157. *Saba*] i.e. the Queen of Sheba. See 1 Kings x. As Greg remarks,
'Saba' is the form of the name 'Sheba' found in the Vulgate and certain
other editions of the Bible.
160. *iterating*] repetition.
162. *lightning*] a trisyllable.
164. *harness*] armour.
169. There turn to them] Mephostophilis shows Faustus that the in-
structions he seeks are to be found in the book already given to him. The
process is repeated at ll. 173 and 179.
172. *dispositions*] situations. An astrological term.

Fau. Nay, let me have one book more, and then I have done,
    wherein I might see all plants, herbs, and trees that grow   175
    upon the earth.
Meph. Here they be.
Fau. O, thou art deceived.
Meph. Tut, I warrant thee.   *Turn to them. Exeunt.*

[*Here a scene is probably lost. It may well have shown the Clown,
Robin, after stealing one of Faustus' books of magic, leaving
Wagner's service to become an ostler at an inn.*]

[Scene vi]

    Enter FAUSTUS *in his study and* MEPHOSTOPHILIS.

Fau. When I behold the heavens, then I repent
    And curse thee, wicked Mephostophilis,
    Because thou hast depriv'd me of those joys.
Meph. 'Twas thine own seeking, Faustus, thank thyself.
    But think'st thou heaven is such a glorious thing?   5
    I tell thee, Faustus, it is not half so fair

179. *Exeunt.*] *B1; not in A1.*   179.1–3. *Here . . . inn.*] *based on Greg; not
in A1, B1; B1 inserts: Enter Wagner solus. | Wag. Learned Faustus | To
know the secrets of Astronomy | Grauen in the booke of Ioues high firma-
ment, | Did mount himselfe to scale Olympus top, | Being seated in a
chariot burning bright, | Drawne by the strength of yoaky Dragons necks, |
He now is gone to proue Cosmography, | And as I gesse will first arriue at
Rome, | To see the Pope and manner of his Court; | And take some part of
holy Peters feast, | That to [on B2] this day is highly solemnized. Exit
Wagner.*

vi. 0.1. *Enter . . . MEPHOSTOPHILIS.*] *B1; not in A1.*   4. 'Twas . . .
thyself.] *B1; why Faustus, A1.*   5. But] *B1; not in A1.*   6. Faustus, it
is] *B1; tis A1.*   6–7. fair / As thou or] *B1; faire as thou, / Or A1.*

179. *warrant thee*] i.e. assure you that the book contains all that I say.
    Here . . . inn] Dyce and subsequent editors suspect the loss of something
between scenes v and vi. Greg's suggestion as to the nature of the missing
material is accepted here.

    vi. 6–7.] To encourage Faustus not to repent of his bargain, Mephosto-
philis extols the 'manly' values which Faustus himself upheld in iii. 87.

As thou or any man that breathes on earth.

Fau. How prov'st thou that?

Meph. 'Twas made for man; then he's more excellent.

Fau. If heaven was made for man, 'twas made for me: 10
I will renounce this magic and repent.

Enter the two Angels.

Good Ang. Faustus, repent; yet God will pity thee.

Bad Ang. Thou art a spirit; God cannot pity thee.

Fau. Who buzzeth in mine ears I am a spirit?

Be I a devil, yet God may pity me;   15

Yea, God will pity me if I repent.

Bad Ang. Ay, but Faustus never shall repent.   *Exeunt* Angels.

Fau. My heart is harden'd, I cannot repent.

Scarce can I name salvation, faith, or heaven,

But fearful echoes thunders in mine ears,   20

'Faustus, thou art damn'd!' Then guns and knives,

Swords, poison, halters, and envenom'd steel

Are laid before me to dispatch myself;

And long ere this I should have done the deed

Had not sweet pleasure conquer'd deep despair.   25

Have not I made blind Homer sing to me

Of Alexander's love and Oenon's death?

And hath not he, that built the walls of Thebes

---

7. breathes] *A1, B2;* breathe *B1.*   9. 'Twas] *B1;* It was *A1.*   then
he's] *B1;* therefore is man *A1.*   10. heaven was] *B1;* it were *A1.*   11.1.
Enter . . . Angels.] *B1; Enter good Angel, and euill Angel. A1.*   16. Yea]
B1; I *A1.*   17. *Exeunt* Angels.] *B3; Exit Angels. B1; exeunt A1.*
18. heart is] *B1;* hearts so *A1.*   20-1. But . . . knives,] *A1; not in B1.*
20. thunders] *A1;* thunder *Dyce.*   21. guns] *Greg;* swordes *A1.*
22. Swords, poison] *B1;* Poyson, gunnes *A1.*   24. done the deed] *B1;*
slaine my selfe *A1.*

---

12. *yet*] even now.   14. *buzzeth*] mutters.

18.] See note on p. 105.

21-3.] This prepares for the dramatized temptation to suicide at xviii.
56.1.

27. *Alexander*] Paris, the lover of Oenone, is usually so named by 'blind
Homer' in the *Iliad.*

28-9. *he . . . harp*] Amphion played with such skill that the stones moved

With ravishing sound of his melodious harp,
Made music with my Mephostophilis?   30
Why should I die, then, or basely despair?
I am resolv'd Faustus shall not repent.—
Come, Mephostophilis, let us dispute again,
And reason of divine astrology.
Speak, are there many spheres above the moon?   35
Are all celestial bodies but one globe
As is the substance of this centric earth?
Meph. As are the elements, such are the heavens,
Even from the moon unto the empyreal orb,
Mutually folded in each other's spheres,   40
And jointly move upon one axle-tree,
Whose termine is term'd the world's wide pole;

32. not] *B1;* nere *A1.*   34. reason] *B1;* argue *A1.*   35. Speak] *B1;*
Tel me *A1.*   spheres] *B1;* heauens *A1.*   38. heavens] *B1;* spheares *A1.*
39. Even ... orb,] *B1; not in A1.*   40. spheres] *B1;* orbe *A1.*   41. And]
B1; And *Faustus* all *A1.*

---

of their own accord to form the walls of Thebes. The last six words are
repeated, with reference to another musician, in the anonymous *Taming of
a Shrew* (ed. Boas), III. vi. 31–2: 'As once did *Orpheus* with his harmony, /
And ravishing sound of his melodious harpe'.

34. *astrology*] astronomy applied to human uses.

35–61.] Marlowe evidently thinks of 'this centric earth' (l. 37) as enclosed
within nine concentric 'spheres' (ll. 35, 40, 59) or 'heavens' (ll. 38, 59), the
first eight of which are in motion. The nearest is the sphere of the moon
(ll. 35, 39). Beyond it, there are the spheres of the six other 'erring stars'
(l. 44) or 'planets' (l. 51), all seven of which are named in ll. 53–5. The
'firmament' (l. 60), or sphere of the fixed stars, then completes the visible
universe. Outside all eight of these, there is the immovable 'empyreal
heaven' (ll. 60–1) or 'empyreal orb' (l. 39) where God sits 'High Thron'd
above all highth' (*Paradise Lost*, iii. 58).

36–44.] Faustus wishes to know whether the entire universe is spherical
as is the earth at the centre of it. Mephostophilis tells him that it is, explaining that just as in the sublunary, elemental part of the universe the
element of fire encloses that of air, which in turn encloses the elements of
water and earth, so in the celestial part each sphere is enclosed by the sphere
which is beyond it, the moving spheres having all a single axle-tree. Since
Saturn, Mars, Jupiter, and the rest have their separate planetary spheres
within the 'empyreal orb', it is not wrong, he concludes, to give them individual names. See Kocher, *C.M.*, pp. 214–16.

37. *centric*] central.

42. *termine*] This word, here used to mean 'end' or 'extremity', occurs

Nor are the names of Saturn, Mars, or Jupiter
Feign'd, but are erring stars.

Fau.   But have they all

One motion, both *situ et tempore*?   45

Meph. All move from east to west in four-and-twenty hours
upon the poles of the world, but differ in their motions
upon the poles of the zodiac.

Fau. These slender questions Wagner can decide:

Hath Mephostophilis no greater skill?   50

Who knows not the double motion of the planets?

That the first is finish'd in a natural day;

The second thus: Saturn in thirty years,

Jupiter in twelve, Mars in four, the sun, Venus, and Mer-

cury in a year, the moon in twenty-eight days. These are   55

freshmen's suppositions. But tell me, hath every sphere a

dominion or *intelligentia*?

Meph. Ay.

Fau. How many heavens or spheres are there?

---

44. erring] *A1*; euening *B1*.   44–5. But ... tempore?] *verse as here Boas;*
prose A1, B1.   44. have] *B1*; tell me, haue *A1*.   46. All] *B1*; All
ioyntly *A1*.   47. motions] *B1*; motion *A1*.   49. These] *B1*; Tush, these
A1.   questions] *B1*; trifles *A1*.   52. That] *B1*; *not in A1*.   53–7.]
Prose from Jupiter *Boas; prose from* The second *A1*; *verse divided after*
years, and, days, every *B1*.   53. thus:] *B1*; thus, as *A1*.   55. These]
B1; Tush these *A1*.   56. suppositions] *A1*; questions *B1*.

---

in a more technical, astrological sense in the 'Beaumont and Fletcher' play
Rollo, Duke of Normandy (ed. Jump), IV. ii. 189. There, too, it is a trisyllable.

45. *both* situ et tempore] both in position and in time. The sentence as a
whole means, 'But do they all move in the same direction and revolve round
the earth in the same time?'

48. *poles of the zodiac*] the common axle-tree on which all the spheres
revolve.

53–5. *Saturn ... days*] These figures are approximately correct, with one
exception: that for Mars is about twice what it should be.

56. *suppositions*] In scholastic logic, a supposition is something held to
be true and taken as the basis of an argument.

57. *dominion or* intelligentia] It was believed that angels or intelligences
directed the turning of the celestial spheres. Donne uses the belief in the
opening lines of his 'Goodfriday, 1613. Riding Westward': 'Let mans Soule
be a Spheare, and then, in this, / The intelligence that moves, devotion
is'.

Meph. Nine: the seven planets, the firmament, and the em-   60
    pyreal heaven.

Fau. But is there not *coelum igneum* ? *et crystallinum* ?

Meph. No, Faustus, they be but fables.

Fau. Resolve me then in this one question:
    Why are not conjunctions, oppositions, aspects, eclipses   65
    all at one time, but in some years we have more, in some
    less ?

Meph. *Per inaequalem motum respectu totius.*

Fau. Well, I am answered. Now tell me who made the world.

Meph. I will not.   70

Fau. Sweet Mephostophilis, tell me.

Meph. Move me not, Faustus.

60–1. empyreal] *B1;* imperiall *A1.*   62–3. *Fau.* But . . . fables.] *B1; not
in A1.*   62. et] *B1;* and *Greg.*   64. Resolve me then] *B1;* Well, resolue
me *A1.*   one] *B1; not in A1.*   64–5. question: / Why] *B1;* question,
why *A1.*   65. are] *B1;* haue wee *A1.*   69. Now] *B1; not in A1.*
72. Faustus] *B1;* for I will not tell thee *A1.*

62–3.] The *coelum crystallinum,* or crystalline sphere, was a tenth celestial
sphere which had been introduced into astronomical theory to account
for the 'trepidation of the spheares' (Donne, 'A Valediction: forbidding
mourning'), i.e. the supposed variation in the rate of precession of the
equinoxes. Some thinkers held that there was also a *coelum igneum,* or fiery
sphere; but Mephostophilis was not alone in denying its existence. In re-
stricting himself to eight moving spheres, he was in line with certain sceptical, empirical Renaissance writers on astronomy, who refused to believe
in moving spheres unfurnished with visible bodies by which their motions
could be directly observed. See F. R. Johnson, 'Marlowe's "Imperiall
Heaven"', *E.L.H.,* XII (1945), pp. 35–44, and 'Marlowe's Astronomy and
Renaissance Skepticism', *E.L.H.,* XIII (1946), pp. 241–54; also Kocher,
C.M., pp. 217–19.

65. *conjunctions, oppositions, aspects, eclipses*] A conjunction is an apparent
proximity to each other of two heavenly bodies. An opposition is an extreme
apparent divergence. These and certain other relative positions are called
aspects. Astrologers ascribe special significance to the various aspects and
to eclipses.

66. *all at one time*] all during the same stretch of time (and all recurring
during each subsequent period of the same length). In other words, at
regular intervals.

68. Per . . . totius] on account of their unequal motion with respect to
the whole. Mephostophilis means that the heavenly bodies do not all have
the same speed and direction of movement.

72. *Move*] anger.

Fau. Villain, have not I bound thee to tell me any thing ?

Meph. Ay, that is not against our kingdom.

     This is. Thou art damn'd; think thou of hell.   75

Fau. Think, Faustus, upon God, that made the world.

Meph. Remember this!   *Exit.*

Fau. Ay, go, accursed spirit, to ugly hell!

     'Tis thou hast damn'd distressed Faustus' soul.

     Is't not too late ?   80

Enter the two Angels.

Bad Ang. Too late.

Good Ang. Never too late, if Faustus will repent.

Bad Ang. If thou repent, devils will tear thee in pieces.

Good Ang. Repent, and they shall never raze thy skin.

                            Exeunt Angels.

Fau. O Christ, my saviour, my saviour,   85

     Help to save distressed Faustus' soul.

Enter LUCIFER, BEELZEBUB, *and* MEPHOSTOPHILIS.

Luc. Christ cannot save thy soul, for he is just;

     There's none but I have interest in the same.

Fau. O, what art thou that look'st so terribly ?

Luc. I am Lucifer,   90

     And this is my companion prince in hell.

Fau. O Faustus, they are come to fetch thy soul.

---

73. not I] *B1;* I not *A1.*   74–5. kingdom. / This . . . hell.] *B1;* kingdome, but this is, / Thinke thou on hell *Faustus,* for thou art damnd. *A1.* 79–80.] *Verse as here A1; one line B1.*   80.1. *Enter . . .* Angels.] *B1; Enter good Angell and euill. A1.*   82. will] *B1;* can *A1.*   83. will] *B1;* shall *A1.*   84.1. Angels] *B1; not in A1.*   85–6.] *Verse as here B1; prose A1.*   85. O] *B1;* Ah *A1.*   saviour, my saviour] *B1;* Sauiour *A1.*   86. Help] *B1;* seeke *A1.*   89. what] *B1;* who *A1.*   terribly] *B1;* terrible *A1.*   90–1.] *Verse as here Dilke; prose A1, B1.*   92. fetch] *B1;* fetch away *A1.*

---

77. *this*] i.e. my previous speech.

84. *raze*] graze.

86.] a deliberate echo of l. 79.

88. *interest in*] a legal claim upon.

Beel. We are come to tell thee thou dost injure us.

Luc. Thou call'st on Christ contrary to thy promise.

Beel. Thou shouldst not think on God.

Luc.   Think on the devil.   95

Beel. And his dam too.

Fau. Nor will I henceforth; pardon me in this,
        And Faustus vows never to look to heaven,
        Never to name God or to pray to him,
        To burn his scriptures, slay his ministers,   100
        And make my spirits pull his churches down.

Luc. So shalt thou show thyself an obedient servant,
        And we will highly gratify thee for it.

Beel. Faustus, we are come from hell in person to show thee
        some pastime. Sit down, and thou shalt behold the Seven   105
        Deadly Sins appear to thee in their own proper shapes
        and likeness.

Fau. That sight will be as pleasant to me as paradise was to
        Adam the first day of his creation.

Luc. Talk not of paradise or creation, but mark the show. Go,   110
        Mephostophilis, fetch them in.

            Enter the Seven Deadly Sins *[led by a* Piper].

93–6.] *Five speeches as here B1; a single speech, assigned to Lucifer, A1.*
93. are] *B1; not in A1.*   94. call'st on] *B1; talkst of A1.*   95. on] *B1;
of A1 (twice).*   96. And] *B1;* And of *A1.*   97. I] *A1; Faustus B1.*
me in] *A1;* him for *B1.*   99–101. Never . . . down.] *A1; not in B1.*
102–3. So . . . it.] *B1;* Do so, and we will highly gratifie thee: (*one line
of verse*) *A1.*   104. *Beel.*] *B1; not in A1.*   in person] *B1; not in A1.*
105. behold] *B1;* see al *A1.*   106. to thee] *B1; not in A1.*   own] *B1;
not in A1.*   107. and likeness] *B1; not in A1.*   108. pleasant to] *B1;*
pleasing vnto *A1.*   110. or] *B1;* nor *A1.*   the] *B1;* this *A1.*   110–
11. Go . . . in.] *B1;* talke of the diuel, and nothing else: come away. *A1.*
111.1. led by a *Piper*] *Greg; not in A1, B1.*

96. *And his dam too*] Several editors suspect that this short line is an
addition to Marlowe's text.

99–101.] These lines, which echo *The Jew of Malta*, v. i. 64–5, evidently
scared the editor of B1; who omitted them.

105–6. *pastime . . . the Seven Deadly Sins*] The 'pastime' takes a different
form in the *Damnable Life*. See Appendix II.

111.1. led by a *Piper*] Greg's addition of this phrase is authorized by
Lucifer's last words before the Sins leave.

Beel. Now, Faustus, question them of their names and dispo-
    sitions.

Fau. That shall I soon. What art thou, the first?

Pride. I am Pride. I disdain to have any parents. I am like to   115
    Ovid's flea; I can creep into every corner of a wench:
    sometimes, like a periwig, I sit upon her brow; next, like
    a necklace, I hang about her neck; then, like a fan of
    feathers, I kiss her lips; and then, turning myself to a
    wrought smock, do what I list. But fie, what a smell is   120
    here! I'll not speak another word, unless the ground be
    perfumed and covered with cloth of arras.

Fau. Thou art a proud knave indeed. What art thou, the
    second?

Covetousness. I am Covetousness, begotten of an old churl in   125
    a leather bag; and, might I now obtain my wish, this
    house, you and all, should turn to gold, that I might lock
    you safe into my chest. O my sweet gold!

Fau. And what art thou, the third?

Envy. I am Envy, begotten of a chimney-sweeper and an   130
    oyster-wife. I cannot read and therefore wish all books

112. *Beel.*] *B1; not in A1.*   question] *B1;* examine *A1.*   their] *B1;*
their seuerall *A1.*   114. That . . . soon.] *B1; not in A1.*   117–18. next
. . . neck] *B1; not in A1.*   118. then] *B1;* or *A1.*   119. lips] *A1; not in
B1.*   119–20. and . . . list.] *B1;* indeede I doe, what doe I not? *A1.*
120. smell] *B1;* scent *A1.*   121. another word] *A1;* a word more for a
Kings ransome *B1.*   unless] *B1;* except *A1.*   be] *B1;* were *A1.*
123. Thou . . . indeed.] *B1; not in A1.*   126. a leather] *E1;* an olde
leatherne *A1.*   now obtain] *B1;* haue *A1.*   126–7. this . . . turn] *B1;*
I would desire, that this house, and all the people in it were turnd *A1.*
128. safe into my] *B1;* vppe in my good *A1.*   129. And] *B1; not in A1.*
130–7.] *In A1 these lines follow, instead of preceding, 138–44.*

114. *soon*] at once.

116. *Ovid's flea*] In an *Elegia de Pulice,* a poem of uncertain date which
was at one time wrongly ascribed to Ovid, the poet says enviously to the
flea, 'Is quocumque placet; nil tibi, saeve, latet', i.e. You go wherever you
wish; nothing, savage, is hidden from you. See *Poetae Latini Minores* (ed.
N. E. Lemaire, Paris, 1826), vii. 275–8.

120. *wrought*] embroidered.

122. *cloth of arras*] To cover a floor with this rich tapestry fabric, as Pride
demands, would be extravagantly ostentatious.

130–1. *begotten . . . oyster-wife*] therefore black and stinking.

burned. I am lean with seeing others eat. O, that there
would come a famine over all the world, that all might
die, and I live alone! then thou shouldst see how fat I'd
be. But must thou sit and I stand? Come down, with a   135
vengeance!

Fau. Out, envious wretch! But what art thou, the fourth?

Wrath. I am Wrath. I had neither father nor mother; I leaped
out of a lion's mouth when I was scarce an hour old, and
ever since have run up and down the world with these   140
case of rapiers, wounding myself when I could get none
to fight withal. I was born in hell; and look to it, for some
of you shall be my father.

Fau. And what art thou, the fifth?

Gluttony. I am Gluttony. My parents are all dead, and the   145
devil a penny they have left me but a small pension, and
that buys me thirty meals a day and ten bevers—a small
trifle to suffice nature. I come of a royal pedigree: my
father was a gammon of bacon, and my mother was a
hogshead of claret wine; my godfathers were these, Peter   150
Pickled-herring and Martin Martlemas-beef. But my
godmother, O, she was a jolly gentlewoman, and well
beloved in every good town and city; her name was

132. burned] *B1;* were burnt *A1.*   133. over] *B1;* through *A1.*   134.
I'd] *B1;* I would *A1.*   137. Out] *B1;* Away *A1.*   wretch] *B1;* rascall
A1.   But] *B1; not in A1.*   fourth] *B1;* fift *A1 (see note on 130–7).*
139. scarce] *B1;* scarce half *A1.*   140. have] *B1;* I haue *A1.*   these]
B1; this *A1.*   141. could get none] *B1;* had no body *A1.*   144. And]
B1; not in A1.   fifth] *B1;* fourth *A1 (see note on 130–7).*   145. I] *B1;*
who I sir, I *A1.*   146. small] *B1;* bare *A1.*   147. buys me] *B1;* is *A1.*
148. I] *B1;* O I *A1.*   pedigree] *B1;* parentage *A1.*   149. father] *B1;*
grandfather *A1.*   and] *B1; not in A1.*   mother was] *B1;* grandmother
A1.   151. But] *B1;* O but *A1.*   152. O] *B1; not in A1.*   152–3. a ...
city] *A1;* an ancient Gentlewoman *B1.*

---

141. *case*] pair.

142–3. *some . . . be*] one of you is sure to prove.

147. *bevers*] light snacks.

151. *Martlemas-beef*] Martinmas, 11 November, was the customary
time for the annual slaughter of cattle for salting and winter consump-
tion.

Margery March-beer. Now, Faustus, thou hast heard
all my progeny; wilt thou bid me to supper?   155

Fau. No, I'll see thee hanged; thou wilt eat up all my victuals.

Glut. Then the devil choke thee.

Fau. Choke thyself, glutton! What art thou, the sixth?

Sloth. Heigh-ho! I am Sloth. I was begotten on a sunny bank,   160
where I have lain ever since; and you have done me great
injury to bring me from thence: let me be carried thither
again by Gluttony and Lechery. Heigh-ho! I'll not speak
a word more for a king's ransom.

Fau. And what are you, Mistress Minx, the seventh and last?   165

Lechery. Who, I, sir? I am one that loves an inch of raw
mutton better than an ell of fried stockfish, and the first
letter of my name begins with Lechery.

Luc. Away, to hell, away! On, piper!

Exeunt the Seven Sins [*and the* Piper].

Fau. O, how this sight doth delight my soul!   170

Luc. But, Faustus, in hell is all manner of delight.

Fau. O, might I see hell and return again safe, how happy
were I then!

Luc. Faustus, thou shalt; at midnight I will send for thee.

154. Margery] *B1;* mistresse Margery *A1.*   156–7. No . . . victuals.] *A1;*
Not I. *B1.*   160. Heigh-ho!] *B1; not in A1.*   161–3. where . . . Lechery]
A1; not in B1.   163. Heigh-ho!] *B1; not in A1.*   164. a word more]
B1; an other word *A1.*   165. And] *B1; not in A1.*   166. Who, I] *A1;*
Who I I *B1.*   169. *Luc.*] *B1; not in A1.*   away! On, piper!] *B1;* to
hel. *A1.*   169.1. Seven] *B1; not in A1.*   *and the* Piper] *This ed.; not in
A1, B1.*   170. *Fau.* O . . . delight] *B1; Lu.* Now Faustus, how dost thou
like this? / *Fau:* O this feedes *A1.*   171. But] *B1;* Tut *A1.*   172. safe]
B1; not in A1.   174–80.] *Verse as here B1; prose A1.*   174. Faustus]
B1; not in A1.   174–5. at . . . view] *B1;* I wil send for thee at midnight,
in mean time take this booke, peruse *A1.*

154. *March-beer*] a strong beer brewed in March.
155. *progeny*] lineage.
167. *mutton*] a cant term for a prostitute.
stockfish] dried codfish.
167–8. *the first . . . Lechery*] a well-known facetious form of words. Compare Lyly, *Euphues and his England* (ed. Bond, ii. 111), 'the first letter of
whose name . . . is *Camilla*'. See P. A. Daniel, quoted by Ward.

Meanwhile peruse this book and view it throughly,   175
And thou shalt turn thyself into what shape thou wilt.
Fau. Thanks, mighty Lucifer.
    This will I keep as chary as my life.
Luc. Now, Faustus, farewell.
Fau. Farewell, great Lucifer. Come, Mephostophilis.   180
                                    Exeunt omnes several ways.

[Scene vii]
                        Enter the Clown [ROBIN].

Rob. What, Dick, look to the horses there till I come again. I
    have gotten one of Doctor Faustus' conjuring books, and
    now we'll have such knavery as 't passes.

                            Enter DICK.

Dick. What, Robin, you must come away and walk the horses.
Rob. I walk the horses! I scorn 't, 'faith, I have other matters   5
    in hand; let the horses walk themselves and they will.
    [*Reading*] *A per se, a; t, h, e, the; o per se, o; deny orgon,
    gorgon.* Keep further from me, O thou illiterate and un-
    learned ostler.

177. Thanks] *B1*; Great thankes *A1*.   179. Now . . . farewell.] *B1*;
Farewel Faustus, and thinke on the diuel. *A1*.   180.1. *several ways*] *B1*;
not in A1.

Scene vii.] *A1 introduces its version of this scene immediately before scene x.
This version is given in Appendix I (see section 5 of the 'Introduction').*
0.1. ROBIN] *Dyce; not in B1*.   1. Rob.] *Dyce; not in B1*.   7. Reading]
This ed.; not in B1.

178. *chary*] carefully.
180.1. several] different.

vii. 3. *as 't passes*] as beats everything.
7. A per se, a; t, h, e, the; o per se, o] As Greg makes clear, Robin is
reading from his book with difficulty. He means, 'A, by itself, spells a;
t, h, e, spells the; o, by itself, spells o'.
7–8. deny orgon, gorgon] Robin is struggling to read the name 'Demogorgon', which has already figured in Faustus' invocation at iii. 19.

Dick. 'Snails, what hast thou got there, a book? Why, thou   10
    canst not tell ne'er a word on't.

Rob. That thou shalt see presently. Keep out of the circle, I
    say, lest I send you into the hostry with a vengeance.

Dick. That's like, 'faith! You had best leave your foolery, for
    an my master come he'll conjure you, 'faith.   15

Rob. My master conjure me! I'll tell thee what, an my master
    come here, I'll clap as fair a pair of horns on's head as e'er
    thou sawest in thy life.

Dick. Thou needest not do that, for my mistress hath done it.

Rob. Ay, there be of us here that have waded as deep into   20
    matters as other men, if they were disposed to talk.

Dick. A plague take you! I thought you did not sneak up and
    down after her for nothing. But I prithee tell me in good
    sadness, Robin, is that a conjuring book?

Rob. Do but speak what thou'lt have me to do, and I'll do 't.   25
    If thou'lt dance naked, put off thy clothes, and I'll con-
    jure thee about presently. Or if thou'lt go but to the tavern
    with me, I'll give thee white wine, red wine, claret wine,
    sack, muscadine, malmsey, and whippincrust, hold-belly-
    hold, and we'll not pay one penny for it.   30

---

10. *'Snails*] God's nails. An oath.

13. *hostry*] inn, hostelry.

15. *an*] if.

20–1. *waded . . . matters*] Boas explains the *double entendre* by quoting *Julius Caesar*, I. i. 24–5: 'I meddle with no tradesman's matters, nor women's matters'.

23–4. *in good sadness*] in earnest.

27. *to the tavern*] from which they emerge at the beginning of scene x.

28. *claret wine*] wine of light red colour. About 1600 the term came to be used for red wines generally.

29. *sack*] the name of a class of strong light-coloured wines imported from Spain and the Canaries.

muscadine] muscatel.

malmsey] another strong sweet wine.

whippincrust] a humorous distortion of 'hippocras', which appears in its usual form in the corresponding scene in A1. Hippocras, named after Hippocrates (see comment on i. 19), was a cordial drink made of wine flavoured with spices. Greg suggests that the present form contains a suggestion of 'whipping-cheer', i.e. flogging.

29–30. *hold-belly-hold*] a belly-full.

Dick. O brave! prithee let's to it presently, for I am as dry as a
     dog.
Rob. Come, then, let's away.   *Exeunt.*

[Chorus 1]

               Enter the Chorus.

Cho. Learned Faustus,
         To find the secrets of astronomy,
         Graven in the book of Jove's high firmament,
         Did mount him up to scale Olympus' top,
         Where, sitting in a chariot burning bright   5
         Drawn by the strength of yoked dragons' necks,
         He views the clouds, the planets, and the stars,
         The tropics, zones, and quarters of the sky,
         From the bright circle of the horned moon
         Even to the height of *primum mobile*;   10
         And, whirling round with this circumference
         Within the concave compass of the pole,
         From east to west his dragons swiftly glide
         And in eight days did bring him home again.
         Not long he stay'd within his quiet house   15

Chorus 1. 0.1. *the* Chorus] *B1; Wagner solus A1.*   1. *Cho.*] *Oxberry;*
Wag. A1; not in B1.   1–2.] *Verse as here A1; one line B1.*   2. find] *B1;*
know *A1.*   4. him up] *B1;* himselfe *A1.*   5. Where, sitting] *B1;* Being
seated *A1.*   6. yoked] *B1;* yoky *A1.*   7–19. He . . . air,] *B1; not in A1.*
8. tropics] *Greg;* Tropick *B1.*

31–2. *as dry as a dog*] a current proverbial saying. See Tilley, D433.

Chorus 1. 8. *tropics . . . sky* 'the tropics (of Cancer and Capricorn) and
the five zones in which they (and the polar circles) divide or 'quarter' the
heavens—for it is the sky, rather than the earth, that is in question' (Greg).

9–10.] from the lowest to the highest of the moving spheres. The *primum
mobile*, i.e. the first moving thing, was a sphere which imparted motion to
each sphere or 'circle' that it enclosed. Marlowe, acknowledging only nine
spheres altogether, identifies the *primum mobile* with the firmament.

11. *this circumference*] beyond which lay only the empyrean. In other
words, Faustus was able to go everywhere short of the abode of God.

12. *the concave . . . pole*] Kocher explains this as referring to the concave
outer limits of all that revolves upon the axis of the universe.

To rest his bones after his weary toil,
But new exploits do hale him out again,
And, mounted then upon a dragon's back,
That with his wings did part the subtle air,
He now is gone to prove cosmography,   20
That measures coasts and kingdoms of the earth,
And as I guess will first arrive at Rome
To see the Pope and manner of his court
And take some part of holy Peter's feast,
The which this day is highly solemniz'd.   *Exit.* 25

[Scene viii]

Enter FAUSTUS *and* MEPHOSTOPHILIS.

Fau. Having now, my good Mephostophilis,
Pass'd with delight the stately town of Trier,
Environ'd round with airy mountain-tops,
With walls of flint, and deep-entrenched lakes,
Not to be won by any conquering prince;   5
From Paris next, coasting the realm of France,
We saw the river Main fall into Rhine,
Whose banks are set with groves of fruitful vines;
Then up to Naples, rich Campania,
With buildings fair and gorgeous to the eye,   10
Whose streets straight forth and pav'd with finest brick

---

21. That . . . earth,] *B1; not in A1.*   25. The which] *B1;* That to *A1.*
Exit.] *B1; exit Wagner A1.*

viii. 9. up to] *A1, B1;* vnto *B3.*   10. With] *Greg;* Whose *A1, B1.*   11.
Whose] *Greg;* The *A1, B1.*

---

19. *subtle*] tenuous, rarified.
20. *prove*] put to the test.
24. *take some part of*] share in. See *O.E.D., part, sb.*, 23.

viii. 4. *lakes*] moats.
9. *Naples, rich Campania*] The *Damnable Life*, here misrepresenting the
original German, seems to have betrayed Marlowe into this erroneous
identification of Campania with Naples. See Appendix II.
11. *straight forth*] in straight lines.

Quarters the town in four equivalents.
There saw we learned Maro's golden tomb,
The way he cut, an English mile in length,
Thorough a rock of stone in one night's space.   15
From thence to Venice, Padua, and the rest,
In midst of which a sumptuous temple stands,
That threats the stars with her aspiring top,
Whose frame is pav'd with sundry colour'd stones
And roof'd aloft with curious work in gold.   20
Thus hitherto hath Faustus spent his time.
But tell me now, what resting-place is this?
Hast thou, as erst I did command,
Conducted me within the walls of Rome?

Meph. I have, my Faustus, and for proof thereof   25
This is the goodly palace of the Pope,
And 'cause we are no common guests
I choose his privy chamber for our use.

Fau. I hope his Holiness will bid us welcome.

Meph. All's one, for we'll be bold with his venison.   30
But now, my Faustus, that thou may'st perceive

12. Quarters . . . equivalents.] *A1; not in B1.*   equivalents] *Dyce;*
equiuolence *A1.*   15. Thorough] *A1;* Through *B1.*   16. rest] *A1;*
East *B1.*   17. midst] *A1;* one *B1.*   19–20. Whose . . . gold.] *B1;*
not in A1.   25–8. I . . . his] *B1;* Faustus I haue, and because we wil
not be vnprouided, I haue taken vp his holinesse *A1.*   30. All's one,
for] *B1;* Tut, tis no matter man, *A1.*   venison] *B1;* good cheare *A1.*
31. But] *B1;* And *A1.*

13–15.] Publius Vergilius Maro, who died in 19 B.C., was buried at
Naples. During the Middle Ages, he acquired a surprising reputation as a
necromancer, and an ancient passageway running through the promon-
tory of Posillipo between Naples and Pozzuoli was ascribed to his arts.
See J. W. Spargo, *Virgil the Necromancer* (Cambridge, Mass., 1934),
pp. 292–5.

17–20.] This 'temple' is St Mark's, Venice. It has not, in fact, the 'aspiring top' which Marlowe here attributes to it. In all probability, he simply
fell back upon one of his favourite terms to describe a building which the
Damnable Life told him was 'sumptuous'. See comment on iii. 70.

31–46.] The 'sittie of Rome' (*Henslowe Papers*, p. 116), which appears
among the properties belonging to the Admiral's Men in 1598, may perhaps have been a backcloth for use at this point.

What Rome contains for to delight thine eyes,
Know that this city stands upon seven hills
That underprop the groundwork of the same:
Just through the midst runs flowing Tiber's stream,   35
With winding banks that cut it in two parts,
Over the which four stately bridges lean,
That make safe passage to each part of Rome.
Upon the bridge call'd Ponte Angelo
Erected is a castle passing strong,   40
Where thou shalt see such store of ordinance
As that the double cannons forg'd of brass
Do match the number of the days contain'd
Within the compass of one complete year;
Beside the gates, and high pyramides   45
That Julius Caesar brought from Africa.

32. contains . . . eyes] *B1;* containeth to delight thee with *A1.*   34. under-
prop] *B1;* vnderprops *A1.*   35–6. Just . . . parts,] *B1; not in A1.*   37.
four] *A1;* two *B1.*   38. make] *B1;* makes *A1.*   41. Where thou shalt
see] *B1;* Within whose walles *A1.*   ordinance] *B1;* ordonance are *A1.*
42. As that the] *B1;* And *A1.*   forg'd of] *B1;* fram'd of carued *A1.*
43–4. Do . . . year;] *B1;* As match the dayes within one compleate yeare, *A1.*
43. match] *A1;* watch *B1.*   45. Beside] *B1;* Besides *A1.*   46. That]
B1; Which *A1.*

---

37. *lean*] bend, incline.

39–40.] In reality, the bridge leads to the castle, which stands upon the
bank of the Tiber. The *Damnable Life* seems to have misled Marlowe. See
Appendix II.

42. *double cannons*] probably cannons of very large calibre. In 1536, the
brothers John and Robert Owen cast a 'fair double cannon' at Calais which
aroused the interest of Henry VIII. But this Great Piece, presumably an
outsize bombard, could not be brought to Westminster for his inspection
in 1537 because Harry Johnson, the master gunner at Calais, failed to
provide an axle-tree for it. See C. ffoulkes, *The Gun-Founders of England*
(Cambridge, 1937), pp. 30–1, 48–9, 110. A 'double Canon' is mentioned
in the anonymous comedy *Wily Beguiled* (ed. Greg), l. 562. Clifford Leech
refers privately to *Macbeth*, I. ii. 37, 'cannons overcharg'd with double
cracks', commenting that here presumably a quart is put into a pint pot.

45. *Beside*} besides.

pyramides] the obelisk which the emperor Caligula brought from Helio-
polis in the first century A.D. and which was moved to the Piazza San Pietro,
where it still stands, in 1586. Boas points out that Marlowe again uses
'pyramides' as a singular in *The Massacre at Paris*, ii. 43–6.

Fau. Now, by the kingdoms of infernal rule,
    Of Styx, of Acheron, and the fiery lake
    Of ever-burning Phlegethon, I swear
    That I do long to see the monuments   50
    And situation of bright-splendent Rome.
    Come, therefore, let's away.
Meph. Nay, stay, my Faustus; I know you'd see the Pope
    And take some part of holy Peter's feast,
    The which in state and high solemnity   55
    This day is held through Rome and Italy
    In honour of the Pope's triumphant victory.
Fau. Sweet Mephostophilis, thou pleasest me:
    Whilst I am here on earth let me be cloy'd
    With all things that delight the heart of man.   60
    My four-and-twenty years of liberty
    I'll spend in pleasure and in dalliance,
    That Faustus' name, whilst this bright frame doth stand,
    May be admired through the furthest land.
Meph. 'Tis well said, Faustus; come, then, stand by me   65
    And thou shalt see them come immediately.
Fau. Nay, stay, my gentle Mephostophilis,
    And grant me my request, and then I go.
    Thou know'st within the compass of eight days

---

48. of] *B1; not in A1.*   53. stay, my Faustus] *B1;* Faustus stay *A1.*
you'd] *B1;* youd faine *A1.*   55–7. The . . . victory.] *B1;* Where thou
shalt see a troupe of bald-pate Friers, / Whose *summum bonum* is in belly-
cheare. *A1.*   55. in state and] *B2;* this day with *B1.*   58–201.] *A1
contains no version either of these lines or of the first eight lines of scene ix. It
makes a single scene out of what it retains of scenes viii and ix.*

47–51.] 'To Mephostophilis' account of the wonders of Rome Faustus
replies with an extraordinary piece of rodomontade, swearing by the three
rivers of Hades—that he wants to see the sights!' (Greg). One of the rivers
is here called a 'lake': compare l. 4.

51. *situation*] lay-out. See section 8 of the 'Introduction', p. xlv.
bright-splendent] brilliantly magnificent.

53–6.] These lines echo the last three lines of Chorus 1.

57. *the Pope's triumphant victory*] See comment on ll. 90–6.

69–75.] These lines refer again to the travels described in the first fourteen lines of Chorus 1.

We view'd the face of heaven, of earth, and hell. 70
So high our dragons soar'd into the air
That looking down the earth appear'd to me
No bigger than my hand in quantity.
There did we view the kingdoms of the world,
And what might please mine eye I there beheld. 75
Then in this show let me an actor be,
That this proud Pope may Faustus' cunning see.
Meph. Let it be so, my Faustus, but first stay
And view their triumphs as they pass this way;
And then devise what best contents thy mind, 80
By cunning in thine art to cross the Pope
Or dash the pride of this solemnity,
To make his monks and abbots stand like apes
And point like antics at his triple crown,
To beat the beads about the friars' pates 85
Or clap huge horns upon the cardinals' heads,
Or any villainy thou canst devise,
And I'll perform it, Faustus. Hark, they come!
This day shall make thee be admir'd in Rome.

Enter the Cardinals *and* Bishops, *some bearing crosiers, some the
pillars;* Monks *and* Friars *singing their procession. Then the* Pope
and RAYMOND, KING OF HUNGARY, *with* BRUNO *led in chains.*

Pope. Cast down our footstool.
Ray.   Saxon Bruno, stoop, 90

77, 81. cunning] *B4;* comming *B1.*

---

79. *triumphs*] spectacular festivities.
84. *antics*] grotesques.
89. *admir'd*] marvelled at.
89.2. pillars] portable pillars carried as symbols of dignity or office.
Wolsey, followed by Pole, seems to have substituted a pair of them for the
silver mace to which a cardinal had a right. There is no other record of
their use.

procession] form of prayer or worship sung in a religious procession.
90–6.] Pope Adrian's victory over the imperial forces and his treatment
of the captured Bruno, the rival pope elected by the Emperor, seem to have
been suggested by passages in John Foxe's *Acts and Monuments,* better
known as Foxe's Book of Martyrs. From this, the playwright could have

    Whilst on thy back his Holiness ascends
    Saint Peter's chair and state pontifical.
Bru. Proud Lucifer, that state belongs to me:
    But thus I fall to Peter, not to thee.
Pope. To me and Peter shalt thou grovelling lie   95
    And crouch before the papal dignity:
    Sound trumpets, then, for thus Saint Peter's heir
    From Bruno's back ascends Saint Peter's chair.

                                 A flourish while he ascends.

    Thus as the gods creep on with feet of wool
    Long ere with iron hands they punish men,   100
    So shall our sleeping vengeance now arise
    And smite with death thy hated enterprise.
    Lord Cardinals of France and Padua,
    Go forthwith to our holy consistory

---

103. France] *B1;* Florence *conj. Greg.*

---

learned how Adrian IV (1154–9) came into conflict with the Empire, 'blustering and thundering against Frederic, the emperor' (ed. Pratt, ii. 189). After his account of Adrian IV, Foxe continues: 'Although this Adrian was bad enough, yet came the next much worse, one Alexander III., who yet was not elected alone; for beside him the emperor, with nine cardinals, . . . did set up another pope, named Victor IV. Between these two popes arose a foul schism and great discord' (ii. 195). Eventually Alexander, having captured Frederick's son, forced the Emperor to submit. Frederick was ordered to kneel at the Pope's feet. 'The proud pope, setting his foot upon the emperor's neck, said the verse of the psalm, "Super aspidem et basiliscum ambulabis, et conculcabis leonem et draconem:" that is, "Thou shalt walk upon the adder and on the basilisk, and shalt tread down the lion and the dragon." To whom the emperor answering again, said, "Non tibi sed Petro:" that is, "Not to thee, but to Peter." The pope again, "Et mihi et Petro;" "Both to me and to Peter." The emperor . . . held his peace' (ii. 195–6). This is apparently the source both of the present passage—though there is a similar incident in 1 *Tamburlaine,* IV. ii—and of ll. 136–42. It is also conceivable that the playwright named his pope after Adrian VI (1522–3), who was contemporary with the historical Faustus. See L. M. Oliver, 'Rowley, Foxe, and the *Faustus* Additions', *M.L.N.*, LX (1945), pp. 391–4.

92. *state*] throne.

98.1. flourish] fanfare of trumpets.

99–100.] The Pope refers to the proverb, 'God comes with leaden (woollen) feet but strikes with iron hands'. See Tilley, G182.

104. *consistory*] i.e. the meeting-place of the papal consistory or senate.

And read amongst the statutes decretal   105
What, by the holy council held at Trent,
The sacred synod hath decreed for him
That doth assume the papal government
Without election and a true consent.
Away, and bring us word with speed.   110
1 Card. We go, my lord.   *Exeunt* Cardinals.
Pope. Lord Raymond—
Fau. Go, haste thee, gentle Mephostophilis,
  Follow the cardinals to the consistory,
  And, as they turn their superstitious books,   115
  Strike them with sloth and drowsy idleness;
  And make them sleep so sound that in their shapes
  Thyself and I may parley with this Pope,
  This proud confronter of the Emperor,
  And in despite of all his holiness   120
  Restore this Bruno to his liberty
  And bear him to the states of Germany.
Meph. Faustus, I go.
Fau.   Dispatch it soon:
  The Pope shall curse that Faustus came to Rome.

                     Exeunt FAUSTUS *and* MEPHOSTOPHILIS.

Bru. Pope Adrian, let me have some right of law;   125
  I was elected by the Emperor.
Pope. We will depose the Emperor for that deed

110. word] *B1;* word again *Greg.*   124.1. *Exeunt*] *Oxberry; Exit B1.*

---

105. *statutes decretal*] 'properly the collection of papal decrees that con-
stituted one part of canon law; here evidently applied to the whole of eccle-
siastical law, including the decrees of councils' (Greg).

106. *council held at Trent*] The Council of Trent sat with interruptions
from 1545 to 1563. This means that, like the reign of Philip II (see i. 131),
it opened after the death of the historical Faustus (c. 1540).

107. *synod*] general council.

112.] The Pope and Raymond converse apart.

125. *let . . . law*] allow that I have some legal claim.

126.] Bruno's defence against the charge that he has assumed 'the papal
government / Without election' (ll. 108–9).

127–31.] Early in 1570, Pius V issued a famous bull declaring that Elizabeth I was excommunicated, depriving her of her right to the throne, and

And curse the people that submit to him;
Both he and thou shalt stand excommunicate
And interdict from church's privilege   130
And all society of holy men.
He grows too proud in his authority,
Lifting his lofty head above the clouds,
And like a steeple overpeers the church.
But we'll pull down his haughty insolence;   135
And, as Pope Alexander, our progenitor,
Trod on the neck of German Frederick,
Adding this golden sentence to our praise,
'That Peter's heirs should tread on emperors
And walk upon the dreadful adder's back,   140
Treading the lion and the dragon down,
And fearless spurn the killing basilisk',
So will we quell that haughty schismatic
And by authority apostolical
Depose him from his regal government.   145
Bru. Pope Julius swore to princely Sigismund,
For him and the succeeding popes of Rome,
To hold the emperors their lawful lords.
Pope. Pope Julius did abuse the church's rights,
And therefore none of his decrees can stand.   150
Is not all power on earth bestow'd on us?
And therefore though we would we cannot err.
Behold this silver belt, whereto is fix'd
Seven golden keys fast seal'd with seven seals

149. rights] *Dyce;* Rites *B1.*   154. keys] *Oxberry;* seales *B1.*

commanding her people on pain of anathema to cease to obey her. This
may well have been in the playwright's mind.
   130. *interdict*] authoritatively cut off.
   136–42.] See comment on ll. 90–6.
   136. *progenitor*] predecessor.
   142. *basilisk*] a fabulous reptile which kills by its look.
   143. *schismatic*] accented on the first and third syllables.
   146–8.] This is fictitious. There was no Pope Julius during the lifetime
of the Emperor Sigismund.
   154. *keys*] of St Peter.

In token of our sevenfold power from heaven,   155
To bind or loose, lock fast, condemn, or judge,
Resign or seal, or whatso pleaseth us.
Then he and thou and all the world shall stoop,
Or be assured of our dreadful curse
To light as heavy as the pains of hell.   160

Enter FAUSTUS *and* MEPHOSTOPHILIS *like the cardinals.*

Meph. Now tell me, Faustus, are we not fitted well?
Fau. Yes, Mephostophilis, and two such cardinals
Ne'er serv'd a holy pope as we shall do.
But whilst they sleep within the consistory
Let us salute his reverend Fatherhood.   165
Ray. Behold, my lord, the cardinals are return'd.
Pope. Welcome, grave fathers, answer presently,
What have our holy council there decreed
Concerning Bruno and the Emperor,
In quittance of their late conspiracy   170
Against our state and papal dignity?
Fau. Most sacred patron of the church of Rome,
By full consent of all the synod
Of priests and prelates, it is thus decreed:
That Bruno and the German Emperor   175
Be held as lollards and bold schismatics
And proud disturbers of the church's peace.
And if that Bruno by his own assent,
Without enforcement of the German peers,
Did seek to wear the triple diadem   180
And by your death to climb Saint Peter's chair,
The statutes decretal have thus decreed,

173. the] *B1;* the holy *conj. Dyce.*

_____

157. *Resign*] 'The word here, in its contrast with "seal", seems to have almost the meaning of the Latin "resignare", unseal' (Boas).

170. *quittance of*] requital for.

176. *lollards*] heretics. The name was given to the followers of Wyclif and to others holding similar views.

179. *enforcement of*] compulsion by.

He shall be straight condemn'd of heresy
And on a pile of faggots burnt to death.

Pope. It is enough. Here, take him to your charge   185
And bear him straight to Ponte Angelo,
And in the strongest tower enclose him fast.
Tomorrow, sitting in our consistory
With all our college of grave cardinals,
We will determine of his life or death.   190
Here, take his triple crown along with you
And leave it in the church's treasury.
Make haste again, my good lord cardinals,
And take our blessing apostolical.

Meph. So, so; was never devil thus blest before.   195

Fau. Away, sweet Mephostophilis, be gone:
The cardinals will be plagu'd for this anon.

Exeunt FAUSTUS *and* MEPHOSTOPHILIS [*with* BRUNO].

Pope. Go presently and bring a banquet forth,
That we may solemnize Saint Peter's feast
And with Lord Raymond, King of Hungary,   200
Drink to our late and happy victory.   *Exeunt.*

[Scene ix]

The banquet is brought in; and then enter FAUSTUS *and*
MEPHOSTOPHILIS *in their own shapes.*

Meph. Now, Faustus, come, prepare thyself for mirth:
The sleepy cardinals are hard at hand

197.1. *with* BRUNO] *Dyce; not in* B1.

ix. 0.1. *The*] *Greg; A Senit while the* B1.

---

186. *to Ponte Angelo*] i.e. to the castle which stands on (or by) the bridge.
See comment on ll. 39–40.

189. *college of grave cardinals*] the assembled cardinals of the Roman
Catholic Church, who constitute the Pope's council.

191. *his*] Bruno had assumed the tiara.

193. *again*] i.e. to return.

  To censure Bruno, that is posted hence,
  And on a proud-pac'd steed as swift as thought
  Flies o'er the Alps to fruitful Germany,   5
  There to salute the woeful Emperor.
Fau. The Pope will curse them for their sloth today,
  That slept both Bruno and his crown away.
  But now, that Faustus may delight his mind
  And by their folly make some merriment,   10
  Sweet Mephostophilis, so charm me here
  That I may walk invisible to all
  And do whate'er I please, unseen of any.
Meph. Faustus, thou shalt; then kneel down presently,
    Whilst on thy head I lay my hand   15
    And charm thee with this magic wand.
    First wear this girdle, then appear
    Invisible to all are here:
    The planets seven, the gloomy air,
    Hell, and the Furies' forked hair,   20
    Pluto's blue fire, and Hecate's tree
    With magic spells so compass thee
    That no eye may thy body see.
  So, Faustus, now, for all their holiness,
  Do what thou wilt, thou shalt not be discern'd.   25

9–13. But . . . any.] *B1; Fau.* Well, I am content, to compasse then [them
Wagner] some sport, / And by their folly make vs merriment, / Then
charme me that I may be inuisible, to do what I please vnseene of any
whilst I stay in Rome. *A1 (continuing the scene opened by its version of viii.
1–57: see note on viii. 58–201).* 14–23. *Meph.* Faustus . . . *see.*] *B1; not
in A1.* 21. tree] *B1; three conj. Boas.* 24–5.] *Verse as here B1; prose
A1.* 24. for all their holiness] *B1; not in A1.*

---

 3. *censure*] pronounce judgement on.
 20. forked 'hair] Greg suggests that the author was thinking of the
forked tongues of the snakes that are shown as forming the hair of the
Furies.
 21. Pluto's blue fire] the sulphurous flames associated with the god of
the nether world.
 Hecate's tree] 'Hecate was Trivia, the goddess of the cross-ways, so con-
ceivably the gallows-tree may be meant' (Greg). Boas suggests that the
reading should be 'three', in allusion to Hecate's triform divinity.

Fau. Thanks, Mephostophilis; now, friars, take heed
    Lest Faustus make your shaven crowns to bleed.
Meph. Faustus, no more; see where the cardinals come.

     Sound a sennet. Enter Pope *and all the* Lords. *Enter the*
                 Cardinals *with a book.*

Pope. Welcome, lord cardinals; come, sit down.
    Lord Raymond, take your seat. Friars, attend,   30
    And see that all things be in readiness,
    As best beseems this solemn festival.
1 Card. First, may it please your sacred Holiness
    To view the sentence of the reverend synod
    Concerning Bruno and the Emperor?   35
Pope. What needs this question? Did I not tell you
    Tomorrow we would sit i' th' consistory
    And there determine of his punishment?
    You brought us word even now, it was decreed
    That Bruno and the cursed Emperor   40
    Were by the holy council both condemn'd
    For loathed lollards and base schismatics:
    Then wherefore would you have me view that book?
1 Card. Your Grace mistakes; you gave us no such charge.
Ray. Deny it not; we all are witnesses   45
    That Bruno here was late deliver'd you,
    With his rich triple crown to be reserv'd
    And put into the church's treasury.
Ambo Card. By holy Paul, we saw them not.

26–8. *Fau.* Thanks . . . come.] *B1; not in A1.*   28.1. *Sound a sennet.*] *A1;
not in B1.*   28.1–2. *Enter* Pope . . . *book.*] *B1; enter the Pope and the Cardinall of Lorraine to the banket, with Friers attending. A1.*   29–58. *Pope.*
Welcome . . . Holiness.] *B1;* Pope My Lord of *Lorraine,* wilt please you
draw neare. *A1.*

    28.1. a sennet] a set of notes on the trumpet as the signal for a ceremonial
entrance or exit.
    Lords] including Raymond, King of Hungary, and the Archbishop of
Rheims.
    47. *reserv'd*] preserved, kept safe.
    49. Ambo Card.] both cardinals.

Pope. By Peter, you shall die,   50
  Unless you bring them forth immediately.
  Hale them to prison, lade their limbs with gyves!
  False prelates, for this hateful treachery
  Curs'd be your souls to hellish misery.

                 [*Exeunt* Attendants *with the two* Cardinals.]

Fau. So, they are safe. Now, Faustus, to the feast: 55
  The Pope had never such a frolic guest.

Pope. Lord Archbishop of Rheims, sit down with us.

Arch. I thank your Holiness.

Fau. Fall to, the devil choke you an you spare!

Pope. Who's that spoke ? Friars, look about.   60

Fri. Here's nobody, if it like your Holiness.

Pope. Lord Raymond, pray fall to: I am beholding
  To the Bishop of Milan for this so rare a present.

Fau. I thank you, sir.   *Snatch it.*

Pope. How now! Who snatch'd the meat from me ?   65
  Villains, why speak you not ?—
  My good Lord Archbishop, here's a most dainty dish ——
  Was sent me from a cardinal in France.

Fau. I'll have that too.   [*Snatch it.*]

Pope. What lollards do attend our Holiness   70
  That we receive such great indignity ?
  Fetch me some wine.

54.1. *Exeunt* . . . Cardinals.] *Dyce; not in B1.*   58. *Arch.] Dyce; Bish. B1.*
59. to,] *B1; too, and A1.*   60. Who's that spoke ?] *B1; How now, whose
that which spake ? A1.*   61–2. *Fri.* Here's . . . Holiness. | *Pope.] A1; not
in B1.*   62–3. Lord . . . present.] *B1; My Lord, here is a daintie dish was
sent me from the Bishop of Millaine. A1.*   64. *Snatch it.] A1; not in B1.*
65. Who] *B1; whose that which A1.*   65–6. me ? | Villains . . . not ?] *B1;
me ? will no man looke ? A1.*   66–7.] *Between these lines, Greg inserts 61,
not having introduced it earlier.*   67–8. My . . . France.] *B1; My Lord,
this dish was sent me from the Cardinall of Florence. A1.*   69. I'll . . .
too.] *B1; You say true, Ile hate. A1.   Snatch it.] Dyce (subs.); not in A1,
B1.*   70–3. *Pope.* What . . . adry.] *B1; not in A1.*   71–2.] *Verse as here
Oxberry; one line B1.*

---

59. *Fall to*] set to work, make a start; used especially of eating.
the devil choke you] Compare Gluttony's words, vi. 158.

Fau. Ay, pray do, for Faustus is adry.

Pope. Lord Raymond, I drink unto your Grace.

Fau. I pledge your Grace.   [*Snatch it.*] 75

Pope. My wine gone too? Ye lubbers, look about
    And find the man that doth this villainy,
    Or by our sanctitude you all shall die.—
    I pray, my lords, have patience at this
    Troublesome banquet.   80

Arch. Please it your Holiness, I think it be
    Some ghost crept out of purgatory, and now
    Is come unto your Holiness for his pardon.

Pope. It may be so:
    Go, then, command our priests to sing a dirge   85
    To lay the fury of this same troublesome ghost.—
    Once again, my lord, fall to.   *The* Pope *crosseth himself.*

Fau. How now?
    Must every bit be spiced with a cross?
    Well, use that trick no more, I would advise you. *Cross again.*
    Well, there's the second time; aware the third: 91
    I give you fair warning.   *Cross again.*

74. Lord Raymond, I] *B1;* What againe? my Lord Ile *A1.*   unto] *B1;*
to *A1.*   75. I] *B1;* Ile *A1.*   Snatch it.] *Dyce (subs.); not in A1, B1.*
76-80. *Pope. My ... banquet.] B1; not in A1.*   81-3.] *Verse as here Boas;*
prose B1; My Lord, it may be some ghost newly crept out of Purgatory
come to begge a pardon of your holinesse. *A1.*   81. *Arch.] Dyce; Bish.*
B1; Lor. A1.   84-6.] *Verse as here B1; prose A1.*   85. Go ... dirge]
B1; Friers prepare a dirge *A1.*   86. same troublesome] *B1; not in A1.*
87. Once ... *himself.] A1; not in B1.*   88-9.] *Verse as here Bullen; one*
line B1; What, are you crossing of your selfe? *A1.*   90-2. Well ...
warning.] *A1; not in B1.*

---

73. *adry*] dry, thirsty.

76. *lubbers*] clumsy, stupid fellows.

83. *pardon*] indulgence.

85. *dirge*] requiem mass. The word is used less appropriately in ll. 99.1,
108.

86. *fury*] Greg points out that this word here seems to mean little more
than 'importunity', and·that it is used in much the same sense in xvii. 37,
and 'furious' in xvii. 67.

91. *aware*] beware.

Nay, then, take that!

FAUSTUS *hits him a box of the ear.*

Pope. O, I am slain! help me, my lords;

O, come and help to bear my body hence.

Damn'd be this soul for ever for this deed.   95

Exeunt the Pope *and his train.*

Meph. Now, Faustus, what will you do now? for I can tell you

you'll be cursed with bell, book, and candle.

Fau. Bell, book, and candle; candle, book, and bell;

Forward and backward, to curse Faustus to hell!

Enter the Friars, *with bell, book, and candle, for the dirge.*

1 Fri. Come, brethren, let's about our business with good   100

devotion.   *Sing this.*

Cursed be he that stole his Holiness' meat from the table.

Maledicat Dominus!

Cursed be he that struck his Holiness a blow on the face.

Maledicat Dominus!   105

Cursed be he that took Friar Sandelo a blow on the pate.

Maledicat Dominus!

92, 92.1.] *Stage-directions placed as here Greg; Crosse againe, and Faustus*
hits him a boxe of the eare, and they all runne away. A*1; not in* B*1.*   92. Nay
. . . that!] B*1; not in* A*1.*   93–95.1. Pope. O . . . train.] B*1; not in* A*1.*
95. this] B*1; his* B*2.*   96–7.] *Prose as here* B*3; verse divided after* tell you
B*1; Fau:* Come on Mephastophilis, what shall we do? / Me. Nay I know
not, we shalbe curst with bell, booke, and candle. A*1.*   98. Bell] B*1;*
How? bell A*1.*   99–99.1.] *Between these lines,* A*1 inserts:* Anon you shal
heare a hogge grunt, a calfe bleate, and an asse braye, because it is S. *Peters*
holy day.   99.1. *Enter . . . dirge.*] B*1; Enter all the Friers to sing the Dirge.*
A*1.*   101. *Sing this.*] A*1; not in* B*1.*   102. stole] B*1; stole away* A*1.*
104. on] A*1; not in* B*1.*   106. took] A*1; strucke* B*1.*

---

95. *this soul*] the 'troublesome ghost' (l. 86).

97. *cursed . . . candle*] referring to a form of excommunication at the
end of which the bell was tolled, the book closed, and the candle extin-
guished.

103. Maledicat Dominus] May the Lord curse him.

106. *took . . . a blow*] gave . . . a blow. Greg suggests that Sandelo receives his blow during the dirge.

Sandelo] evidently a name suggested by the sandals worn by friars.

> Cursed be he that disturbeth our holy dirge.
> *Maledicat Dominus !*
> Cursed be he that took away his Holiness' wine.   110
> *Maledicat Dominus !*
> *Et omnes sancti ! Amen.*
> [FAUSTUS *and* MEPHOSTOPHILIS] *beat the* Friars, *and
> fling fireworks among them, and so exeunt.*

[Scene x]

Enter Clown [ROBIN] *and* DICK *with a cup.*

Dick. Sirrah Robin, we were best look that your devil can answer the stealing of this same cup, for the vintner's boy
follows us at the hard heels.

Rob. 'Tis no matter, let him come! An he follow us, I'll so conjure him as he was never conjured in his life, I warrant   5
him. Let me see the cup.

Enter Vintner.

Dick. Here 'tis. Yonder he comes. Now, Robin, now or never
show thy cunning.

Vint. O, are you here ? I am glad I have found you. You are a

112. *Et . . . Amen.*] *A1; not in B1.*   112.1. FAUSTUS *and* MEPHOSTO-
PHILIS] *Dyce; not in A1, B1.*   112.1–2. Friars . . . exeunt.] *A1;* Friers,
fling fire worke among them, and *Exeunt. Exeunt. B1.*

*After this scene, A1 inserts Chorus 2, which in the present edition imme-
diately precedes scene xi; it is not in B1. A1 then introduces its version of
scene vii.*

Scene x.] *The A-version of this scene is given in Appendix I (see section 5 of
the 'Introduction').*   0.1. ROBIN] *Dyce; not in B1.*

112. Et omnes sancti] and all the saints.

Scene x.] The similarity of the business of the stolen goblet in this scene
to that of the stolen pot of ale in *Mucedorus* (printed 1598), III. v, has been
pointed out by C. F. Tucker Brooke in 'Notes on Marlowe's *Doctor
Faustus*', *P.Q.*, XII (1933), pp. 17–23. Perhaps the scene in *Mucedorus* was
written in imitation of the present scene.

3. *at the hard heels*] right at our heels.

couple of fine companions! Pray, where's the cup you   10
stole from the tavern?

Rob. How, how? we steal a cup! Take heed what you say; we
look not like cup-stealers, I can tell you.

Vint. Never deny 't, for I know you have it, and I'll search you.

Rob. Search me? Ay, and spare not. [*Aside to Dick*] Hold the   15
cup, Dick. [*To the Vintner*] Come, come, search me,
search me.   [Vintner *searches him.*]

Vint. [*To Dick*] Come on, sirrah, let me search you now.

Dick. Ay, ay, do, do. [*Aside to Robin*] Hold the cup, Robin.
[*To the Vintner*] I fear not your searching; we scorn to   20
steal your cups, I can tell you.   [Vintner *searches him.*]

Vint. Never outface me for the matter, for sure the cup is between you two.

Rob. Nay, there you lie; 'tis beyond us both.

Vint. A plague take you! I thought 'twas your knavery to take   25
it away. Come, give it me again.

Rob. Ay, much! when, can you tell? Dick, make me a circle,
and stand close at my back, and stir not for thy life. Vintner, you shall have your cup anon. Say nothing, Dick.
O per se, o; Demogorgon, Belcher, and Mephostophilis!   30

Enter MEPHOSTOPHILIS.

Meph. You princely legions of infernal rule,

---

15. *Aside to Dick*] *Oxberry; not in* B1.   16. *To the Vintner*] *This ed.; not
in* B1.   17, 21. *Vintner . . . him.*] *Dyce; not in* B1.   18. *To Dick*] *Boas;
not in* B1.   19. *Aside to Robin*] *Oxberry; not in* B1.   20. *To the Vintner*]
This ed.; not in B1.

---

10. *companions*] fellows. Contemptuous as used here, though not as used
in Cho. 2, 5.

22. *outface . . . matter*] brazen the matter out with me.

24. *beyond us*] out of our hands. Robin has now disposed of it.

27. *Ay, much!*] a derisive exclamation conveying incredulity.

when, can you tell?] a defiant retort, used also in S. Rowley, *When You
See Me You Know Me* (ed. Wilson), l. 880.

29. *Say nothing*] because speech is dangerous in the presence of spirits.
Compare xii. 44–8, xviii. 27.

30. O per se, o; Demogorgon] echoing vii. 7–8.
Belcher] one of the devils summoned by Wagner in iv. 32–8.

How am I vexed by these villains' charms!
From Constantinople have they brought me now
Only for pleasure of these damned slaves.   [*Exit* Vintner.]

Rob. By lady, sir, you have had a shrewd journey of it. Will it   35
please you to take a shoulder of mutton to supper, and a
tester in your purse, and go back again?

Dick. Ay, I pray you heartily, sir; for we called you but in jest,
I promise you.

Meph. To purge the rashness of this cursed deed,   40
First be thou turned to this ugly shape,
For apish deeds transformed to an ape.

Rob. O brave, an ape! I pray, sir, let me have the carrying of
him about to show some tricks.

Meph. And so thou shalt: be thou transformed to a dog, and   45
carry him upon thy back. Away, be gone!

Rob. A dog! that's excellent: let the maids look well to their
porridge-pots, for I'll into the kitchen presently. Come,
Dick, come.   *Exeunt the two* Clowns.

Meph. Now with the flames of ever-burning fire   50
I'll wing myself and forthwith fly amain
Unto my Faustus, to the Great Turk's court.   *Exit.*

[Chorus 2]

Enter Chorus.

Cho. When Faustus had with pleasure ta'en the view
Of rarest things and royal courts of kings,

34. *Exit* Vintner.] *Dyce; not in* B1.

Chorus 2.] *This speech is placed as here in Boas; it follows scene ix in* A1; *it is
not in* B1.   1. *Cho.*] *Dyce; not in* A1.

31–4.] A1 replaces l. 31 by three lines of bombast and then reproduces
the remaining lines of this speech with little change. Only here does its
version of the scene closely parallel B1's. See Appendix I.

32–4.] These lines are in flat contradiction to iii. 46–56. They are presumably the work of a different author.

35. *shrewd*] poor, unsatisfactory.

37. *tester*] a slang term for a sixpence.

42. *apish*] fantastically foolish.

He stay'd his course and so returned home,
Where such as bare his absence but with grief—
I mean his friends and nearest companions—   5
Did gratulate his safety with kind words;
And in their conference of what befell
Touching his journey through the world and air
They put forth questions of astrology,
Which Faustus answer'd with such learned skill   10
As they admir'd and wonder'd at his wit.
Now is his fame spread forth in every land:
Amongst the rest the Emperor is one,
Carolus the Fifth, at whose palace now
Faustus is feasted 'mongst his noblemen.   15
What there he did in trial of his art
I leave untold, your eyes shall see perform'd.   *Exit.*

[Scene xi]

> *Enter* MARTINO *and* FREDERICK *at several doors.*

Mar. What ho, officers, gentlemen!
Hie to the presence to attend the Emperor.
Good Frederick, see the rooms be voided straight,
His Majesty is coming to the hall;
Go back, and see the state in readiness.   5
Fre. But where is Bruno, our elected Pope,
That on a fury's back came post from Rome?
Will not his Grace consort the Emperor?

---

4. bare] *Greg;* beare *A1;* bear *Dyce.*
Scene xi.] *This scene is not in A1.*

Chorus 2. 3. stay'd his course] stopped his travelling.
6. *gratulate*] express joy at.
14. *Carolus the Fifth*] Charles V was Emperor from 1519 until his retirement in 1556, that is, for a period which included the last twenty years or so of the life of the historical Faustus.

xi. 2. *presence*] presence-chamber.
3. *voided straight*] cleared at once.
8. *consort*] accompany.

Mar. O yes, and with him comes the German conjuror,
  The learned Faustus, fame of Wittenberg,   10
  The wonder of the world for magic art;
  And he intends to show great Carolus
  The race of all his stout progenitors,
  And bring in presence of his Majesty
  The royal shapes and warlike semblances   15
  Of Alexander and his beauteous paramour.
Fre. Where is Benvolio?
Mar.   Fast asleep, I warrant you.
  He took his rouse with stoups of Rhenish wine
  So kindly yesternight to Bruno's health
  That all this day the sluggard keeps his bed.   20
Fre. See, see, his window's ope; we'll call to him.
Mar. What ho, Benvolio!

    Enter BENVOLIO *above at a window, in his nightcap,*
          buttoning.

Ben. What a devil ail you two?
Mar. Speak softly, sir, lest the devil hear you;
  For Faustus at the court is late arriv'd,   25
  And at his heels a thousand furies wait
  To accomplish whatsoever the doctor please.
Ben. What of this?
Mar. Come, leave thy chamber first, and thou shalt see
  This conjuror perform such rare exploits   30

---

15. warlike] *B1;* perfect *B2.*   26. a] *B1;* ten *B2.*

---

10. *fame*] the glory. *O.E.D.* gives no other instance of this use of the word; but see *Edward III* (*The Shakespeare Apocrypha*, ed. C. F. Tucker Brooke, Oxford, 1908), v. i. 179.

13. *progenitors*] Here the meaning may be either 'predecessors', as in viii. 136, or 'ancestors'.

18. *took his rouse*] had a drinking-bout. With the whole line, compare *Hamlet*, I. iv. 8–10, 'The king ... takes his rouse ... drains his draughts of Rhenish down'.

 stoups] measures.

22.2. buttoning] buttoning up his clothes.

  Before the Pope and royal Emperor
  As never yet was seen in Germany.
Ben. Has not the Pope enough of conjuring yet?
  He was upon the devil's back late enough;
  And if he be so far in love with him   35
  I would he would post with him to Rome again.
Fre. Speak, wilt thou come and see this sport?
Ben.   Not I.
Mar. Wilt thou stand in thy window and see it then?
Ben. Ay, and I fall not asleep i' th' meantime.
Mar. The Emperor is at hand, who comes to see 40
  What wonders by black spells may compass'd be.
Ben. Well, go you attend the Emperor. I am content for this
  once to thrust my head out at a window, for they say if a
  man be drunk overnight the devil cannot hurt him in the
  morning. If that be true, I have a charm in my head shall 45
  control him as well as the conjuror, I warrant you.
           [*Exeunt* FREDERICK *and* MARTINO.]

[Scene xii]

 A sennet. CHARLES *the* GERMAN EMPEROR, BRUNO, [DUKE OF]
SAXONY, FAUSTUS, MEPHOSTOPHILIS, FREDERICK, MARTINO,
   and Attendants. [BENVOLIO *remains at his window.*]

Emp. Wonder of men, renown'd magician,
  Thrice-learned Faustus, welcome to our court.
  This deed of thine, in setting Bruno free

46.1. *Exeunt . . .* MARTINO.] *Dyce; Exit.* B*1*.

*Scene xii.] The A-version of this scene is given in Appendix I (see section 5 of
the 'Introduction').* 0.1. DUKE OF] *Oxberry; not in* B*1*. 0.3. BENVOLIO
. . . window.] Greg; not in B*1*.

―――――――――――――――――――――――――――――――――――――――

  31. *Pope*] In the scenes at the Emperor's court, this naturally means
Bruno.
  46. *control*] overpower.

  xii. 0.3. *Benvolio . . .* window] He is there, without having re-entered, at
l. 24.

From his and our professed enemy,
Shall add more excellence unto thine art   5
Than if by powerful necromantic spells
Thou couldst command the world's obedience.
For ever be belov'd of Carolus;
And if this Bruno thou hast late redeem'd
In peace possess the triple diadem   10
And sit in Peter's chair despite of chance,
Thou shalt be famous through all Italy
And honour'd of the German Emperor.

Fau. These gracious words, most royal Carolus,
Shall make poor Faustus to his utmost power   15
Both love and serve the German Emperor
And lay his life at holy Bruno's feet.
For proof whereof, if so your Grace be pleas'd,
The doctor stands prepar'd by power of art
To cast his magic charms, that shall pierce through   20
The ebon gates of ever-burning hell
And hale the stubborn furies from their caves
To compass whatsoe'er your Grace commands.

Ben. Blood! he speaks terribly. But, for all that, I do not great-
ly believe him; he looks as like a conjuror as the Pope to a   25
costermonger.

Emp. Then, Faustus, as thou late didst promise us,
We would behold that famous conqueror,
Great Alexander, and his paramour
In their true shapes and state majestical   30
That we may wonder at their excellence.

Fau. Your Majesty shall see them presently.—
Mephostophilis, away,
And with a solemn noise of trumpets' sound
Present before this royal Emperor   35

25. a conjuror] *B2;* Coniurer *B1.*

---

4. *professed*] openly declared.
9. *redeem'd*] set free.
11. *chance*] fortune.

Great Alexander and his beauteous paramour.

Meph. Faustus, I will.   *Exit* MEPHOSTOPHILIS.

Ben. Well, master doctor, an your devils come not away quick-
    ly, you shall have me asleep presently. Zounds, I could eat
    myself for anger to think I have been such an ass all this   40
    while to stand gaping after the devil's governor, and can
    see nothing.

Fau. I'll make you feel something anon, if my art fail me not.—
    My lord, I must forewarn your Majesty
    That when my spirits present the royal shapes   45
    Of Alexander and his paramour
    Your Grace demand no questions of the King,
    But in dumb silence let them come and go.

Emp. Be it as Faustus please; we are content.

Ben. Ay, ay, and I am content too. And thou bring Alexander   50
    and his paramour before the Emperor, I'll be Actaeon and
    turn myself to a stag.

Fau. And I'll play Diana and send you the horns presently.

Sennet. Enter at one door the EMPEROR ALEXANDER, *at the other*
DARIUS; *they meet;* DARIUS *is thrown down;* ALEXANDER *kills him,
takes off his crown, and, offering to go out, his* Paramour *meets him;
he embraceth her and sets* DARIUS' *crown upon her head; and coming
back both salute the* Emperor, *who, leaving his state, offers to embrace
them, which* FAUSTUS *seeing suddenly stays him. Then trumpets cease
and music sounds.*

My gracious lord, you do forget yourself;
These are but shadows, not substantial.   55

Emp. O, pardon me, my thoughts are ravish'd so
    With sight of this renowned Emperor

---

37. *Exit* MEPHOSTOPHILIS.] *A1; not in B1.*   53.1. *door*] *B2; not in B1.*
56. ravish'd so] *Greg;* so rauished *B1.*

---

    41. *governor*] tutor.
    51. *Actaeon*] He came upon Diana and her nymphs bathing. The goddess
punished him for his intrusion by changing him into a stag with the result
that his own dogs tore him to pieces. See ll. 94–9.

That in mine arms I would have compass'd him.
But, Faustus, since I may not speak to them
To satisfy my longing thoughts at full,　　　　　　　60
Let me this tell thee: I have heard it said
That this fair lady, whilst she liv'd on earth,
Had on her neck a little wart or mole;
How may I prove that saying to be true?

Fau. Your Majesty may boldly go and see.　　　　65

Emp. Faustus, I see it plain,
And in this sight thou better pleasest me
Than if I gain'd another monarchy.

Fau. Away, be gone!　　　　　　　　　　*Exit* Show.
See, see, my gracious lord, what strange beast is yon, that　70
thrusts his head out at the window.

Emp. O, wondrous sight! See, Duke of Saxony,
Two spreading horns most strangely fastened
Upon the head of young Benvolio.

Sax. What, is he asleep, or dead?　　　　　75

Fau. He sleeps, my lord, but dreams not of his horns.

Emp. This sport is excellent: we'll call and wake him.
What ho, Benvolio!

Ben. A plague upon you! let me sleep awhile.

Emp. I blame thee not to sleep much, having such a head of　80
thine own.

Sax. Look up, Benvolio, 'tis the Emperor calls.

Ben. The Emperor! where? O, zounds, my head!

Emp. Nay, and thy horns hold, 'tis no matter for thy head, for
that's armed sufficiently.　　　　　　　85

Fau. Why, how now, sir knight? what, hanged by the horns?
This is most horrible. Fie, fie, pull in your head for shame,
let not all the world wonder at you.

71. the] *B2; not in B1.*　　　87. is] *B2; not in B1.*

---

58. *compass'd*] embraced.
79. *A plague upon you!*] Benvolio has not yet recognized the Emperor.
80. *I . . . much*] I do not much blame you for sleeping.
83–9.] Benvolio's horns prevent him from pulling his head back through
the window.

Ben. Zounds, doctor, is this your villainy?

Fau. O, say not so, sir: the doctor has no skill,   90
 No art, no cunning to present these lords
 Or bring before this royal Emperor
 The mighty monarch, warlike Alexander.
 If Faustus do it, you are straight resolv'd
 In bold Actaeon's shape to turn a stag.   95
 And therefore, my lord, so please your Majesty,
 I'll raise a kennel of hounds shall hunt him so
 As all his footmanship shall scarce prevail
 To keep his carcase from their bloody fangs.
 Ho, Belimote, Argiron, Asterote!   100

Ben. Hold, hold! Zounds, he'll raise up a kennel of devils, I
 think, anon. Good my lord, entreat for me. 'Sblood, I
 am never able to endure these torments.

Emp. Then, good master doctor,
 Let me entreat you to remove his horns;   105
 He has done penance now sufficiently.

Fau. My gracious lord, not so much for injury done to me,
 as to delight your Majesty with some mirth, hath Faustus justly requited this injurious knight; which being all
 I desire, I am content to remove his horns.—Mephosto-   110
 philis, transform him.—And hereafter, sir, look you
 speak well of scholars.

Ben. [*Aside*] Speak well of ye! 'Sblood, and scholars be such
 cuckold-makers to clap horns of honest men's heads o'
 this order, I'll ne'er trust smooth faces and small ruffs   115
 more. But, an I be not revenged for this, would I might

98. As] *B1;* And *B2.*   113. *Aside*] *Dyce; not in B1.*

---

 98. *footmanship*] skill in running.

 100. *Belimote, Argiron, Asterote*] Two of these names recur, in slightly
different forms, in xiii. 78. '*Asterote* or *Asteroth* is obviously the Phoenician
Ashtaroth or Astarte; *Belimote* or *Belimoth* may possibly have been suggested by Behemoth; about *Argiron* I can make no suggestion, unless it is
a perversion of Acheron' (Greg).

 109. *injurious*] insulting.

 114–15. *o' this order*] in this fashion.

 115. *smooth . . . ruffs*] 'beardless scholars in academical garb' (Boas).

be turned to a gaping oyster and drink nothing but salt
water.

Emp. Come, Faustus, while the Emperor lives,
    In recompense of this thy high desert,   120
    Thou shalt command the state of Germany
    And live belov'd of mighty Carolus.   *Exeunt omnes.*

[Scene xiii]

        Enter BENVOLIO, MARTINO, FREDERICK, *and* Soldiers.

Mar. Nay, sweet Benvolio, let us sway thy thoughts
    From this attempt against the conjuror.
Ben. Away, you love me not, to urge me thus.
    Shall I let slip so great an injury,
    When every servile groom jests at my wrongs   5
    And in their rustic gambols proudly say,
    'Benvolio's head was grac'd with horns today'?
    O, may these eyelids never close again
    Till with my sword I have that conjuror slain.
    If you will aid me in this enterprise,   10
    Then draw your weapons and be resolute:
    If not, depart: here will Benvolio die
    But Faustus' death shall quit my infamy.
Fre. Nay, we will stay with thee, betide what may,
    And kill that doctor if he come this way.   15
Ben. Then, gentle Frederick, hie thee to the grove
    And place our servants and our followers
    Close in an ambush there behind the trees.
    By this, I know, the conjuror is near:
    I saw him kneel and kiss the Emperor's hand   20

Scene xiii.] *This scene is not in A1.*

---

xiii. 4. *let slip*] overlook.
5. *groom*] low fellow.
13. *But*] unless.
quit] repay, make a return for.
18. *Close*] hidden.

And take his leave laden with rich rewards.
Then, soldiers, boldly fight; if Faustus die,
Take you the wealth, leave us the victory.
Fre. Come, soldiers, follow me unto the grove:
Who kills him shall have gold and endless love.   25
                      Exit FREDERICK *with the* Soldiers.

Ben. My head is lighter than it was by th' horns,
But yet my heart's more ponderous than my head
And pants until I see that conjuror dead.
Mar. Where shall we place ourselves, Benvolio?
Ben. Here will we stay to bide the first assault.   30
O, were that damned hell-hound but in place,
Thou soon shouldst see me quit my foul disgrace.

              Enter FREDERICK.

Fre. Close, close! the conjuror is at hand
And all alone comes walking in his gown;
Be ready then and strike the peasant down.   35
Ben. Mine be that honour, then: now, sword, strike home;
For horns he gave, I'll have his head anon.

         Enter FAUSTUS *with the false head.*

Mar. See, see, he comes.
Ben.   No words; this blow ends all.
Hell take his soul, his body thus must fall.   [*Strikes.*]
Fau. O!   40
Fre. Groan you, master doctor?
Ben. Break may his heart with groans. Dear Frederick, see,
Thus will I end his griefs immediately.

---

27. heart's] *B2;* heart *B1.*   33. conjuror] *B1;* hated conjuror *Greg.*
39. Strikes.] *Dyce (subs.); not in B1.*

31. *in place*] on the spot.
35. *peasant*] low fellow, rascal.
37.1. with the false head] *the* false head which the author knew the company to possess or knew that it would acquire. Similar knowledge on the prompter's part explains the stage-direction, '*Enter Piramus with the Asse head*' in the First Folio text of *A Midsummer-Night's Dream,* III. i.
43. *griefs*] mischiefs.

Mar. Strike with a willing hand. His head is off.

                   [*Strikes;* FAUSTUS' *head falls off.*]

Ben. The devil's dead; the furies now may laugh.   45

Fre. Was this that stern aspect, that awful frown,
     Made the grim monarch of infernal spirits
     Tremble and quake at his commanding charms?

Mar. Was this that damned head whose heart conspir'd
     Benvolio's shame before the Emperor?   50

Ben. Ay, that's the head, and here the body lies,
     Justly rewarded for his villainies.

Fre. Come, let's devise how we may add more shame
     To the black scandal of his hated name.

Ben. First, on his head, in quittance of my wrongs,   55
     I'll nail huge forked horns and let them hang
     Within the window where he yok'd me first,
     That all the world may see my just revenge.

Mar. What use shall we put his beard to?

Ben. We'll sell it to a chimney-sweeper: it will wear out ten   60
birchen brooms, I warrant you.

Fre. What shall his eyes do?

Ben. We'll put out his eyes, and they shall serve for buttons
to his lips to keep his tongue from catching cold.

Mar. An excellent policy. And now, sirs, having divided him,   65
what shall the body do?   [FAUSTUS *gets up.*]

Ben. Zounds, the devil's alive again!

Fre. Give him his head, for God's sake!

Fau. Nay, keep it; Faustus will have heads and hands,
     Ay, all your hearts, to recompense this deed.   70

44.1. *Strikes . . . off.*] Dyce (*subs.*)*; not in B1.*   49. heart] *B1;* art Dilke.
62. his] *B2; not in B1.*   63. put] *B1;* pull B3.   66. FAUSTUS *gets up.*]
Robinson; *not in B1.*   70. Ay, all] Oxberry; I call *B1.*

---

     49. *heart*] Most of the editors have adopted Dilke's emendation. No
doubt the line is inept. But it is no more so than others which this author
apparently contributed to the play, and even if 'heart' is changed to 'art'
it remains inept.

     57. *yok'd*] held fast, as with a yoke.

     65. *policy*] device, trick.

Knew you not, traitors, I was limited
For four-and-twenty years to breathe on earth ?
And had you cut my body with your swords,
Or hew'd this flesh and bones as small as sand,
Yet in a minute had my spirit return'd   75
And I had breath'd a man made free from harm.
But wherefore do I dally my revenge ?
Asteroth, Belimoth, Mephostophilis!

Enter MEPHOSTOPHILIS *and other* Devils.

Go, horse these traitors on your fiery backs
And mount aloft with them as high as heaven;   80
Thence pitch them headlong to the lowest hell.
Yet stay, the world shall see their misery,
And hell shall after plague their treachery.
Go, Belimoth, and take this caitiff hence
And hurl him in some lake of mud and dirt;   85
Take thou this other, drag him through the woods,
Amongst the pricking thorns and sharpest briers,
Whilst with my gentle Mephostophilis
This traitor flies unto some steepy rock
That rolling down may break the villain's bones   90
As he intended to dismember me.
Fly hence, dispatch my charge immediately.

Fre. Pity us, gentle Faustus, save our lives!
Fau. Away!
Fre.   He must needs go that the devil drives.

Exeunt Spirits *with the* Knights.

Enter the ambushed Soldiers.

71–2. *limited . . . years*] accorded the fixed period of twenty-four years.

73–4.] These lines seem to be echoed in the anonymous *Taming of a Shrew* (ed. Boas), IV. ii. 60–1: 'This angrie sword should rip thy hatefull chest, / And hewd thee smaller than the *Libian* sands'.

77. *dally*] trifle with.

94. *He . . . drives*] a well-known proverb. See Tilley, D278.

94.2. the ambushed *Soldiers*] who left the stage at l. 25.1.

1 Sold. Come, sirs, prepare yourselves in readiness,   95
  Make haste to help these noble gentlemen;
  I heard them parley with the conjuror.
2 Sold. See where he comes; dispatch, and kill the slave.
Fau. What's here ? an ambush to betray my life!
  Then, Faustus, try thy skill. Base peasants, stand!   100
  For lo, these trees remove at my command
  And stand as bulwarks 'twixt yourselves and me
  To shield me from your hated treachery:
  Yet to encounter this your weak attempt
  Behold an army comes incontinent.   105

FAUSTUS *strikes the door, and enter a* Devil *playing on a drum, after him another bearing an ensign, and divers with weapons;* MEPHOSTO-PHILIS *with fireworks; they set upon the* Soldiers *and drive them out.*
              [*Exit* FAUSTUS.]

[Scene xiv]

Enter at several doors BENVOLIO, FREDERICK, *and* MARTINO, *their heads and faces bloody, and besmeared with mud and dirt, all having horns on their heads.*

Mar. What ho, Benvolio!
Ben.   Here! What, Frederick, ho!
Fre. O help me, gentle friend. Where is Martino ?
Mar. Dear Frederick, here,
  Half smother'd in a lake of mud and dirt,

105.4. *Exit* FAUSTUS.] *Boas; not in* B*1*.

Scene xiv.] *This scene is not in* A*1*.

---

  101. *remove*] change their places.
  105. *incontinent*] immediately.
  105.1. the door] of the stage. The imagined setting is a wood.

 xiv. 4–5.] In *The Merry Wives of Windsor*, IV. v. 65–9, Bardolph apparently compares his own sufferings with those of these three knights: 'so soon as I came beyond Eton, they threw me off, from behind one of them, in a slough of mire; and set spurs and away, like three German devils, three Doctor Faustuses'. *The Merry Wives* was probably written in 1600–1.

      Through which the furies dragg'd me by the heels.   5

Fre. Martino, see! Benvolio's horns again.

Mar. O misery! How now, Benvolio?

Ben. Defend me, heaven, shall I be haunted still?

Mar. Nay, fear not, man, we have no power to kill.

Ben. My friends transformed thus! O hellish spite,   10

      Your heads are all set with horns.

Fre.   You hit it right:

      It is your own you mean, feel on your head.

Ben. Zounds, horns again!

Mar.   Nay, chafe not, man, we all are sped.

Ben. What devil attends this damn'd magician,

      That, spite of spite, our wrongs are doubled?   15

Fre. What may we do that we may hide our shames?

Ben. If we should follow him to work revenge,

      He'd join long asses' ears to these huge horns

      And make us laughing-stocks to all the world.

Mar. What shall we then do, dear Benvolio?   20

Ben. I have a castle joining near these woods,

      And thither we'll repair and live obscure

      Till time shall alter these our brutish shapes.

      Sith black disgrace hath thus eclips'd our fame,

      We'll rather die with grief than live with shame.   25

                              Exeunt omnes.

6.] *One line as here Oxberry; divided after* see *B1*.   23. these] *B2;* this *B1*.

There would seem to be confirmation here for the view that the present scene and the others most closely associated with it were not, as used to be believed, added to the play by Birde and Rowley in 1602. See section 4 of the 'Introduction'.

    9. *we . . . kill*] 'Martino means that though Benvolio has been partly transformed into animal likeness, his companions are not equipped for hunting him to death. There is probably a play upon "haunted"' (Boas).

    13. *sped*] done for (by being furnished with horns).

    15. *spite of spite*] despite everything.

    doubled] a trisyllable.

    24. *Sith*] seeing that.

    25.] a variant of the proverb, 'It is better to die with honour than to live with shame'. See Tilley, H576.

[Scene xv]

Enter FAUSTUS *and the* Horse-courser.

Hor. I beseech your worship, accept of these forty dollars.

Fau. Friend, thou canst not buy so good a horse for so small
a price. I have no great need to sell him; but if thou likest
him for ten dollars more, take him, because I see thou
hast a good mind to him.   5

Hor. I beseech you, sir, accept of this. I am a very poor man
and have lost very much of late by horse-flesh, and this
bargain will set me up again.

Fau. Well, I will not stand with thee; give me the money.
Now, sirrah, I must tell you that you may ride him o'er   10
hedge and ditch and spare him not; but, do you hear? in
any case ride him not into the water.

Hor. How, sir, not into the water? Why, will he not drink of
all waters?

Fau. Yes, he will drink of all waters. But ride him not into the   15
water; o'er hedge and ditch, or where thou wilt, but not
into the water. Go, bid the ostler deliver him unto you;
and remember what I say.

Hor. I warrant you, sir. O, joyful day! now am I a made man
for ever.   *Exit.*   20

Fau. What art thou, Faustus, but a man condemn'd to die?
Thy fatal time draws to a final end;
Despair doth drive distrust into my thoughts.
Confound these passions with a quiet sleep.
Tush, Christ did call the thief upon the cross;   25

Scene xv.] *The A-version of this scene is given in Appendix I (see section 5 of
the 'Introduction'*).   0.1. Horse-courser.] *Oxberry; Horse-courser, and
Mephostophilis. B1.*

---

xv. 0.1. *Horse-courser*] horse-dealer. As such, he has a ready-made reputation for dishonesty.
  9. *stand*] dispute, haggle.
  13–14. *will . . . waters?*] Boas paraphrases, 'Will he not be ready for anything?' and quotes *Twelfth Night*, IV. ii. 66, 'Nay, I am for all waters'. But
Greg suspects that the question means, 'Will he not go anywhere?'
  22. *fatal time*] time allotted by fate.
  24. *Confound*] disperse.

Then rest thee, Faustus, quiet in conceit.   *He sits to sleep.*

Enter the Horse-courser, *wet.*

Hor. O, what a cozening doctor was this! I, riding my horse
   into the water, thinking some hidden mystery had been
   in the horse, I had nothing under me but a little straw and
   had much ado to escape drowning. Well, I'll go rouse him   30
   and make him give me my forty dollars again. Ho, sirrah
   doctor, you cozening scab! Master doctor, awake, and
   rise, and give me my money again, for your horse is turned
   to a bottle of hay. Master doctor!   *He pulls off his leg.*
   Alas, I am undone! what shall I do? I have pulled off his   35
   leg.

Fau. O, help, help! the villain hath murdered me.

Hor. Murder or not murder, now he has but one leg I'll out-
   run him and cast this leg into some ditch or other.   [*Exit.*]

Fau. Stop him, stop him, stop him!—Ha, ha, ha! Faustus   40
   hath his leg again, and the horse-courser a bundle of hay
   for his forty dollars.

Enter WAGNER.

How now, Wagner, what news with thee?

Wag. If it please you, the Duke of Vanholt doth earnestly entreat your company and hath sent some of his men to at-   45
   tend you with provision fit for your journey.

Fau. The Duke of Vanholt's an honourable gentleman, and
   one to whom I must be no niggard of my cunning. Come
   away!   *Exeunt.*

39. *Exit.*] Oxberry; not in B1.   44, 47. Vanholt] B1; Anholt Boas.

26. *in conceit*] in mind.
32. *scab*] rascal, scoundrel.
34. *bottle*] bundle. Dryden refers to this transformation in *An Evening's
Love* (ed. Scott and Saintsbury), III. i: 'A witch's horse, you know, when
he enters into water, returns into a bottle of hay again'.

[Scene xvi]

Enter Clown [ROBIN], DICK, Horse-courser, *and a* Carter.

Cart. Come, my masters, I'll bring you to the best beer in
Europe. What ho, hostess! Where be these whores?

Enter Hostess.

Host. How now, what lack you? What, my old guests, welcome.

Rob. Sirrah Dick, dost thou know why I stand so mute?   5

Dick. No, Robin, why is't?

Rob. I am eighteen pence on the score. But say nothing; see if
she have forgotten me.

Host. Who's this that stands so solemnly by himself? What,
my old guest!   10

Rob. O, hostess, how do you? I hope my score stands still.

Host. Ay, there's no doubt of that, for methinks you make no
haste to wipe it out.

Dick. Why, hostess, I say, fetch us some beer.

Host. You shall presently. Look up into th' hall there, ho!   *Exit.*

Dick. Come, sirs, what shall we do now till mine hostess   16
comes?

Cart. Marry, sir, I'll tell you the bravest tale how a conjuror
served me. You know Doctor Fauster?

Hor. Ay, a plague take him! Here's some on's have cause to   20
know him. Did he conjure thee too?

Cart. I'll tell you how he served me. As I was going to Witten-

---

Scene xvi.] *This scene is not in A1.*   0.1. ROBIN] *Dyce; not in B1.*   5, 7,
11, etc. Rob.] *Dyce; Clo. or Clow. throughout this scene B1.*   15. into th'
hall there] *B1;* in th' hall there *Boas;* into th' hall. There *Greg.*

---

xvi. 11–13] Robin hopes that his debt stands 'still', i.e. without increas-
ing. The Hostess gives 'still' another meaning, i.e. always, and retorts that
he is in no hurry to pay what he owes her.

15. *Look . . . ho!*] an instruction to her staff. Compare 1 *Henry IV*, II.
iv. 37–8, 'Look down into the Pomgarnet, Ralph'. The emendations of
Boas and Greg are unnecessary.

19, 38. *Fauster*] a clownish corruption of 'Faustus'.

berg t'other day with a load of hay, he met me and asked
me what he should give me for as much hay as he could
eat. Now, sir, I, thinking that a little would serve his turn,   25
bade him take as much as he would for three farthings. So
he presently gave me my money and fell to eating; and, as
I am a cursen man, he never left eating till he had eat up all
my load of hay.

All. O monstrous, eat a whole load of hay!   30

Rob. Yes, yes, that may be, for I have heard of one that has eat
a load of logs.

Hor. Now, sirs, you shall hear how villainously he served me.
I went to him yesterday to buy a horse of him, and he
would by no means sell him under forty dollars. So, sir,   35
because I knew him to be such a horse as would run over
hedge and ditch and never tire, I gave him his money. So,
when I had my horse, Doctor Fauster bade me ride him
night and day and spare him no time. 'But', quoth he, 'in
any case ride him not into the water.' Now, sir, I, thinking   40
the horse had had some rare quality that he would not
have me know of, what did I but rid him into a great river?
and when I came just in the midst my horse vanished
away, and I sat straddling upon a bottle of hay.

All. O brave doctor!   45

Hor. But you shall hear how bravely I served him for it. I went
me home to his house, and there I found him asleep. I
kept a hallooing and whooping in his ears, but all could
not wake him. I, seeing that, took him by the leg and never
rested pulling till I had pulled me his leg quite off; and   50
now 'tis at home in mine hostry.

41. rare] *B2; not in B1.*

28. *cursen*] a dialectal form of 'christen', i.e. Christian.

31–2. *eat . . . logs*] Perhaps this means 'wastefully consumed the timber
standing on his estate'. None of the editors has tried to explain it.

45, 46. *brave . . . bravely*] excellent . . . well.

51. *'tis . . . hostry*] It appears that the Horse-courser did not carry out
his intention of casting the leg 'into some ditch or other' (xv. 39).

Dick. And has the doctor but one leg then? That's excellent,
for one of his devils turned me into the likeness of an ape's
face.

Cart. Some more drink, hostess!   55

Rob. Hark you, we'll into another room and drink awhile, and
then we'll go seek out the doctor.   *Exeunt omnes.*

[Scene xvii]

> *Enter the* DUKE OF VANHOLT, *his* DUCHESS, FAUSTUS, *and*
> MEPHOSTOPHILIS.

Duke. Thanks, master doctor, for these pleasant sights.
Nor know I how sufficiently to recompense your great de-
serts in erecting that enchanted castle in the air, the sight
whereof so delighted me,
As nothing in the world could please me more.   5

Fau. I do think myself, my good lord, highly recompensed in
that it pleaseth your Grace to think but well of that which
Faustus hath performed. But, gracious lady, it may be
that you have taken no pleasure in those sights; therefore
I pray you tell me what is the thing you most desire to   10
have: be it in the world, it shall be yours. I have heard
that great-bellied women do long for things are rare and
dainty.

Duch. True, master doctor, and, since I find you so kind, I will
make known unto you what my heart desires to have; and   15

52. Dick.] *Boas; Clow. B1.*

xvii. 0.1-2. *Enter . . .* MEPHOSTOPHILIS.] *B1; Enter to them the Duke, and
the Dutches, the Duke speakes. A1.*   0.1. VANHOLT] *B1;* ANHOLT *Boas.*
1-13. *Duke.* Thanks . . . dainty.] *B1; Du: Beleeue me maister Doctor, this
merriment hath much pleased me. / Fau: My gratious Lord, I am glad it
contents you so wel: but it may be Madame, you take no delight in this,
I haue heard that great bellied women do long for some dainties or other,
what is it Madame? tell me, and you shal haue it. A1.*   3-4. sight . . . me,]
as verse-line B1.   14. Duch.] *A1; Lady. B1.*   14-15. True . . . what]
B1; Thankes, good maister doctor, / And for I see your curteous intent to
pleasure me, I wil not hide from you the thing *A1.*   15. to have] *B1;*
not in *A1.*

---

xvii. 12. *are*] which are.

were it now summer, as it is January, a dead time of the
winter, I would request no better meat than a dish of ripe
grapes.

Fau. This is but a small matter. Go, Mephostophilis, away!

                              Exit MEPHOSTOPHILIS.

Madam, I will do more than this for your content.   20

   Enter MEPHOSTOPHILIS *again with the grapes.*

Here, now taste ye these; they should be good,
For they come from a far country, I can tell you.

Duke. This makes me wonder more than all the rest,
That at this time of the year, when every tree
Is barren of his fruit, from whence you had   25
These ripe grapes.

Fau. Please it your Grace, the year is divided into two circles
over the whole world, so that, when it is winter with us,
in the contrary circle it is likewise summer with them, as
in India, Saba, and such countries that lie far east, where   30
they have fruit twice a year. From whence, by means of a
swift spirit that I have, I had these grapes brought as you
see.

---

16. a] *B1;* and the *A1.*   17. request] *B1;* desire *A1.*   19. This . . .
away!] *B1;* Alas Madame, thats nothing, *Mephastophilis,* be gone: *A1.*
20. Madam . . . content.] *B1;* were it a greater thing then this, so it would
content you, you should haue it *A1.*   20.1. again] *B1; not in A1.*   21–2.
Here . . . you.] *B1; prose Dilke;* here they be madam, wilt please you taste
on them. *A1.*   23–6.] *Verse as here Boas; prose B1;* Beleeue me master
Doctor, this makes me wonder aboue the rest, that being in the dead time
of winter, and in the month of Ianuary, how you shuld come by these
grapes. *A1.*   27. Please it] *B1;* If it like *A1.*   28. so] *B1; not in A1.*
is] *B1;* is heere *A1.*   29. likewise] *B1; not in A1.*   30–1. such . . .
whence,] *B1;* farther countries in the East, and *A1.*   32–3. these . . . see.]
B1; them brought hither, as ye see, how do you like them Madame, be they
good? *A1.*

---

17. *meat*] food.
27–30. *the year . . . lie far east*] The 'two circles' ought to have been de-
fined as the northern and southern hemispheres. Instead, the dramatist
muddles the account by distinguishing between a western circle and one
containing 'India, Saba, and such countries that lie far east'.
30. *Saba*] Sheba. Compare v. 157.

Duch. And, trust me, they are the sweetest grapes that e'er I
    tasted.   *The* Clowns *bounce at the gate within.*   35
Duke. What rude disturbers have we at the gate ?
    Go, pacify their fury, set it ope,
    And then demand of them what they would have.
                    They knock again and call out to talk with FAUSTUS.
A Servant. Why, how now, masters, what a coil is there!
    What is the reason you disturb the Duke ?   40
Dick. We have no reason for it, therefore a fig for him!
Ser. Why, saucy varlets, dare you be so bold ?
Hor. I hope, sir, we have wit enough to be more bold than wel-
    come.
Ser. It appears so: pray be bold elsewhere,   45
    And trouble not the Duke.
Duke.   What would they have ?
Ser. They all cry out to speak with Doctor Faustus.
Cart. Ay, and we will speak with him.
Duke. Will you, sir ? Commit the rascals.
Dick. Commit with us! He were as good commit with his   50
    father as commit with us.
Fau. I do beseech your Grace, let them come in;
    They are good subject for a merriment.
Duke. Do as thou wilt, Faustus; I give thee leave.
Fau. I thank your Grace.

    Enter the Clown [ROBIN], DICK, Carter, *and* Horse-courser.

                    Why, how now, my good friends ?   55

34. *Duch.*] *A1; Lady B1.*   And . . . sweetest] *B1; Beleeue me Maister*
doctor, they be the best *A1.*   35. tasted.] *B1; tasted in my life before. /*
Fau: I am glad they content you so Madam. *A1.*   35–116. *The . . .*
Hostess.] *A1 contains no version of these lines.*   35. Clowns] *Dyce;*
Clowne *B1.*   55. ROBIN] *Dyce; not in B1.*

---

35. bounce] knock loudly.
39. *coil*] noisy disturbance, row.
41.] See note on p. 105.
49–51.] The Duke means, 'Take the rascals to prison'; but Dick gives
'commit' the meaning 'have sexual intercourse'.

'Faith, you are too outrageous; but come near,
I have procur'd your pardons. Welcome all!

Rob. Nay, sir, we will be welcome for our money, and we will
pay for what we take. What ho! give's half-a-dozen of
beer here, and be hanged.   60

Fau. Nay, hark you, can you tell me where you are?

Cart. Ay, marry, can I; we are under heaven.

Ser. Ay, but, sir sauce-box, know you in what place?

Hor. Ay, ay, the house is good enough to drink in. Zounds,
fill us some beer, or we'll break all the barrels in the house   65
and dash out all your brains with your bottles.

Fau. Be not so furious; come, you shall have beer.
My lord, beseech you give me leave awhile;
I'll gage my credit, 'twill content your Grace.

Duke. With all my heart, kind doctor, please thyself;   70
Our servants and our court's at thy command.

Fau. I humbly thank your Grace. Then fetch some beer.

Hor. Ay, marry, there spake a doctor indeed; and, 'faith, I'll
drink a health to thy wooden leg for that word.

Fau. My wooden leg! what dost thou mean by that?   75

Cart. Ha, ha, ha! Dost hear him, Dick? He has forgot his leg.

Hor. Ay, ay, he does not stand much upon that.

Fau. No, 'faith, not much upon a wooden leg.

Cart. Good Lord, that flesh and blood should be so frail with
your·worship! Do not you remember a horse-courser you   80
sold a horse to?

Fau. Yes, I remember I sold one a horse.

Cart. And do you remember you bid he should not ride him
into the water?

---

58. *Rob.*] *Dyce; Clow.* B*1*.   83. him] B*2; not in* B*1*.

---

56. *outrageous*] violent.
63. *sir sauce-box*] a name given to a person who makes saucy or imper-
tinent remarks.
69. *gage*] stake.
77. *stand much upon*] attach much importance to. In his reply, Faustus
exploits the literal meaning of the words.

Fau. Yes, I do very well remember that.   85

Cart. And do you remember nothing of your leg ?

Fau. No, in good sooth.

Cart. Then I pray remember your curtsy.

Fau. I thank you, sir.

Cart. 'Tis not so much worth. I pray you tell me one thing.   90

Fau. What's that ?

Cart. Be both your legs bedfellows every night together ?

Fau. Wouldst thou make a colossus of me, that thou askest me
    such questions ?

Cart. No, truly, sir, I would make nothing of you; but I would   95
    fain know that.

Enter Hostess *with drink.*

Fau. Then I assure thee certainly they are.

Cart. I thank you, I am fully satisfied.

Fau. But wherefore dost thou ask ?

Cart. For nothing, sir; but methinks you should have a   100
    wooden bedfellow of one of 'em.

Hor. Why, do you hear, sir, did not I pull off one of your legs
    when you were asleep ?

Fau. But I have it again now I am awake: look you here, sir.

All. O horrible! Had the doctor three legs ?   105

Cart. Do you remember, sir, how you cozened me and eat up
    my load of—   FAUSTUS *charms him dumb.*

Dick. Do you remember how you made me wear an ape's—
                                    [FAUSTUS *charms him dumb.*]

Hor. You whoreson conjuring scab, do you remember how
    you cozened me with a ho—   [FAUSTUS *charms him dumb.*]

108.1, 110, 113, 116. FAUSTUS . . . dumb.] *Dyce (subs.); not in B1.*

---

88. *curtsy*] The Carter alludes to a second meaning of 'leg', i.e. obeisance,
bow.

93. *colossus*] the Colossus of Rhodes, here (as commonly) imagined as
straddling the harbour entrance.

95. *make nothing of*] The Carter uses the words not only in the literal
sense but also colloquially to mean 'make light of'.

Rob. Ha' you forgotten me? You think to carry it away with   111
　　your 'hey-pass' and 're-pass'. Do you remember the
　　dog's fa—　　[FAUSTUS *charms him dumb.*] *Exeunt* Clowns.
Host. Who pays for the ale? Hear you, master doctor, now
　　you have sent away my guests, I pray who shall pay me   115
　　for my a—　　[FAUSTUS *charms her dumb.*] *Exit* Hostess.
Duch. My lord,
　　We are much beholding to this learned man.
Duke. So are we, madam, which we will recompense
　　With all the love and kindness that we may.　　　120
　　His artful sport drives all sad thoughts away.　　*Exeunt.*

[Scene xviii]

Thunder and lightning. Enter Devils *with covered dishes.* MEPHO-
STOPHILIS *leads them into* FAUSTUS' *study. Then enter* WAGNER.

Wag. I think my master means to die shortly:
　　He has made his will and given me his wealth,
　　His house, his goods, and store of golden plate,
　　Besides two thousand ducats ready coin'd.
　　I wonder what he means. If death were nigh,　　　5
　　He would not banquet and carouse and swill

111. Rob.] Dyce; *Clow. B1.*　　117–21. *Duch.* My . . . *Exeunt.*] *B1; Du:*
Come Madame, let vs in, where you must wel reward this learned man for
the great kindnes he hath shewd to you. / *Dut:* And so I wil my Lord, and
whilst I liue, / Rest beholding for this curtesie. / *Fau:* I humbly thanke
your Grace. / *Du:* Come, maister Doctor follow vs, and receiue your reward. *exeunt. A1.*　　117. *Duch.*] *A1; Lady. B1.*

xviii. 0.1–2. *Thunder . . .* WAGNER.] *B1; enter Wagner solus. A1.*　　1–5.]
Verse as here Boas; prose B1; Wag. I thinke my maister meanes to die
shortly, / For he hath giuen to me al his goodes, / And yet me thinkes, if
that death were neere, *A1.*　　6–10. He . . . ended.] *A1;* he would not
frolick thus: hee's now at supper with the schollers, where ther's such belly-
cheere, as *Wagner* in his life nere saw the like: and see where they come,
belike the feast is done. *B1 (verse Boas).*

111. *carry it away*] carry it off, have the advantage.
112. *'hey-pass' and 're-pass'*] exclamations employed by jugglers and
conjurors when commanding articles to move. Compare xv. 53–4 in
Appendix I.

Amongst the students, as even now he doth,
Who are at supper with such belly-cheer
As Wagner ne'er beheld in all his life.
See where they come; belike the feast is ended.   *Exit.* 10

Enter FAUSTUS, MEPHOSTOPHILIS, *and two or three* Scholars.

1 Sch. Master Doctor Faustus, since our conference about fair
ladies, which was the beautifullest in all the world, we have
determined with ourselves that Helen of Greece was the
admirablest lady that ever lived. Therefore, master doctor, if you will do us that favour, as to let us see that peer-   15
less dame of Greece, whom all the world admires for
majesty, we should think ourselves much beholding unto
you.

Fau. Gentlemen,
For that I know your friendship is unfeign'd,   20
And Faustus' custom is not to deny
The just requests of those that wish him well,
You shall behold that peerless dame of Greece,
No otherways for pomp and majesty
Than when Sir Paris cross'd the seas with her   25
And brought the spoils to rich Dardania.
Be silent, then, for danger is in words.

10. *Exit.*] *B1; not in A1.*   10.1. MEPHOSTOPHILIS] *B1; not in A1.*   *and*]
B1; with A1.   15. us that] *A1;* vs so much *B1.*   19–27.] *Verse as here
(except that 19–20 is one line) B1; prose A1.*   21. And . . . not] *A1;* It is
not *Faustus* custome *B1.*   22. requests] *A1;* request *A2, A3, B1.*   24.
otherways] *A1;* otherwise *B1.*   and] *A1;* or *B1.*   25. with] *A1, B1;*
for *Greg.*

---

13. *determined with ourselves*] settled among ourselves.
15–17. *that peerless . . . majesty*] These words anticipate ll. 23 and 29.
Perhaps this prose speech was inserted after the completion of the verse
speeches which follow it.
25. *Sir*] This title assimilates Paris to a hero of mediaeval romance. Compare l. 109.
26. *the spoils*] the booty, including Helen, acquired during his expedition
to Sparta.
Dardania] Troy. Poets often refer to it, as here, by the name of the city
which Dardanus built upon the Hellespont.

Music sounds. MEPHOSTOPHILIS *brings in* HELEN; *she*
passeth over the stage.

2 Sch. Too simple is my wit to tell her praise
　　　Whom all the world admires for majesty.
3 Sch. No marvel though the angry Greeks pursu'd　　　　　30
　　　With ten years' war the rape of such a queen,
　　　Whose heavenly beauty passeth all compare.
1 Sch. Since we have seen the pride of nature's works
　　　And only paragon of excellence,
　　　Let us depart, and for this glorious deed　　　　　35
　　　Happy and blest be Faustus evermore.
Fau. Gentlemen, farewell; the same wish I to you.
　　　　　　　　　　　　　　　　Exeunt Scholars.

Enter an Old Man.

Old Man. O gentle Faustus, leave this damned art,
　　　This magic, that will charm thy soul to hell
　　　And quite bereave thee of salvation.　　　　　40

27.1. sounds] *A1*; sound *B1*.　　MEPHOSTOPHILIS ... *she*] *B1*; *and Helen*
A1.　　27.2–28.] *Between these lines, B1 inserts:* 2 Was this faire *Hellen*,
whose admired worth / Made *Greece* with ten yeares warres afslict poore
Troy?　　28. 2 *Sch.*] *A1*; 3 *B1*.　　praise] *A1*; worth *B1*.　　30–2. *3 Sch.*
No ... compare.] *A1; not in B1*.　　33. Since] *A1*; Now *B1*.　　works] *A1*;
worke *B1*.　　34. And ... excellence,] *A1; not in B1*.　　35. Let us depart]
A1; Wee'l take our leaues *B1*.　　glorious deed] *A1*; blessed sight *B1*.
37. wish I] *B1*; I wish *A1*.　　37.1.] *Stage-direction placed as here A1; after*
36 B1.　　37.2.] *Stage-direction placed as here B1; in right-hand margin,*
34–5, A1.　　38–54. Old Man. O ... soul.] *B1*; *Old*. Ah Doctor Faustus,
that I might preuaile, / To guide thy steps vnto the way of life, / By which
sweete path thou maist attaine the gole / That shall conduct thee to celestial
rest. / Breake heart, drop bloud, and mingle it with teares, / Teares falling
from repentant heauinesse / Of thy most vilde and loathsome filthinesse, /
The stench whereof corrupts the inward soule / With such flagitious crimes
of hainous sinnes, / As no commiseration may expel, / But mercie Faustus
of thy Sauiour sweete, / Whose bloud alone must wash away thy guilt. *A1*.

───────────────────────

27.2. passeth over the stage] This form of words recurs frequently in the
stage-directions of the period. Allardyce Nicoll understands by it a movement from the yard, across the stage, and out by the yard on the other side.
See his 'Passing over the Stage', *Shakespeare Survey*, XII (1959), pp. 47–55.
Alternatively, Helen simply enters by one door and leaves by the other.
　　30. *pursu'd*] campaigned to avenge.

Though thou hast now offended like a man,
Do not persever in it like a devil.
Yet, yet, thou hast an amiable soul,
If sin by custom grow not into nature:
Then, Faustus, will repentance come too late,   45
Then thou art banish'd from the sight of heaven;
No mortal can express the pains of hell.
It may be this my exhortation
Seems harsh and all unpleasant; let it not,
For, gentle son, I speak it not in wrath   50
Or envy of thee, but in tender love
And pity of thy future misery;
And so have hope that this my kind rebuke,
Checking thy body, may amend thy soul.

Fau. Where art thou, Faustus? wretch, what hast thou done?   55
Damn'd art thou, Faustus, damn'd; despair and die!

                    MEPHOSTOPHILIS *gives him a dagger.*

Hell claims his right and with a roaring voice
Says, 'Faustus, come; thine hour is almost come';
And Faustus now will come to do thee right.

                [FAUSTUS *goes to use the dagger.*]

Old. O, stay, good Faustus, stay thy desperate steps!   60
I see an angel hovers o'er thy head
And with a vial full of precious grace
Offers to pour the same into thy soul:

---

56. Damn'd . . . die!] *A1; not in B1.*   57. claims his] *B1;* calls for *A1.*
58. almost] *B1; not in A1.*   59. now] *B1; not in A1.*   59.1. FAUSTUS
. . . *dagger.] This ed.; not in A1, B1.*   60. O] *B1;* Ah *A1.*   61. hovers]
A1; houer *B1.*

---

42. *persever*] accented on the second syllable.
43–4.] You have still a soul that is worthy of love so long as sin does not
by habit become natural to you.
51. *envy of*] ill-will towards.
54. *Checking*] reproving.
56.1. *Mephostophilis . . . dagger*] Compare Lodge and Greene, *A Looking-
Glass for London and England* (ed. Greg), ll. 2064–5, where the Evil Angel
tempts the Usurer, '*offering the knife and rope*'; and Spenser, *The Faerie
Queene,* I. ix. 29, 51, where Despair makes the same offer.
59. *do thee right*] pay you your due.

Then call for mercy, and avoid despair.

Fau. O friend, I feel   65
　　Thy words to comfort my distressed soul.
　　Leave me awhile to ponder on my sins.

Old. Faustus, I leave thee, but with grief of heart,
　　Fearing the enemy of thy hapless soul.   *Exit.*

Fau. Accursed Faustus, where is mercy now?   70
　　I do repent, and yet I do despair;
　　Hell strives with grace for conquest in my breast.
　　What shall I do to shun the snares of death?

Meph. Thou traitor, Faustus, I arrest thy soul
　　For disobedience to my sovereign lord: 75
　　Revolt, or I'll in piecemeal tear thy flesh.

Fau. I do repent I e'er offended him.
　　Sweet Mephostophilis, entreat thy lord
　　To pardon my unjust presumption,
　　And with my blood again I will confirm   80
　　The former vow I made to Lucifer.

Meph. Do it, then, Faustus, with unfeigned heart,
　　Lest greater dangers do attend thy drift.

Fau. Torment, sweet friend, that base and aged man
　　That durst dissuade me from thy Lucifer,   85
　　With greatest torment that our hell affords.

65. O] *B1;* Ah my sweete *A1.*   65–6. feel / Thy words to] *Oxberry;* feele
thy words to *B1;* feele thy words / To *A1.*   68. Faustus . . . thee] *B1;*
I goe sweete Faustus *A1.*   grief of heart] *B1;* heauy cheare *A1.*   69.
enemy] *B1;* ruine *A1.*   hapless] *B1;* hopelesse *A1.*   *Exit.*] *B1; not in*
A1.   70. where . . . now?] *A1;* wretch what hast thou done? *B1.*   77.
I . . . him.] *B1; not in A1.*   81. The] *B1;* My *A1.*   82. *Meph.*] *A1; not*
in B1.   Faustus] *B1;* quickely *A1.*   83. dangers] *B1;* danger *A1.*
84. *Fau.*] *A1; not in B1.*   aged man] *B1;* crooked age *A1.*   86. torment]
B1; torments *A1.*

---

76. *Revolt*] return to your allegiance.

77.] The opening words of this line ironically echo those of l. 71. Faustus'
'repentance' has now taken 'a new turn: he repents that he has ever wavered
in his allegiance to the powers of evil' (P. Simpson, 'The 1604 Text of
Marlowe's *Doctor Faustus*', *Essays and Studies*, VII (1921), p. 147).

83. *drift*] drifting, shilly-shallying. This is Greg's explanation; it makes
better sense than does Ward's 'intention'.

86.] See note on p. 105.

Meph. His faith is great; I cannot touch his soul;
    But what I may afflict his body with
    I will attempt, which is but little worth.

Fau. One thing, good servant, let me crave of thee   90
    To glut the longing of my heart's desire:
    That I may have unto my paramour
    That heavenly Helen which I saw of late,
    Whose sweet embraces may extinguish clear
    Those thoughts that do dissuade me from my vow,   95
    And keep mine oath I made to Lucifer.

Meph. This or what else my Faustus shall desire
    Shall be perform'd in twinkling of an eye.

    Enter HELEN *again, passing over between two* Cupids.

Fau. Was this the face that launch'd a thousand ships
    And burnt the topless towers of Ilium?   100
    Sweet Helen, make me immortal with a kiss.
    Her lips suck forth my soul: see where it flies!
    Come, Helen, come, give me my soul again.
    Here will I dwell, for heaven is in these lips,
    And all is dross that is not Helena.   105

    Enter Old Man.

---

92. may] *B1;* might *A1.* 94. embraces] *B1;* imbracings *A1.* clear] *B1;*
cleane *A1.* 95. Those] *B1;* These *A1.* 96. mine oath] *A1;* my vow
B1. 97. This] *B1; Faustus,* this *A1.* my Faustus shall] *B1;* thou shalt
A1. 98 1. *again . . .* Cupids] *B1; not in A1.* 102. suck] *B1;* suckes
A1. 104. is] *B1;* be *A1.* 105.1. *Enter* Old Man.] *A1; not in B1.*

---

94. *clear*] entirely.

98.1. *passing over*] See comment on l. 27.2. If Allardyce Nicoll's in-
terpretation of this phrase is correct, Faustus at the end of his speech
goes with Helen and her Cupids down from the stage and out by the
yard.

99–100.] Compare 2 *Tamburlaine,* II. iv. 87–8: 'Helen, whose beauty
summoned Greece to arms, / And drew a thousand ships to Tenedos'.

100. *topless*] immeasurably high.

101.] Compare *Dido, Queen of Carthage,* IV. iv. 122–3: 'For in his looks
I see eternity, / And he'll make me immortal with a kiss'.

105.1.] In B1, the Old Man does not re-enter, and the scene ends with
l. 118. Greg surmises that the editor of B1 made the cut because he felt

> I will be Paris, and for love of thee
> Instead of Troy shall Wittenberg be sack'd,
> And I will combat with weak Menelaus
> And wear thy colours on my plumed crest,
> Yea, I will wound Achilles in the heel   110
> And then return to Helen for a kiss.
> O, thou art fairer than the evening's air
> Clad in the beauty of a thousand stars,
> Brighter art thou than flaming Jupiter
> When he appear'd to hapless Semele,   115
> More lovely than the monarch of the sky
> In wanton Arethusa's azur'd arms,
> And none but thou shalt be my paramour.

Exeunt [FAUSTUS, HELEN, *and the* Cupids].

Old Man. Accursed Faustus, miserable man,
> That from thy soul exclud'st the grace of heaven   120
> And fliest the throne of his tribunal seat!

Enter the Devils.

---

112. evening's] *B1;* euening *A1.*   117. azur'd] *A1, B2;* azure *B1.*   118.1.
FAUSTUS . . . Cupids] *Boas; not in A1, B1.*   119–27. *Old Man.* Accursed . . . God. *Exeunt.*] *A1; not in B1.*

---

that an eavesdropper would impair the theatrical effect of Faustus' rhapsody.

106–7.] Compare Dido's words to Aeneas in *Dido, Queen of Carthage*, v. i. 146–8: 'So thou wouldst prove as true as Paris did, / Would, as fair Troy was, Carthage might be sack'd, / And I be call'd a second Helena!'

108. *Menelaus*] Homer describes how Menelaus, the husband of Helen, would have defeated Paris in single combat but for the intervention of the goddess Aphrodite (*Iliad*, iii).

115. *Semele*] She asked Zeus to visit her in his divine splendour and was consumed by his lightning.

116–17.] more beautiful than the sun when it is reflected in the blue waters of the spring Arethusa. Marlowe seems not to be referring here to any specific incident in classical mythology.

119–27.] 'The Old Man is, of course, a real character, but here at the end, where his triumph over the diabolic power is set in contrast to Faustus' defeat, he takes on some of the abstract or allegorical character of the Angels in the "morality" set-up' (Greg). See section 9 of the 'Introduction'.

Satan begins to sift me with his pride:
As in this furnace God shall try my faith,
My faith, vile hell, shall triumph over thee.
Ambitious fiends, see how the heavens smiles   125
At your repulse and laughs your state to scorn!
Hence, hell! for hence I fly unto my God.   *Exeunt.*

[Scene xix]

   Thunder. Enter LUCIFER, BEELZEBUB, *and* MEPHOSTOPHILIS
                  [*above*].

Luc. Thus from infernal Dis do we ascend
    To view the subjects of our monarchy,
    Those souls which sin seals the black sons of hell,
    'Mong which as chief, Faustus, we come to thee,
    Bringing with us lasting damnation   5
    To wait upon thy soul; the time is come
    Which makes it forfeit.
Meph.   And this gloomy night
    Here in this room will wretched Faustus be.
Beel. And here we'll stay
    To mark him how he doth demean himself.   10
Meph. How should he but in desperate lunacy?

xix. 0.1–25. *Thunder . . . changed.*] *B1; not in A1.*   0.2. *above*] *Boas; not
in B1.*

---

122. *sift*] Compare Luke xxii. 31: 'Satan hath desired to have you, that
he may sift you as wheat'.

   pride] 'display of power' (Boas).

127. *I fly unto my God*] It is not certain whether the Old Man's faith gives
him physical immunity or a martyr's spiritual victory. In either case, he
triumphs over hell. If the dramatist followed the *Damnable Life*, the Old
Man was physically unharmed. See Appendix II.

xix. 1–19.] In this scene, as in scene iii, diabolical characters watch
Faustus without being perceived by him. Presumably they are 'above'. If
so, it seems reasonable to suppose that the A1 reporter omitted these lines
because his company could not count upon having the theatrical means for
their performance. See section 4 of the 'Introduction'.

1. *Dis*] a name sometimes given to Pluto, and hence also, as here, to the
lower world.

Fond worldling, now his heart-blood dries with grief,
His conscience kills it, and his labouring brain
Begets a world of idle fantasies
To overreach the devil; but all in vain: 15
His store of pleasures must be sauc'd with pain.
He and his servant Wagner are at hand,
Both come from drawing Faustus' latest will.
See where they come.

Enter FAUSTUS *and* WAGNER.

Fau. Say, Wagner, thou hast perus'd my will: 20
      How dost thou like it ?
Wag.   Sir, so wondrous well
      As in all humble duty I do yield
      My life and lasting service for your love.

Enter the Scholars.

Fau. Gramercies, Wagner. Welcome, gentlemen. [*Exit* WAGNER.]
1 Sch. Now, worthy Faustus, methinks your looks are changed. 25
Fau. Ah, gentlemen!
2 Sch. What ails Faustus ?
Fau. Ah, my sweet chamber-fellow, had I lived with thee,
      then had I lived still, but now must die eternally. Look,
      sirs, comes he not ? comes he not ?   30
1 Sch. O my dear Faustus, what imports this fear ?
2 Sch. Is all our pleasure turned to melancholy ?

---

24. *Exit* WAGNER.] *Oxberry; not in B1.*   26.] *Before this line, with which
it opens the scene, A1 inserts: Enter Faustus with the Schollers.*   Ah] *A1;*
Oh *B1.*   27. 2] *B1;* 1 *A1.*   28–30.] *Prose as here A1; verse divided after
thee, eternally B1.*   29. must] *B1;* I *A1.*   30. sirs] *B1; not in A1.*
31–3. *1 Sch.* O . . . with] *B1;* 2. *Sch:* what meanes Faustus ? / 3. *Scholler
Belike he is growne into some sickenesse, by A1.*

---

24. *Gramercies*] thank you.
26. *Ah*] Greg points out that in the present scene B1 almost invariably
uses the exclamation 'O' where A1 uses sometimes 'O' but more often 'ah'.
He may well be right in diagnosing a mannerism of the compositor.
28. *chamber-fellow*] Ward explains that it was customary at this time for
two or more university students to occupy the same room.

3 Sch. He is not well with being over-solitary.

2 Sch. If it be so, we'll have physicians, and Faustus shall be
cured.   35

3 Sch. 'Tis but a surfeit, sir; fear nothing.

Fau. A surfeit of deadly sin, that hath damned both body and
soul.

2 Sch. Yet, Faustus, look up to heaven and remember God's
mercy is infinite.   40

Fau. But Faustus' offence can ne'er be pardoned: the serpent
that tempted Eve may be saved, but not Faustus. Ah,
gentlemen, hear me with patience, and tremble not at my
speeches. Though my heart pants and quivers to remember that I have been a student here these thirty years, O,   45
would I had never seen Wittenberg, never read book! and
what wonders I have done all Germany can witness, yea,
all the world, for which Faustus hath lost both Germany
and the world, yea, heaven itself—heaven, the seat of
God, the throne of the blessed, the kingdom of joy—and   50
must remain in hell for ever. Hell, ah, hell for ever! Sweet
friends, what shall become of Faustus, being in hell for
ever?

3 Sch. Yet, Faustus, call on God.

Fau. On God, whom Faustus hath abjured? on God, whom   55
Faustus hath blasphemed? Ah, my God, I would weep,
but the devil draws in my tears. Gush forth blood, instead
of tears, yea, life and soul! O, he stays my tongue! I would

---

34. *2*] *B1;* 1 *A1.*   34–6. and . . . nothing.] *B1;* to cure him, tis but a
surffet, neuer feare man. *A1.*   39. and] *B1; not in A1.*   God's] *A1;*
not in B1.   40. mercy is] *B1;* mercies are *A1.*   41–2. But . . . saved]
Prose as here Dilke; verse divided after pardoned, saved *A1, B1.*   42. Ah]
A1; O *B1.*   43. me] *A1; not in B1.*   44. pants and quivers] *A1;* pant
& quiuer *B1.*   51. ah] *A1;* O *B1.*   54. *3*] *A1;* 2 *B1.*   56. Ah] *A1;*
O *B1.*

---

39. *God's*] The editor of B1 seems to have felt that the name of God
occurred far too often in this scene and to have begun to put things right
by cutting it out here. For further signs of his bowdlerizing, see textual
notes on ll. 145, 146, 150–1, 153, 165–7, and 187.

lift up my hands, but see, they hold them, they hold them.

All. Who, Faustus?   60

Fau. Why, Lucifer and Mephostophilis. Ah, gentlemen, I
gave them my soul for my cunning.

All. God forbid!

Fau. God forbade it, indeed; but Faustus hath done it. For
the vain pleasure of four-and-twenty years hath Faustus   65
lost eternal joy and felicity. I writ them a bill with mine
own blood: the date is expired, this is the time, and he will
fetch me.

1 Sch. Why did not Faustus tell us of this before, that divines
might have prayed for thee?   70

Fau. Oft have I thought to have done so; but the devil threat-
ened to tear me in pieces if I named God, to fetch me body
and soul if I once gave ear to divinity; and now 'tis too late.
Gentlemen, away, lest you perish with me!

2 Sch. O, what may we do to save Faustus?   75

Fau. Talk not of me, but save yourselves and depart.

3 Sch. God will strengthen me. I will stay with Faustus.

1 Sch. Tempt not God, sweet friend; but let us into the next
room and there pray for him.

Fau. Ay, pray for me, pray for me; and, what noise soever ye   80
hear, come not unto me, for nothing can rescue me.

2 Sch. Pray thou, and we will pray, that God may have mercy
upon thee.

Fau. Gentlemen, farewell. If I live till morning, I'll visit you;
if not, Faustus is gone to hell.   85

All. Faustus, farewell.   *Exeunt* Scholars.

---

59. them ... them] *A1;* 'em ... 'em *B1.*   61–2.] *Prose as here B1; Lucifer
and Mephastophilis. (as a line of verse) A1.*   61. Why] *B1; not in A1.*
Ah] *A1;* O *B1.*   63. God] *A1;* O God *B1.*   65. the] *B1; not in A1.*
67. this is the time] *B1;* the time wil come *A1.*   72. fetch me] *B1;*
fetch both *A1.*   75. may] *B1;* shal *A1.*   save] *B1; not in A1.*   79.
there] *A1; not in A3, B1.*   80. ye] *A1;* you *B1.*   82. pray,] *B1;* pray
A1.

---

66. *bill*] deed.

Meph. Ay, Faustus, now thou hast no hope of heaven;
　　Therefore despair, think only upon hell,
　　For that must be thy mansion, there to dwell.

Fau. O thou bewitching fiend, 'twas thy temptation   90
　　Hath robb'd me of eternal happiness.

Meph. I do confess it, Faustus, and rejoice.
　　'Twas I that, when thou wert i' the way to heaven,
　　Damm'd up thy passage; when thou took'st the book
　　To view the scriptures, then I turn'd the leaves   95
　　And led thine eye.
　　What, weep'st thou? 'tis too late, despair, farewell!
　　Fools that will laugh on earth must weep in hell.   *Exit.*

　　Enter the Good Angel *and the* Bad Angel *at several doors.*

Good Ang. O Faustus, if thou hadst given ear to me,
　　Innumerable joys had follow'd thee;   100
　　But thou didst love the world.

Bad Ang.　　　　　　　　　　Gave ear to me,
　　And now must taste hell's pains perpetually.

Good Ang. O, what will all thy riches, pleasures, pomps
　　Avail thee now?

Bad Ang.　　　　　Nothing but vex thee more,
　　To want in hell, that had on earth such store.   105
　　　　　　　　　　　Music while the throne descends.

Good Ang. O, thou hast lost celestial happiness,
　　Pleasures unspeakable, bliss without end.

87–132. *Meph.* Ay . . . confusion. *Exit.*] *B1; not in A1.*　　98. must] *B2;*
most *B1.*　　99. O] *B1;* Ah *Greg.*

　　87–132.] This passage presupposes a theatre well equipped with stage
machinery. It seems likely that the reporter responsible for A1 omitted it
because he had to envisage production with less elaborate facilities than it
assumed. See comment on ll. 1–19 and section 4 of the 'Introduction'.

　　87.] Mephostophilis here becomes visible to Faustus. He probably descends, leaving Lucifer and Beelzebub 'above'.

　　96. *led thine eye*] for example, to the texts juxtaposed in i. 39–43.

　　102.] anticipates l. 135.

　　105.1. the throne] This could be let down from the theatrical 'heavens'
by means of cords and pulleys. See Chambers, *E.S.*, iii. 77. Here the
throne represents that which Faustus might have occupied in heaven.

Hadst thou affected sweet divinity,
Hell or the devil had had no power on thee.
Hadst thou kept on that way, Faustus, behold   110
In what resplendent glory thou hadst sit
In yonder throne, like those bright shining saints,
And triumph'd over hell; that hast thou lost.
And now, poor soul, must thy good angel leave thee;
The jaws of hell are open to receive thee.   *Exit.*   115
                                                Hell is discovered.

Bad Ang. Now, Faustus, let thine eyes with horror stare
Into that vast perpetual torture-house.
There are the furies, tossing damned souls
On burning forks; their bodies boil in lead:
There are live quarters broiling on the coals,   120
That ne'er can die: this ever-burning chair
Is for o'er-tortur'd souls to rest them in:
These that are fed with sops of flaming fire
Were gluttons and lov'd only delicates
And laugh'd to see the poor starve at their gates.   125
But yet all these are nothing; thou shalt see
Ten thousand tortures that more horrid be.
Fau. O, I have seen enough to torture me.
Bad Ang. Nay, thou must feel them, taste the smart of all:
He that loves pleasure must for pleasure fall: 130
And so I leave thee, Faustus, till anon;
Then wilt thou tumble in confusion.   *Exit.*
                                                The clock strikes eleven.

111. sit] *B2;* set *B1.*   119. boil] *B3;* broyle *B1.*

---

108. *affected*] been drawn to, preferred.
115–115.1.] The throne is raised, and the Good Angel retires. Perhaps the drawing of a curtain reveals a painted backcloth representing the horrors of hell. An alternative would be a trap uncovered with smoke etc. arising. Clifford Leech, who privately suggests this second method, observes that it would produce a stronger antithesis to the descending throne.
132. Exit] The Bad Angel retires either behind the curtain, drawing it so as to conceal both himself and the painted backcloth representing hell, or by way of the trap.

Fau. Ah, Faustus,
　　　Now hast thou but one bare hour to live,
　　　And then thou must be damn'd perpetually.   135
　　　Stand still, you ever-moving spheres of heaven,
　　　That time may cease, and midnight never come;
　　　Fair nature's eye, rise, rise again, and make
　　　Perpetual day; or let this hour be but
　　　A year, a month, a week, a natural day,   140
　　　That Faustus may repent and save his soul.
　　　O lente lente currite noctis equi !
　　　The stars move still, time runs, the clock will strike,
　　　The devil will come, and Faustus must be damn'd.
　　　O, I'll leap up to my God! Who pulls me down?   145
　　　See, see where Christ's blood streams in the firmament!
　　　One drop would save my soul, half a drop. Ah, my Christ!—
　　　Rend not my heart for naming of my Christ;
　　　Yet will I call on him. O, spare me, Lucifer!—

133. Ah] *A1;* O *B1*.   139–40. be but / A year, a] *Oxberry;* be but a yeare, /
A *A1, B1;* but be / A year, a *Greg*.   145. my God] *A1;* heauen *B1*.
146. See . . . firmament!] *A1; not in B1*.   147. would . . . Ah] *A1;* of
bloud will saue me; oh *B1*.   148. Rend] *B1;* Ah rend *A1*.

136–44.] Compare *Edward II*, v. i. 64–70: 'Continue ever thou celestial
sun; / Let never silent night possess this clime: / Stand still you watches
of the element; / All times and seasons, rest you at a stay, / That Edward
may be still fair England's king. / But day's bright beams doth vanish fast
away, / And needs I must resign my wished crown.'
　140. *a natural day*] 'a mere day' (Clifford Leech, privately).
　142.] quoted from Ovid, *Amores*, I. xiii. 40, '"clamares: "lente currite,
noctis equi!"'', a line which Marlowe himself translates in his *Ovid's
Elegies*, 'Then would'st thou cry, "Stay night, and run not thus"'', and to
which there are allusions in *Dido, Queen of Carthage*, I. i. 26, and *Arden of
Feversham* (ed. Macdonald), ll. 60–4. Ovid wishes to prolong the night he
is spending with his lover. Marlowe's transference of Ovid's words to the
doomed Faustus adds immeasurably to their power and poignancy.
　146.] T. S. Eliot points to this as a triumphantly successful remodelling
of the earlier line, 'And set black streamers in the firmament' (2 *Tamburlaine*, v. iii. 49). See his 'Christopher Marlowe', *Selected Essays* (London,
1932), pp. 118–25.
　148.] 'Faustus remembers the previous violations of his vow and the
consequences [vi. 85–95 and xviii. 71–6]' (Boas). The words 'Rend not my
heart' open *Edward II*, I. iv. 117.

Where is it now? 'Tis gone: and see where God
Stretcheth out his arm and bends his ireful brows
Mountains and hills, come, come, and fall on me,
And hide me from the heavy wrath of God!
No, no:
Then will I headlong run into the earth.   155
Earth, gape! O, no, it will not harbour me.
You stars that reign'd at my nativity,
Whose influence hath allotted death and hell,
Now draw up Faustus like a foggy mist
Into the entrails of yon labouring cloud,   160
That, when you vomit forth into the air,

---

150. gone: and] *Dyce;* gone.] And *A1, B1.*   150-1. where God / Stretcheth ... brows.] *Dyce;* where ... arme, / And ... browes: *A1;* a threatning
Arme, an angry Brow. *B1.*   153. God] *A1;* heauen *B1.*   154-5.] *Verse
as here Dyce; one line A1, B1.*   154. No, no:] *A1;* No ? *B1.*   156. Earth,
gape] *A1;* Gape earth *B1.*   160. cloud] *A1, B1;* clouds *Dyce 2.*   161-2.
you ... your] *A1, B1;* they ... their *Greg, conj. Dyce 2.*

---

150. '*Tis gone*] The vision of Christ's blood has faded because Faustus
in his terror has called on Lucifer.

152-3.] Compare Revelation vi. 16: 'And said to the mountains and
rocks, Fall on us, and hide us from the face of him that sitteth on the
throne, and from the wrath of the Lamb'. See also Hosea x. 8; and the
Damnable Life (in Appendix II).

153. *the heavy wrath of God*] Compare i. 71, 'God's heavy wrath'.

157-63.] 'Faustus begs the planets to exhale him upward into a cloud.
There his gross Earthly parts would be compacted into a thunderstone and
rejected, thus purifying his soul for admission into heaven' (S. K. Henin-
ger, *A Handbook of Renaissance Meteorology* (Durham, North Carolina,
1960), p. 174).

157.] Compare 1 *Tamburlaine*, IV. ii. 33: 'Smile, stars that reign'd at my
nativity'. The phrase is echoed by Ford in the speech with which Anna-
bella opens '*Tis Pity She's a Whore*, v. i: 'Would thou hadst been less subject to those stars / That luckless reign'd at my nativity!' See Clifford
Leech, *John Ford and the Drama of his Time* (London, 1957), p. 56.

158. *influence*] the supposed streaming from the stars of an ethereal fluid
acting upon the characters and destiny of men.

159-62.] Boas understands 'you' and 'your' to refer to 'cloud'. Gram-
matically, they should refer to 'stars' (l. 157); but if Boas is right they h
been attracted by the nearer substantive. Greg, believing the passag
rupt, adopts Dyce's suggestions and reads 'clouds ... they ... t'

160.] Compare 1 *Tamburlaine*, IV. ii. 44: 'Wrapt in the bowel
ing cloud'.

My limbs may issue from your smoky mouths,
So that my soul may but ascend to heaven.   *The watch strikes.*
Ah, half the hour is pass'd: 'twill all be pass'd anon.
O God,   165
If thou wilt not have mercy on my soul,
Yet for Christ's sake, whose blood hath ransom'd me,
Impose some end to my incessant pain;
Let Faustus live in hell a thousand years,
A hundred thousand, and at last be sav'd.   170
O, no end is limited to damned souls.
Why wert thou not a creature wanting soul?
Or why is this immortal that thou hast?
Ah, Pythagoras' *metempsychosis*, were that true,
This soul should fly from me and I be chang'd   175
Unto some brutish beast: all beasts are happy,
For when they die
Their souls are soon dissolv'd in elements;
But mine must live still to be plagu'd in hell.
Curs'd be the parents that engender'd me!   180
No, Faustus, curse thyself, curse Lucifer
That hath depriv'd thee of the joys of heaven.

                                    The clock striketh twelve.

---

163. So . . . but] *A1;* But let my soule mount, and *B1.*   164.] *One line
as here B1; divided after* is pass'd *A1.*   Ah] *A1;* O *B1.*   165-7. O . . .
me] *Verse as here Dyce 2; two lines divided after* soul *A1;* O, if my soule
must suffer for my sinne *B1.*   171. O, no] *A1;* No *B1.*   174. Ah] *A1;*
Oh *B1.*   176-7.] *Verse as here Dyce; one line A1; divided after* beast *B1.*
176. Unto] *A1;* Into *B1.*   182.1. *striketh*] *A1; strikes B1.*

---

163. watch] clock.
171. *limited*] appointed, fixed definitely.
174. *Pythagoras'* metempsychosis] Pythagoras of Samos, who flourished
in the sixth century B.C., was regarded as the author of the doctrine of the
transmigration of souls. Simpson ('The 1604 Text of Marlowe's *Doctor
Faustus'*, *Essays and Studies*, VII (1921), p. 155) would read these two Greek
words 'according to the accent', stressing the third syllable of each, and
would divide the line after them. But F. P. Wilson (*Marlowe and the Early
Shakespeare* (Oxford, 1953), p. 138) shows that the Elizabethans stressed
the second syllable of 'Pythagoras', exactly as we do today.
182. *depriv'd . . . heaven*] words uttered by Faustus in a very different
spirit in iii. 86.

O, it strikes, it strikes! Now, body, turn to air,
Or Lucifer will bear thee quick to hell!

Thunder and lightning.

O soul, be chang'd into little water drops,   185
And fall into the ocean, ne'er be found.

Enter Devils.

My God, my God! Look not so fierce on me!
Adders and serpents, let me breathe awhile!
Ugly hell, gape not! Come not, Lucifer;
I'll burn my books!—Ah, Mephostophilis!   190

Exeunt with him. [*Exeunt* LUCIFER *and* BEELZEBUB.]

[Scene xx]

Enter the Scholars.

1 Sch. Come, gentlemen, let us go visit Faustus,
For such a dreadful night was never seen
Since first the world's creation did begin;
Such fearful shrieks and cries were never heard.
Pray heaven the doctor have escap'd the danger.   5
2 Sch. O, help us, heaven! see, here are Faustus' limbs,
All torn asunder by the hand of death.

183. O] *A1; not in B1.*   184.1, 186.1.] *Two stage-directions placed after
184 and 187 A1; a single stage-direction* Thunder, *and enter the deuils. after
186 B1.*   185. into] *A1, B1; to Greg.*   little] *A1;* small *B1.*   187.
My God, my God!] *A1;* O mercy heauen, *B1.*   190. Ah] *A1;* oh *B1.*
190.1. with him] *A1; not in B1.*   Exeunt ... BEELZEBUB.] *This ed.; not
in A1, B1.*

Scene xx.] *This scene is not in A1.*

184. *quick*] alive.
190. *books*] of magic.
Ah, Mephostophilis] Mephostophilis evidently reappears at this point.
190.1. Exeunt with him] The hell to which the Devils drag Faustus could
be either behind a curtain at the rear of the stage or below the stage. See
comment on ll. 115–115.1.

xx. 6.] Perhaps the Second Scholar draws back the curtain and so dis-
covers Faustus' remains.

3 Sch. The devils whom Faustus serv'd have torn him thus;
  For, 'twixt the hours of twelve and one, methought
  I heard him shriek and call aloud for help,   10
  At which self time the house seem'd all on fire
  With dreadful horror of these damned fiends.
2 Sch. Well, gentlemen, though Faustus' end be such
  As every Christian heart laments to think on,
  Yet, for he was a scholar, once admir'd   15
  For wondrous knowledge in our German schools,
  We'll give his mangled limbs due burial;
  And all the students, cloth'd in mourning black,
  Shall wait upon his heavy funeral.   *Exeunt.*

[Epilogue]

Enter Chorus.

Cho. Cut is the branch that might have grown full straight,
  And burned is Apollo's laurel bough
  That sometime grew within this learned man.
  Faustus is gone: regard his hellish fall,
  Whose fiendful fortune may exhort the wise   5
  Only to wonder at unlawful things,
  Whose deepness doth entice such forward wits
  To practise more than heavenly power permits. [*Exit.*]

Terminat hora diem; terminat Author opus.

FINIS.

Epilogue. 1. *Cho.*] Dyce; *not in A1, B1.* 8. *Exit.*] Dyce 2; *not in A1, B1.*
8.1. *Author*] A1, B1; *Auctor Oxberry.*

---

19. *wait upon*] accompany on its way.
heavy] sad, sorrowful.

Epilogue. 1.] The source of this line appears to be T. Churchyard,
'Shore's Wife', l. 140, in *The Mirror for Magistrates* (ed. Campbell), 'bent
the wand that might have growen ful streight'.

3. *sometime*] at one time.

5. *fiendful*] proceeding from diabolical agency.

6. *Only to wonder*] to be content with merely wondering.

8.1.] The hour ends the day; the author ends his work. Greg holds that this motto was probably added by the printer of A1. B1, which here derives from A3, naturally has it too.

ADDITIONAL NOTES

iii. 1–4.] There is a similar passage in Spenser, *The Faerie Queene*, III. x. 46. See J. D. Jump, 'Spenser and Marlowe', *N. & Q.*, New Series, XI (1964), pp. 261–2.

vi. 18.] This line occurs also in the anonymous play, *A Knack to Know a Knave*. See Hazlitt's Dodsley, vi. 520; and C. A. Zimansky, 'Marlowe's *Faustus:* The Date Again', *P.Q.*, XLI (1962), pp. 181–7.

xvii. 41.] Robin's 'reason : raisin' pun introduces the popular expression of contempt, 'a fig for him!' See J. C. Maxwell, 'Notes on *Dr. Faustus*', *N. & Q.*, New Series, XI (1964), p. 262. Faustus, by his charms, has brought the clowns into the presence of the Duke without disturbing their belief that they have merely passed into 'another room' (xvi. 56) in the tavern.

xviii. 86.] Apparently an echo of Kyd, *The Spanish Tragedy* (ed. Edwards), II. iii. 48, 'With greatest pleasure that our court affords'. See J. C. Maxwell, 'Notes on *Dr. Faustus*', *N. & Q.*, New Series, XI (1964), p. 262.

THE
TRAGICALL

History of D. Faustus.

As it hath bene Acted by the Right
Honorable the Earle of Nottingham his seruants.

Written by Ch. Marl.

LONDON
Printed by V. S. for Thomas Bushell. 1604.

Title-page of the Quarto of 1604

The A-Version of Scenes iv, vii, x, xii, and xv

(See section 5 of the 'Introduction'.)

[Scene iv]

        Enter WAGNER *and the* Clown [ROBIN].

Wag. Sirrah boy, come hither.

Rob. How, boy! zounds, boy! I hope you have seen many boys
    with such pickedevants as I have. Boy, quotha!

Wag. Tell me, sirrah, hast thou any comings in?

Rob. Ay, and goings out too, you may see else.   5

Wag. Alas, poor slave! see how poverty jesteth in his naked-
    ness. The villain is bare and out of service, and so hungry
    that I know he would give his soul to the devil for a shoul-
    der of mutton, though it were blood-raw.

Rob. How, my soul to the devil for a shoulder of mutton,   10
    though 'twere blood-raw? Not so, good friend. By'r lady,
    I had need have it well roasted, and good sauce to it, if I
    pay so dear.

Wag. Well, wilt thou serve me? and I'll make thee go like *Qui*
    mihi discipulus.   15

---

iv. 0.1. ROBIN] *Greg; not in A1.*   2, 5, 10, *etc.* Rob.] *This ed.; Clo. or Clow.*
throughout this scene A1.

    Scene iv.] There are comments on *pickedevants* (l. 3), *comings in* (l. 4),
Qui mihi discipulus (ll. 14–15), *beaten silk* (l. 17), *stavesacre* (l. 17), *familiars*
(l. 27), *take these guilders* (l. 31), *diametrally* (l. 72), and quasi vestigiis
nostris insistere (ll. 72–3) appended to the version of this scene given in
the main body of the text.
    3. *quotha*] indeed. (Literally, 'said he?').

Rob. How, in verse ?

Wag. No, sirrah, in beaten silk and stavesacre.

Rob. How, how, knave's acre! Ay, I thought that was all the
    land his father left him. Do ye hear ? I would be sorry to
    rob you of your living.   20

Wag. Sirrah, I say in stavesacre.

Rob. Oho, oho, stavesacre! Why, then, belike, if I were your
    man, I should be full of vermin.

Wag. So thou shalt, whether thou beest with me or no. But,
    sirrah, leave your jesting and bind yourself presently unto   25
    me for seven years, or I'll turn all the lice about thee into
    familiars and they shall tear thee in pieces.

Rob. Do you hear, sir ? you may save that labour. They are too
    familiar with me already. Zounds, they are as bold with
    my flesh as if they had paid for my meat and drink.   30

Wag. Well, do you hear, sirrah ? hold, take these guilders.

Rob. Gridirons, what be they ?

Wag. Why, French crowns.

Rob. Mass, but for the name of French crowns, a man were as
    good have as many English counters. And what should I   35
    do with these ?

Wag. Why, now, sirrah, thou art at an hour's warning, when-
    soever or wheresoever the devil shall fetch thee.

Rob. No, no; here, take your gridirons again.

---

18. *knave's acre*] 'To go home by knave's acre' means 'to be ruined, to
fail badly'. See E. Partridge, *A Dictionary of Slang* (London, 1949).

30. *as if . . . drink*] 'as if it was they who kept and fatted me up for their
own eating' (Greg).

33, 34. *French crowns*] the name usually given to the French coins called
écus, which had been current in England for many years. They were often
debased and counterfeited. This may explain Robin's disparaging attitude.
But it is possible, as explained in the next comment, that he is disparaging
not French crowns but Dutch guilders. See H. E. Cain, 'Marlowe's
"French Crowns"', *M.L.N.*, XLIX (1934), pp. 380–4.

34–5. *Mass . . . counters*] Robin may mean either that French crowns are
no better than English counters or that Wagner's Dutch guilders are
superior to English counters only in being dignified by the name of French
crowns.

35. *counters*] worthless tokens used in counting money.

Wag. Truly, I'll none of them.   40

Rob. Truly, but you shall.

Wag. Bear witness I gave them him.

Rob. Bear witness I give them you again.

Wag. Well, I will cause two devils presently to fetch thee
   away. Baliol and Belcher!   45

Rob. Let your Balio and your Belcher come here, and I'll
   knock them, they were never so knocked since they were
   devils. Say I should kill one of them, what would folks
   say? 'Do ye see yonder tall fellow in the round slop? He
   has killed the devil.' So I should be called Kill-devil all   50
   the parish over.

   Enter two Devils, *and the* Clown *runs up and down crying.*

Wag. Baliol and Belcher—spirits, away!   *Exeunt* [Devils].

Rob. What, are they gone? A vengeance on them! they have
   vile long nails. There was a he-devil and a she-devil. I'll
   tell you how you shall know them: all he-devils has horns,   55
   and all she-devils has clefts and cloven feet.

Wag. Well, sirrah, follow me.

Rob. But, do you hear? if I should serve you, would you teach
   me to raise up Banios and Belcheos?

Wag. I will teach thee to turn thyself to anything, to a dog, or   60
   a cat, or a mouse, or a rat, or anything.

Rob. How! a Christian fellow to a dog or a cat, a mouse or a
   rat! No, no, sir, if you turn me into anything, let it be in
   the likeness of a little pretty frisking flea, that I may be

---

52. Devils] *Dyce; not in A1.*

---

42. *Bear witness*] Wagner here appeals to the audience.

48–51. *Say . . . over*] This, which has no parallel in B1, seems to have
been borrowed, by the reporter responsible for A1, from Lodge and
Greene, *A Looking-Glass for London and England* (ed. Greg), ll. 1732–5,
where the Clown boasts: 'Then may I count my selfe I thinke a tall man,
that am able to kill a diuell. Now who dare deale with me in the parish,
or what wench in *Niniuie* will not loue me, when they say, there goes he
that beate the diuell.'

49. *tall*] valiant.

slop] wide baggy breeches.

    here and there and everywhere. O, I'll tickle the pretty 65
    wenches' plackets, I'll be amongst them i' faith.

Wag. Well, sirrah, come.

Rob. But, do you hear, Wagner?

Wag. How! Baliol and Belcher!

Rob. O Lord, I pray, sir, let Banio and Belcher go sleep. 70

Wag. Villain, call me Master Wagner, and let thy left eye be
    diametrally fixed upon my right heel, with *quasi vestigiis
    nostris insistere.*   *Exit.*

Rob. God forgive me, he speaks Dutch fustian. Well, I'll fol-
    low him; I'll serve him, that's flat.   *Exit.* 75

         *   *   *

[Scene vii]

Enter ROBIN *the ostler with a book in his hand.*

Rob. O, this is admirable! Here I ha' stolen one of Doctor
    Faustus' conjuring books, and, i' faith, I mean to search
    some circles for my own use. Now will I make all the
    maidens in our parish dance at my pleasure stark naked
    before me, and so by that means I shall see more than e'er 5
    I felt or saw yet.

Enter RALPH, *calling* ROBIN.

Ral. Robin, prithee come away. There's a gentleman tarries to

72–3. *vestigiis nostris*] *Dyce 2; vestigias nostras A1, B1.*

Scene vii.] *In A1, this scene immediately precedes scene x, scene x immediately
precedes scene xii, and scenes xii and xv form a single scene.*

---

    66. *plackets*] a current obscene application of the word for the slit at the
top of a skirt or petticoat for ease of putting on and off.

    72. *with*] The use of this word where B1 has 'that thou maist' indicates
a failure on the part of Robin, or of the reporter responsible for A1, to
understand the Latin phrase which follows.

    74. *fustian*] jargon, gibberish.

    vii. 3. *circles*] Robin refers punningly both to the rings or circles drawn
by magicians and to the female pudenda.

have his horse, and he would have his things rubbed and
made clean; he keeps such a chafing with my mistress
about it, and she has sent me to look thee out. Prithee   10
come away.

Rob. Keep out, keep out, or else you are blown up, you are dis-
membered, Ralph: keep out, for I am about a roaring
piece of work.

Ral. Come, what dost thou with that same book? Thou canst   15
not read.

Rob. Yes, my master and mistress shall find that I can read, he
for his forehead, she for her private study; she's born to
bear with me, or else my art fails.

Ral. Why, Robin, what book is that?   20

Rob. What book! why, the most intolerable book for conjuring
that e'er was invented by any brimstone devil.

Ral. Canst thou conjure with it?

Rob. I can do all these things easily with it: first, I can make
thee drunk with hippocras at any tavern in Europe for   25
nothing—that's one of my conjuring works.

Ral. Our master parson says that's nothing.

Rob. True, Ralph. And more, Ralph, if thou hast any mind to
Nan Spit our kitchenmaid, then turn her and wind her to
thy own use, as often as thou wilt, and at midnight.   30

Ral. O brave, Robin, shall I have Nan Spit, and to mine own
use? On that condition I'll feed thy devil with horse-
bread as long as he lives, of free cost.

15. book?] *Dyce;* booke *A1.*

8–9. *he would have . . . mistress*] further *doubles entendres.*
10. *look thee out*] find you by looking.
12. *out*] outside my circle.
13. *roaring*] riotous, befitting a 'roarer'.
18. *his forehead*] where his cuckold's horns will sprout.
18–19. *she for . . . me*] more *doubles entendres.*
21. *intolerable*] No doubt Robin means 'incomparable'.
25. *hippocras*] a cordial drink made of wine flavoured with spices.
29. *turn her and wind her*] spoken with punning allusion to her surname.
32–3. *horse-bread*] made of beans, bran, etc.
33. *of free cost*] cost free.

Rob. No more, sweet Ralph, let's go and make clean our boots,
    which lie foul upon our hands, and then to our conjuring,   35
    in the devil's name.   *Exeunt.*

*   *   *

[Scene x]

Enter ROBIN *and* RALPH *with a silver goblet.*

Rob. Come, Ralph, did not I tell thee we were for ever made
    by this Doctor Faustus' book? *Ecce signum!* here's a
    simple purchase for horse-keepers: our horses shall eat
    no hay as long as this lasts.

Enter the Vintner.

Ral. But, Robin, here comes the vintner.   5
Rob. Hush, I'll gull him supernaturally. Drawer, I hope all is
    paid. God be with you. Come, Ralph.
Vint. Soft, sir; a word with you. I must yet have a goblet paid
    from you ere you go.
Rob. I, a goblet, Ralph! I, a goblet! I scorn you; and you are   10
    but a etc. I, a goblet! Search me.
Vint. I mean so, sir, with your favour.   [*Searches* ROBIN.]
Rob. How say you now?

x. 12. *Searches* ROBIN.] *Dyce; not in A1.*

Scene x.] In A1, this scene immediately follows scene vii.
2. Ecce signum] See the proof.
3. *simple purchase*] clear piece of gain.
6. *gull*] dupe, cheat.
supernaturally] extraordinarily. 'Or is Robin still thinking in terms of his
magical skill, even though he is not going to use it on this occasion?'
(Clifford Leech, privately).
Drawer] Robin insultingly pretends to mistake the Vintner, the inn-
keeper who sells the wine, for the tapster who merely draws it for the
customers.
11. *etc.*] Here and in l. 29 Greg understands the 'etc.' as primarily a con-
fession of failure of memory on the part of the reporter. In practice, it
authorizes the actor to carry on as best he may. But the same abbreviation
in the A-version of v. 140 was perhaps intended to be spoken. Of course,
this too may well have originated from a failure of memory.

Vint. I must say somewhat to your fellow. You, sir!

Ral. Me, sir! me, sir! search your fill. [*Vintner searches him.*]   15
　　Now, sir, you may be ashamed to burden honest men with
　　a matter of truth.

Vint. Well, t' one of you hath this goblet about you.

Rob. [*Aside*] You lie, drawer, 'tis afore me. [*To the Vintner*]
　　Sirrah you, I'll teach ye to impeach honest men. Stand by.   20
　　I'll scour you for a goblet. Stand aside, you had best, I
　　charge you in the name of Beelzebub. [*Aside to Ralph*]
　　Look to the goblet, Ralph.

Vint. What mean you, sirrah?

Rob. I'll tell you what I mean.   *He reads.*   25
　　Sanctobulorum Periphrasticon—nay, I'll tickle you, vint-
　　ner. [*Aside to Ralph*] Look to the goblet, Ralph. *Polyprag-
　　mos Belseborams framanto pacostiphos tostu Mephostophilis*
　　etc.

　　　　　Enter to them MEPHOSTOPHILIS.

Meph. Monarch of hell, under whose black survey   30
　　Great potentates do kneel with awful fear,
　　Upon whose altars thousand souls do lie,
　　How am I vexed with these villains' charms!

---

15. Vintner . . . *him.*] Dyce; not in *A1*.   19. *Aside*] Dyce; not in *A1*.
To the Vintner] *This ed.; not in A1.*   22, 27. *Aside to Ralph*] Dyce; not
in A1.   29.1.] *Stage-direction placed as here, conj. Simpson; A1 has instead
the stage-direction and dialogue of the revised ending, with the present stage-
direction inserted between its lines 5 and 6.*   30. *Meph.*] Dyce; not in *A1*.

---

17. *matter of truth*] charge affecting their reputation for honesty.

21. *scour*] beat, scourge. Robin is playing on this meaning of 'scour' and
the literal meaning, i.e. polish, which is applicable to a goblet.

26. *tickle*] used ironically to mean 'chastise'.

29.1–44.1.] This ending to the scene is shorter by one-third than the
corresponding passage in B1; and, whereas Robin becomes the dog in B1,
he becomes the ape in this version. Some time after the preparation of the
reported text, a simpler and still shorter ending seems to have been inserted,
presumably in view of the dwindling resources of the company (see section
4 of the 'Introduction'). This ending is printed after the present scene.

30–5.] See note on x. 31–4 in the main body of the text.

31. *awful*] terror-stricken.

33. *villains*] low fellows.

From Constantinople am I hither come
Only for pleasure of these damned slaves.   35

Rob. How, from Constantinople! You have had a great journey. Will you take sixpence in your purse to pay for your
supper and be gone?

Meph. Well, villains, for your presumption, I transform thee
into an ape, and thee into a dog; and so be gone.   *Exit.* 40

Rob. How, into an ape! that's brave: I'll have fine sport with
the boys; I'll get nuts and apples enow.

Ral. And I must be a dog.

Rob. I' faith, thy head will never be out of the pottage-pot.

Exeunt.

[*Revised ending, to replace ll.* 29.1–44.1]

Enter MEPHOSTOPHILIS: *sets squibs at their backs.*
They run about.

Vint. O *nomine Domini!* What meanest thou, Robin? thou
hast no goblet.

Ral. *Peccatum peccatorum!* Here's thy goblet, good vintner.

Rob. *Misericordia pro nobis!* What shall I do? Good devil, forgive me now, and I'll never rob thy library more.   5

Meph. Vanish, villains, th' one like an ape, another like a bear,
the third an ass, for doing this enterprise.   [*Exeunt.*]

*   *   *

Revised ending.] *See note on 29.1 above.*   1. *Domini*] *Dyce; Domine A1.*
7. *Exeunt.*] *This ed.; not in A1.*

Revised ending. 1–4.] The garbled scraps of liturgical Latin are presumably all that the speakers can produce in the language in which it was believed spirits had to be addressed.

[Scene xii]

Enter EMPEROR, FAUSTUS, [MEPHOSTOPHILIS,] *and a* Knight,
with Attendants.

Emp. Master Doctor Faustus, I have heard strange report of
thy knowledge in the black art, how that none in my Empire, nor in the whole world, can compare with thee for
the rare effects of magic. They say thou hast a familiar
spirit by whom thou canst accomplish what thou list.   5
This, therefore, is my request, that thou let me see some
proof of thy skill, that mine eyes may be witnesses to confirm what mine ears have heard reported; and here I
swear to thee, by the honour of mine imperial crown, that,
whatever thou dost, thou shalt be no ways prejudiced or   10
endamaged.

Kni. I' faith, he looks much like a conjuror.   *Aside.*

Fau. My gracious sovereign, though I must confess myself far
inferior to the report men have published, and nothing
answerable to the honour of your imperial Majesty, yet,   15
for that love and duty binds me thereunto, I am content
to do whatsoever your Majesty shall command me.

Emp. Then, Doctor Faustus, mark what I shall say.
As I was sometime solitary set
Within my closet, sundry thoughts arose   20
About the honour of mine ancestors,
How they had won by prowess such exploits,
Got such riches, subdued so many kingdoms,
As we that do succeed, or they that shall
Hereafter possess our throne, shall,   25
I fear me, never attain to that degree

---

xii. o.i. MEPHOSTOPHILIS] *Boas; not in A1.*   18–29.] *Verse as here Dyce;*
prose A1.

Scene xii.] In A1, this scene immediately follows scene x.
11. *endamaged*] harmed.
14–15. *nothing answerable*] quite unequal.
19. *sometime solitary set*] once seated solitarily.
22. *won*] been victorious in.

Of high renown and great authority;
Amongst which kings is Alexander the Great,
Chief spectacle of the world's pre-eminence,
The bright shining of whose glorious acts   30
Lightens the world with his reflecting beams,
As when I hear but motion made of him
It grieves my soul I never saw the man.
If, therefore, thou, by cunning of thine art,
Canst raise this man from hollow vaults below,   35
Where lies entomb'd this famous conqueror,
And bring with him his beauteous paramour,
Both in their right shapes, gesture, and attire
They us'd to wear during their time of life,
Thou shalt both satisfy my just desire   40
And give me cause to praise thee whilst I live.

Fau. My gracious lord, I am ready to accomplish your request, so far forth as by art and power of my spirit I am able to perform.

Kni. I' faith, that's just nothing at all.   *Aside.* 45

Fau. But, if it like your Grace, it is not in my ability to present before your eyes the true substantial bodies of those two deceased princes, which long since are consumed to dust.

Kni. Ay, marry, master doctor, now there's a sign of grace in 50
you, when you will confess the truth.   *Aside.*

Fau. But such spirits as can lively resemble Alexander and his paramour shall appear before your Grace in that manner that they both lived in, in their most flourishing estate, which I doubt not shall sufficiently content your imperial 55
Majesty.

32. motion] *A1;* mention *Wagner.*   54. both] *Dyce 2;* best *A1.*

---

29. *pre-eminence*] pre-eminent men. Ward compares 'nobility', i.e. noblemen.
32. *motion*] mention.
38. *gesture*] bearing.
43. *my spirit*] i.e. Mephostophilis.
52. *lively*] in a lifelike manner, to the life.

Emp. Go to, master doctor, let me see them presently.

Kni. Do you hear, master doctor? you bring Alexander and
    his paramour before the Emperor!

Fau. How then, sir?   60

Kni. I' faith, that's as true as Diana turned me to a stag.

Fau. No, sir, but when Actaeon died he left the horns for you.
    Mephostophilis, be gone!   *Exit* MEPHOSTOPHILIS.

Kni. Nay, and you go to conjuring, I'll be gone.   *Exit* Knight.

Fau. I'll meet with you anon for interrupting me so.—Here 65
    they are, my gracious lord.

    Enter MEPHOSTOPHILIS *with* ALEXANDER *and his* Paramour.

Emp. Master doctor, I heard this lady while she lived had a
    wart or mole in her neck. How shall I know whether it be
    so or no?

Fau. Your Highness may boldly go and see.   70

Emp. Sure these are no spirits but the true substantial bodies
    of those two deceased princes.

                    Exeunt ALEXANDER [*and his* Paramour].

Fau. Will 't please your Highness now to send for the knight
    that was so pleasant with me here of late?

Emp. One of you call him forth.   75

    Enter the Knight *with a pair of horns on his head.*

How now, sir knight? why, I had thought thou hadst
been a bachelor; but now I see thou hast a wife, that not
only gives thee horns but makes thee wear them. Feel on
thy head.

72.1. *Exeunt . . .* Paramour.] *Boas; exit Alex: A1 (at 70).*   76. How]
Dyce 2; emp. How *A1.*

---

    62. *Actaeon*] See comment on xii. 51 in the main body of the text.

    64. Exit *Knight*] B1 requires that the horns be fixed to the Knight's head
while he is at his window in full view of the audience. No window is called
for here; and the Knight leaves the stage to receive his horns. The difference is indicative of the gap between the theatres and companies for which
the two versions seem to have been prepared.

    65. *meet with you*] be even with you. See l. 86.

    74. *pleasant*] facetious.

Kni. Thou damned wretch and execrable dog,⠀⠀⠀⠀⠀⠀⠀⠀⠀80
⠀⠀⠀Bred in the concave of some monstrous rock,
⠀⠀⠀How dar'st thou thus abuse a gentleman ?
⠀⠀⠀Villain, I say, undo what thou hast done.

Fau. O, not so fast, sir, there's no haste but good. Are you
⠀⠀⠀remembered how you crossed me in my conference with⠀⠀85
⠀⠀⠀the Emperor ? I think I have met with you for it.

Emp. Good master doctor, at my entreaty release him. He
⠀⠀⠀hath done penance sufficient.

Fau. My gracious lord, not so much for the injury he offered
⠀⠀⠀me here in your presence, as to delight you with some⠀⠀90
⠀⠀⠀mirth, hath Faustus worthily requited this injurious
⠀⠀⠀knight; which being all I desire, I am content to release
⠀⠀⠀him of his horns: and, sir knight, hereafter speak well of
⠀⠀⠀scholars. Mephostophilis, transform him straight. Now,
⠀⠀⠀my good lord, having done my duty, I humbly take my⠀⠀95
⠀⠀⠀leave.

Emp. Farewell, master doctor; yet, ere you go, expect from
⠀⠀⠀me a bounteous reward.

⠀⠀⠀⠀⠀⠀⠀⠀⠀⠀⠀⠀⠀⠀*Exeunt* EMPEROR [*, Knight, and* Attendants].

[Scene xv]

Fau. Now, Mephostophilis, the restless course

97–8.] *Prose as here A1; verse divided after* go *Dyce.*⠀⠀⠀⠀98.1. *Exeunt . . .*
Attendants.] *Dyce; exit Emperour. A1.*

Scene xv.] *In A1, scenes xii and xv form a single scene, Faustus remaining on
the stage throughout.*⠀⠀⠀1–2, 5–6.] *Verse as here Dyce; prose A1.*

⠀⠀⠀80–3.] The reporter has already imitated Marlowe in ll. 35–6. Now, as
Greg points out, he not only imitates him again but lifts l. 81 from 2 *Tamburlaine*, III. ii. 89, 'Fenc'd with the concave of a monstrous rock'.

⠀⠀⠀81. *concave*] hollow.

⠀⠀⠀84. *there's . . . good*] 'No haste but good (speed)' was a well-known proverb. See Tilley, H199.

⠀⠀⠀84–5. *Are you remembered*] do you remember.

⠀⠀⠀89. *injury*] insult.

⠀⠀⠀98.1. Exeunt . . . *Attendants*] Faustus and Mephostophilis remain on the
stage, where the Horse-courser joins them at xv. 8.1.

⠀⠀⠀*Scene xv.*] In A1, this scene immediately follows scene xii. Indeed, there

That time doth run with calm and silent foot,
Shortening my days and thread of vital life,
Calls for the payment of my latest years.
Therefore, sweet Mephostophilis, let us   5
Make haste to Wittenberg.

Meph.   What, will you go
On horseback or on foot?

Fau.   Nay, till I am past
This fair and pleasant green, I'll walk on foot.

Enter a Horse-courser.

Hor. I have been all this day seeking one master Fustian.
Mass, see where he is! God save you, master doctor.   10

Fau. What, horse-courser! you are well met.

Hor. Do you hear, sir? I have brought you forty dollars for
your horse.

Fau. I cannot sell him so. If thou likest him for fifty, take him.

Hor. Alas, sir, I have no more. [*To Mephostophilis*] I pray you   15
speak for me.

Meph. I pray you let him have him. He is an honest fellow,
and he has a great charge, neither wife nor child.

Fau. Well, come, give me your money; my boy will deliver
him to you. But I must tell you one thing before you have   20
him: ride him not into the water, at any hand.

6–8.] *Verse-division introduced this ed.; prose A1.*   15. *To Mephostophilis*]
Boas; not in A1.

---

is not even a break between them. See comments on xii. 98.1 and xv. 1–8
in this appendix.

There are comments on *Horse-courser* (l. 8.1), *will . . . waters?* (l. 22),
fatal time (l. 36), *Confound* (l. 38), *in conceit* (l. 40), and *bottle* (l. 50) appended to the version of this scene given in the main body of the text.

1–8.] These lines, which have no equivalent in B1, are evidently designed
to produce a smooth transition from scene xii to scene xv in a text which
omits scenes xiii–xiv.

9. *Fustian*] a clownish corruption of 'Faustus'. Compare xvi. 19 and 38,
'Fauster'.

18. *a great . . . child*] spoken ironically.

19. *my boy*] Mephostophilis now appears as Faustus' servant and no
longer as 'an old Franciscan friar' (iii. 27).

21. *at any hand*] on any account.

Hor. Why, sir, will he not drink of all waters?

Fau. O yes, he will drink of all waters. But ride him not into
the water; ride him over hedge or ditch, or where thou
wilt, but not into the water.   25

Hor. Well, sir. [*Aside*] Now am I made man for ever, I'll not
leave my horse for forty: if he had but the quality of hey-
ding-ding, hey-ding-ding, I'd make a brave living on
him; he has a buttock as slick as an eel. [*To Faustus*] Well,
God b' wi' ye, sir, your boy will deliver him me. But,   30
hark ye, sir, if my horse be sick or ill at ease, if I bring
his water to you, you'll tell me what it is?

Fau. Away, you villain! What, dost think I am a horse-
doctor?   *Exit* Horse-courser.
What art thou, Faustus, but a man condemn'd to die?   35
Thy fatal time doth draw to final end;
Despair doth drive distrust unto my thoughts.
Confound these passions with a quiet sleep.
Tush, Christ did call the thief upon the cross;
Then rest thee, Faustus, quiet in conceit.   40

Sleep in his chair.

Enter Horse-courser, *all wet, crying.*

Hor. Alas, alas! Doctor Fustian, quotha? mass, Doctor Lopus
was never such a doctor. Has given me a purgation, has
purged me of forty dollars; I shall never see them more.
But yet, like an ass as I was, I would not be ruled by him,

26. *Aside*] *Dyce; not in A1.*   29. *To Faustus*] *This ed.; not in A1.*   34–5.]
Divided as here Dyce; prose A1.   34.] *Stage-direction placed as here Dyce;
after 32 A1.*

26. *am I made man*] am I a made man.

27. *forty*] used frequently to designate a large though indefinite amount.

27–8. *the quality of hey-ding-ding*] which would make him a valuable
stallion. There is a similar use of the phrase in Nashe's *Have With You*
(ed. McKerrow, iii. 113).

29. *as slick as an eel*] a variant of the well-known expression 'as slippery
as an eel'. See Tilley, E60.

41. *Doctor Lopus*] Roderigo Lopez, private physician to Elizabeth I, was
accused of having entered into a plot to poison her. He was tried in February 1594 and executed the following June.

for he bade me I should ride him into no water. Now I,   45
thinking my horse had had some rare quality that he
would not have had me known of, I, like a venturous
youth, rid him into the deep pond at the town's end. I was
no sooner in the middle of the pond but my horse vanished away and I sat upon a bottle of hay, never so near   50
drowning in my life. But I'll seek out my doctor and have
my forty dollars again, or I'll make it the dearest horse!—
O, yonder is his snipper-snapper. Do you hear? you, hey-
pass, where's your master?

Meph. Why, sir, what would you? You cannot speak with   55
him.

Hor. But I will speak with him.

Meph. Why, he's fast asleep. Come some other time.

Hor. I'll speak with him now, or I'll break his glass-windows
about his ears.   60

Meph. I tell thee he has not slept this eight nights.

Hor. And he have not slept this eight weeks, I'll speak with
him.

Meph. See where he is, fast asleep.

Hor. Ay, this is he. God save ye, master doctor, master doc-   65
tor, master Doctor Fustian. Forty dollars, forty dollars
for a bottle of hay!

Meph. Why, thou seest he hears thee not.

Hor. So-ho, ho! so-ho, ho!   *Hollo in his ear.*

No, will you not wake? I'll make you wake ere I go.   70
                    Pull him by the leg, and pull it away.

Alas, I am undone! What shall I do?

---

47. *known of*] aware of.

53. *snipper-snapper*] conceited young fellow.

53–4. *hey-pass*] The Horse-courser uses, as a name for Faustus' servant,
the exclamation employed by jugglers and conjurors to command an
article to move. Compare xvii. 112.

59. *glass-windows*] of the house or inn where Faustus is now sleeping.
But several of the editors toy with the idea that the reference may be to the
spectacles worn by Faustus.

69. *So-ho*] a call used by huntsmen to direct attention to a hare which
has been discovered.

Fau. O my leg, my leg! Help, Mephostophilis! call the officers! My leg, my leg!

Meph. Come, villain, to the constable.

Hor. O Lord, sir, let me go, and I'll give you forty dollars   75
more.

Meph. Where be they?

Hor. I have none about me. Come to my hostry, and I'll give
them you.

Meph. Be gone quickly.   Horse-courser *runs away*.   80

Fau. What, is he gone? farewell he! Faustus has his leg again,
and the horse-courser, I take it, a bottle of hay for his
labour. Well, this trick shall cost him forty dollars more.

Enter WAGNER.

How now, Wagner, what's the news with thee?

Wag. Sir, the Duke of Vanholt doth earnestly entreat your   85
company.

Fau. The Duke of Vanholt! an honourable gentleman, to
whom I must be no niggard of my cunning. Come,
Mephostophilis, let's away to him.   *Exeunt.*

85, 87. Vanholt] *A 1;* Anholt *Boas.*

---

89. Exeunt] It seems to have been intended that there should be no
break between this scene and scene xvii which immediately follows it in
A1. Such at all events is the implication of the stage-direction which there
opens scene xvii: '*Enter to them the Duke* . . .' If this implication is accepted,
the present '*Exeunt*' should be merely '*Exit* WAGNER'.

The Historie of the Damnable Life, and Deserued Death of Doctor Iohn Faustus

The chief passages of the *Damnable Life* used by the authors of *Doctor Faustus* are reproduced here. The small roman numerals accompanying the abbreviation '*D.L.*' refer to its chapters. The text of 1592 has been followed exactly, except for the silent correction of obvious misprints. See sections 2 and 7 of the 'Introduction'.

Faustus, Prologue, 11–27.

D.L., i. *Iohn Faustus*, borne in the town of *Rhode*, lying in the Prouince of *Weimer* in *Germ[anie,]* his father a poore Husbandman, and not [able] wel to bring him vp: but hauing an Uncle at *Wittenberg*, a rich man, & without issue, took this *I.Faustus* from his father, & made him his heire, in so much that his father was no more troubled with him, for he remained with his Uncle at *Wittenberg*, where he was kept at yᵉ Uniuersitie in the same citie to study diuinity. But *Faustus* being of a naughty minde & otherwise addicted, applied not his studies, but tooke himselfe to other exercises . . . he gaue himself secretly to study Necromancy and Coniuration, in so much that few or none could perceiue his profession.

But to the purpose: *Faustus* continued at study in the Uniuersity, & was by the Rectors and sixteene Masters afterwards examined howe he had profited in his studies; and being found by them, that none for his time were able to argue with him in Diuinity, or for the excellency of his wisedome to compare with him, with one consent they made him Doctor of Diuinitie.

D.L., ii. You haue heard before, that all *Faustus* minde was set to study the artes of Necromancie and Coniuration, the which exercise hee followed day and night: and taking to him the wings of an Eagle, thought to flie ouer the whole world, and to know the secrets of heauen and earth; for his Speculation was so wonderfull, being expert in vsing his *Vocabula*, Figures, Characters, Coniurations, and other Ceremoniall actions.

Faustus, i.

D.L., i. Doctor *Faustus* . . . fell into such fantasies and deepe cogitations, that he was marked of many . . . and sometime he would
throw the Scriptures from him as though he had no care of his former
profession . . . he accompanied himselfe with diuers that were seene
in those diuelish Arts, and that had the *Chaldean, Persian, Hebrew,
Arabian,* and *Greeke* tongues, vsing Figures, Characters, Coniurations, Incantations, with many other ceremonies belonging to these
infernal Arts . . . in so much that hee could not abide to bee called
Doctor of Diuinitie, but waxed a worldly man, and named himselfe
an Astrologian . . . & for a shadow sometimes a Phisitian, and did
great cures.

Faustus, iii. 1–37.

D.L., ii. And taking his way to a thicke Wood neere to *Wittenberg*,
called in the Germane tongue *Spisser Waldt*: that is in English the
Spissers Wood, (as *Faustus* would oftentimes boast of it among his
crue being in his iolitie,) he came into the same wood towards euening
into a crosse way, where he made with a wand a Circle in the dust,
and within that many more Circles and Characters: and thus he past
away the time, vntill it was nine or ten of the clocke in the night, then
began Doctor *Faustus* to call for *Mephostophiles* the Spirite, and to
charge him in the name of *Beelzebub* to appeare there personally without any long stay . . . *Faustus* all this while halfe amazed at the Diuels
so long tarrying, and doubting whether he were best to abide any
more such horrible Coniurings, thought to leaue his Circle and depart; wherevpon the Diuel made him such musick of all sortes, as if
the Nimphes themselues had beene in place: whereat *Faustus* was
reuiued and stoode stoutly in his Circle aspecting his purpose, and
began againe to coniure the spirite *Mephostophiles* in the name of
the Prince of Diuels to appeare in his likenesse: where at sodainly
ouer his head hanged houering in the ayre a mighty Dragon . . . presently not three fadome aboue his head fell a flame in manner of a
lightning, and changed it selfe into a Globe . . . sodainly the Globe
opened and sprang vp in height of a man: so burning a time, in the
end it conuerted to the shape of a fiery man. This pleasant beast ranne
about the circle a great while, and lastly appeared in manner of a gray
Frier, asking *Faustus* what was his request.

Faustus, iii. 38–44 and 95–99.

D.L., iii. . . . then began Doctor *Faustus* anew with him to coniure
him that he should be obedient vnto him, & to answere him certaine
Articles, and to fulfil them in al points.

1 That the Spirit should serue him and be obedient vnto him in all

things that he asked of him from yᵗ houre vntil the houre of his death.

2 Farther, any thing that he desired of him he should bring it to him.

3 Also, that in all *Faustus* his demaunds or Interrogations, the spirit should tell him nothing but that which is true.

Hereupon the Spirit answered and laid his case foorth, that he had no such power of himselfe, vntil he had first giuen his Prince (that was ruler ouer him) to vnderstand thereof, and to know if he could obtaine so much of his Lord: therfore speake farther that I may do thy whole desire to my Prince: for it is not in my power to fulfill without his leaue.

Faustus, iii. 65–75.

D.L., x. Here *Faustus* said: but how came thy Lord and master *Lucifer* to haue so great a fal frõ heauẽ? *Mephostophiles* answered: My Lord *Lucifer* was a faire Angell, created of God as immortal, and being placed in the Seraphins, which are aboue the Cherubins, hee would haue presumed vnto the Throne of God, with intent to haue thrust God out of his seate. Vpon this presumption the Lord cast him downe headlong, and where before he was an Angel of light, now dwels hee in darkenes.

D.L., xiii. . . . my Lord *Lucifer*, (so called now, for that he was banished out of the cleare light of Heauen) was at the first an Angell of God, he sate on the Cherubins, and sawe all the wonderfull works of God, yea he was so of God ordained, for shape, pompe, authority, worthines, & dwelling, that he far exceeded all other the creatures of God . . . but when hee began to be high minded, proude, and so presumptuous that hee would vsurpe the seate of his Maiestie, then was he banished out from amongst the heauenly powers.

Faustus, v. 31–115.

D.L., iv. . . . this swift flying Spirit appeared to *Faustus*, offering himself with al submissiõ to his seruice, with ful authority from his Prince to doe whatsoeuer he would request, if so be *Faustus* would promise to be his . . . Doctor *Faustus* gaue him this answere, though faintly (for his soules sake) That his request was none other but to become a Diuel, or at the least a limme of him, and that the Spirit should agree vnto these Articles as followeth.

1 That he might be a Spirite in shape and qualitie.

2 That *Mephostophiles* should be his seruant, and at his commandement.

3 That *Mephostophiles* should bring him any thing, and doo for him whatsoeuer.

4 That at all times he should be in his house, inuisible to all men,

except onely to himselfe, and at his commandement to shew himselfe.

5 Lastly, that *Mephostophiles* should at all times appeare at his commaund, in what forme or shape soeuer he would.

Upon these poynts the Spirit answered Doctor *Faustus*, that all this should be granted him and fulfilled, and more if he would agree vnto him vpon certaine Articles as followeth.

First, that Doctor *Faustus* should giue himselfe to his Lord *Lucifer*, body and soule.

Secondly, for confirmation of the same, he should make him a writing, written with his owne blood.

Thirdly, that he would be an enemie to all Christian people.

Fourthly, that he would denie his Christian beleefe.

Fiftly, that he let not any man change his opinion, if so bee any man should goe about to disswade, or withdraw him from it.

D.L., v. . . . to confirme it the more assuredly, he tooke a small penknife, and prickt a vaine in his left hand, & for certaintie therevpon, were seene on his hand these words written, as if they had been written with blood, *ô homo fuge*: whereat the Spirit vanished, but *Faustus* continued in his damnable minde, & made his writing as followeth.

D.L., vi. *How Doctor Faustus set his blood in a saucer on warme ashes, and writ as followeth.* . . . now haue I Doctor *Iohn Faustus*, vnto the hellish prince of Orient and his messenger *Mephostophiles*, giuen both bodie & soule, vpon such condition, that they shall learne me, and fulfill my desire in all things, as they haue promised and vowed vnto me, with due obedience vnto me, according vnto the Articles mentioned betweene vs.

Further, I couenant and grant with them by these presents, that at the end of *24.* yeares next ensuing the date of this present Letter, they being expired, and I in the meane time, during the said yeares be serued of them at my wil, they accomplishing my desires to the full in al points as we are agreed, that then I giue them full power to doe with mee at their pleasure, to rule, to send, fetch, or carrie me or mine, be it either body, soule, flesh, blood, or goods, into their habitation, be it wheresoeuer.

Faustus, v. 116–27.

D.L., xi. *How Doctor Faustus . . . questioned with his Spirit of matters as concerning hell, with the Spirits answer.* . . . my *Mephostophiles*, I pray thee resolue me in this doubt: what is hell, what substance is it of, in what place stands it, and when was it made? *Mephostophiles* answered: my *Faustus*, thou shalt knowe, that before the fall of my Lord *Lucifer* there was no hell, but euen then was hell ordained: it is of no substance, but a confused thing . . . in this confused hell is nought to finde but a filthie, Sulphurish, firie, stinking mist or fog. Further, wee Diuels know not what substance it is of, but a confused thing . . . but to bee short with thee *Faustus*, we know that hell hath neither bottome nor end.

Faustus, v. 141–79.

D.L., ix. Doctor *Faustus* . . . bethinking himselfe of a wife, called *Mephostophiles* to counsaile; which would in no wise agree: demanding of him if he would breake the couenant made with him, or if hee had forgot it. Hast not thou (quoth *Mephostophiles*) sworne thy selfe an enemy to God and all creatures? To this I answere thee, thou canst not marry; thou canst not serue two masters, God, and my Prince: for wedlock is a chiefe institution ordained of God, and that hast thou promised to defie, as we doe all, and that hast thou also done: and moreouer thou hast confirmed it with thy blood: perswade thy selfe, that what thou doost in contempt of wedlock, it is all to thine owne delight. Therefore *Faustus*, looke well about thee, and bethinke thy selfe better, and I wish thee to change thy minde: for if thou keepe not what thou hast promised in thy writing, we wil teare thee in peeces like the dust vnder thy feete. Therefore sweete *Faustus*, thinke with what vnquiet life, anger, strife, & debate thou shalt liue in when thou takest a wife: therefore change thy minde. . . .

Then *Faustus* said vnto him, I am not able to resist nor bridle my fantasie, I must and will haue a wife, and I pray thee giue thy consent to it. . . . Hereupon appeared vnto him an ougly Diuell, so fearefull and monstrous to beholde, that *Faustus* durst not looke on him. The Diuell said, what wouldst thou haue *Faustus*? how likest thou thy wedding? what minde art thou in now? *Faustus* answered, he had forgot his promise, desiring him of pardon, and he would talke no more of such things. The diuell answered, thou were best so to doe, and so vanished.

After appeared vnto him his Frier *Mephostophiles* with a bel in his hand, and spake to *Faustus*: It is no iesting with vs, holde thou that which thou hast vowed, and wee will performe as wee haue promised: and more than that, thou shalt haue thy hearts desire of what woman soeuer thou wilt, bee shee aliue or dead, and so long as thou wilt, thou shalt keepe her by thee.

D.L., x. *Mephostophiles* . . . brought with him a booke in his hand of all maner of diuelish and inchanted artes, the which he gaue *Faustus*, saying: hold my *Faustus*, worke now thy hearts desire.

Faustus, vi. 1–105 and 172–80.

D.L., xviii. Doctor *Faustus* . . . called vnto him *Mephostophiles* his spirit, saying: . . . when I conferre *Astronomia* and *Astrologia*, as the

Mathematicians and auncient writers haue left in memory, I finde them to vary and very much to disagree: wherefore I pray thee to teach me the truth in this matter.

D.L., xix. *How Doctor Faustus fell into despaire with himselfe: for hauing put foorth a question vnto his Spirit, they fell at variance, whereupon the whole route of diuels appeared vnto him, threatning him sharply.* Doctor *Faustus* . . . became so wofull and sorrowfull in his cogitations, that he thought himselfe already frying in the hottest flames of hell . . . [Mephostophiles said,] although I am not bound vnto thee in such respects as concerne the hurt of our kingdome, yet was I alwaies willing to answere thee . . . *Faustus* . . . spake in this sorte, *Mephostophiles*, tell me how and after what sorte God made the world . . . The spirit hearing this, answered, *Faustus* thou knowest that all this is in vaine for thee to aske . . . Whereat *Faustus* al sorrowful for that he had put forth such a question, fel to weeping and to howling bitterly . . . And . . . the greatest Diuel in hell appeared vnto him, with certaine of his hideous and infernal companie in the most ougliest shapes that it was possible to think vpon, and . . . spake in this sorte: *Faustus*, I haue seene thy thoughtes, which are not as thou hast vowed vnto me, by vertue of this letter, and shewed him the Obligation that hee had written with his owne blood, wherefore I am come to visite thee and to shewe thee some of our hellish pastimes . . . Saith *Faustus*, I will that thou teach me to transforme my selfe in like sort as thou and the rest haue done: then *Lucifer* put forth his Pawe, and gaue *Faustus* a booke, saying holde, doe what thou wilt.

D.L., xx. Quoth *Faustus*, I would knowe of thee if I may see Hell and take a view thereof? That thou shalt (said the diuell) and at midnight I will fetch thee.

Faustus, Cho. 1, 1–14.

D.L., xxi. [From a letter of Faustus to a friend.] I being once laide on my bed, and could not sleepe for thinking on my Kalender and practise, I marueiled with my selfe how it were possible that the Firmament should bee knowne and so largely written of men, or whether they write true or false, by their owne opinions, or supposition, or by due obseruations and true course of the heauens. Beholde, being in these my muses, sodainly I heard . . . a groning voyce which said, get vp, the desire of thy heart, minde, and thought shalt thou see . . . and beholde, there stoode a Waggon, with two Dragons before it to drawe the same, and all the Waggon was of a light burning fire . . . I got me into the Waggon, so that the Dragons caried me vpright into ye ayre . . . on the Tewsday went I out, and on Tewsday seuennights following I came home againe, that is, eight dayes . . . and like as I shewed before . . . euen so the firmament wherein the Sun and the rest of the Planets are fixed, moued, turned, and carried with the winde, breath, or Spirit of God, for the heauens and firmament are moueable as the Chaos, but the sun is fixed in the firmament. . . . I was thus nigh the heauens, where me thought euery Planet was but as halfe the earth . . . and me thought that the whole length of the earth was not a span long.

Faustus, viii. 1–46.

D.L., xxii. . . . he tooke a little rest at home, and burning in desire to see more at large, and to beholde the secrets of each kingdome, he set forward again on his iourney vpon his swift horse *Mephostophiles*, and came to *Treir*, for that he chiefly desired to see this towne, and the monuments thereof; but there he saw not many wonders, except one fayre Pallace that belonged vnto the Bishop, and also a mighty large Castle that was built of bricke, with three walles and three great trenches, so strong, that it was impossible for any princes power to win it . . . from whence he departed to *Paris*, where hee liked well the Academie; and what place or Kingdome soeuer fell in his minde, the same he visited. He came from *Paris* to *Mentz*, where the riuer of *Mayne* fals into the *Rhine*; notwithstanding he taried not long there, but went to *Campania* in the Kingdome of *Neapolis*, in which he saw an innumerable sort of Cloysters, Nunneries, and Churches, great and high houses of stone, the streetes fayre and large, and straight foorth from one end of the towne to the other as a line, and al the pauement of the Citie was of brick, and the more it rayned in the towne, the fayrer the streetes were; there saw he the Tombe of Virgil; & the high way that hee cutte through that mighty hill of stone in one night, the whole length of an English mile . . . From thence he came to *Venice*, whereas he wondered not a little to see a Citie so famously built standing in the Sea . . . He wondred not a little at the fayrenes of Saint *Markes* place, and the sumptuous Church standing therein called Saint *Markes*; how all the pauement was set with coloured stones, and all the Roode or loft of the Church double gilded ouer. Leauing this, he came to *Padoa* . . . Well, forward he went to *Rome*, which lay, & doth yet lie, on the riuer *Tybris*, the which deuideth the Citie in two parts: ouer the riuer are foure great stone bridges, and vpon the one bridge called *Ponte* S. *Angelo* is the Castle of S. *Angelo*, wherein are so many great cast peeces as there are dayes in a yeare, & such Pieces that will shoote seuen bullets off with one fire . . . Hard by . . . he visited the Church yard of S. *Peters*, where he saw the *Pyramide* that *Iulius Cæsar* brought out of *Africa*.

Faustus, ix. 55–112.

D.L., xxii. . . . amongst the rest he was desirous to see the Popes
N*

Pallace, and his maner of seruice at his table, wherefore he and his Spirit made themselues inuisible, and came into the Popes Court, and priuie chamber where he was, there saw he many seruants attendant on his holines, with many a flattering Sycophant carrying of his meate, and there hee marked the Pope and the manner of his seruice, which hee seeing to bee so vnmeasurable and sumptuous; fie (quoth *Faustus*) why had not the Diuel made a Pope of me? . . . on a time the Pope would haue a feast prepared for the Cardinall of *Pauia*, and for his first welcome the Cardinall was bidden to dinner: and as he sate at meate, the Pope would euer be blessing and crossing ouer his mouth; *Faustus* could suffer it no longer, but vp with his fist and smote the Pope on the face, and withall he laughed that the whole house might heare him, yet none of them sawe him nor knew where he was: the Pope perswaded his company that it was a damned soule, commanding a Masse presently to be said for his deliuerie out of Purgatory, which was done: the Pope sate still at meate, but when the latter messe came in to the Popes boord, Doctor *Faustus* laid hands thereon saying; this is mine: & so he took both dish & meate & fled vnto the Capitol or Campadolia, calling his spirit vnto him and said: come let vs be merry, for thou must fetch me some wine, & the cup that the Pope drinkes of . . . but when the Pope and the rest of his crue perceiued they were robbed, and knew not after what sort, they perswaded themselues that it was the damned soule that before had vexed the Pope so, & that smote him on the face, wherefore he sent commandement through al the whole Citie of *Rome*, that they should say Masse in euery Church, and ring al the bels for to lay the walking Spirit, & to curse him with Bel, Booke, and Candle, that so inuisiblie had misused the Popes holinesse, with the Cardinall of *Pauia*, and the rest of their company.[1]

Faustus, xii. 1–69 (A-version, xii. 1–72).

D.L., xxix. The Emperour *Carolus* the fifth of that name was personally with the rest of his Nobles and gentlemen at the towne of *Inszbruck* where he kept his court, vnto the which also Doctor *Faustus* resorted, and being there well knowne of diuers Nobles & gentlemen, he was inuited into the court to meat, euen in the presence of the Emperour . . . the Emperour held his peace vntill he had taken his repast, after which hee called vnto him *Faustus*, into the priuie chamber, whither being come, he sayd vnto him: *Faustus*, I haue heard much of thee, that thou art excellent in the black Arte, and none like thee in mine Empire, for men say that thou hast a familiar Spirit with thee & that thou canst do what thou list: it is therefore

[1] Towards the end of this chapter, a visit to Constantinople is described. Compare *Faustus*, x. 33.

(saith the Emperour) my request of thee that thou let me see a proofe
of thine experience, and I vowe vnto thee by the honour of mine
Emperiall Crowne, none euill shall happen vnto thee for so dooing.
Herevpon Doctor *Faustus* answered his Maiestie, that vpon those
conditions he was ready in any thing that he could, to doe his highnes
commaundement in what seruice he would appoynt him. Wel, then
heare what I say (quoth the Emperour.) Being once solitarie in my
house, I called to mind mine elders and auncesters, how it was possible for them to attaine vnto so great a degree of authoritie, yea so
high, that wee the successors of that line are neuer able to come neere.
As for example, the great and mighty monarch of the worlde *Alexander magnus*, was such a lanterne & spectacle to all his successors,
as the Cronicles makes mention of so great riches, conquering, and
subduing so many kingdomes, the which I and those that follow me
(I feare) shall neuer bee able to attaine vnto: wherefore, *Faustus*, my
hearty desire is that thou wouldst vouchsafe to let me see that *Alexander*, and his Paramour, the which was praysed to be so fayre, and
I pray thee shew me them in such sort that I may see their personages,
shape, gesture & apparel, as they vsed in their life time, and that here
before my face; to the ende that I may say I haue my long desire
fulfilled, & to prayse thee to be a famous man in thine arte and experience. Doctor *Faustus* answered: My most excellent Lord, I am ready
to accomplish your request in all things, so farre foorth as I and my
Spirit are able to performe: yet your Maiestie shall know, that their
dead bodies are not able substantially to be brought before you, but
such Spirits as haue seene *Alexander* and his Paramour aliue, shall
appeare vnto you in manner and forme as they both liued in their
most florishing time: and herewith I hope to please your imperiall
Maiestie. Then *Faustus* went a little aside to speake to his Spirit, but
he returned againe presently, saying: now if it please your Maiesty
you shall see them, yet vpon this condition that you demaund no
question of them, nor speake vnto them, which the Emperour agreed
vnto. Wherewith Doctor *Faustus* opened the priuy chamber doore,
where presently entred the great and mighty Emperour *Alexander
magnus*, in all things to looke vpon as if he had beene aliue ... and so
passing towards the Emperour *Carolus*, he made lowe and reuerent
curtesie: whereat the Emperour *Carolus* would haue stoode vp to
receiue and greete him with the like reuerence, but *Faustus* tooke
holde of him and would not permit him to doe it. Shortly after *Alexander* made humble reuerence and went out againe, and comming to
the doore his Paramour met him, she comming in, she made the
Emperour likewise reuerence ... the Emperour ... sayd to himselfe:
now haue I seene two persons, which my heart hath long wished for
to beholde, and sure it cannot otherwise be, sayd he to himselfe, but

that the Spirits haue changed themselues into these formes, and haue
not deceiued me . . . and for that the Emperour would be the more
satisfied in the matter, he thought, I haue heard say, that behinde
her necke she had a great wart or wenne, wherefore he tooke *Faustus*
by the hand without any words, and went to see if it were also to be
seen on her or not, but she perceiuing that he came to her, bowed
downe her neck, where he saw a great wart, and hereupon shee vanished, leauing the Emperour and the rest well contented.

Faustus, xii. 70–118.

D.L., xxx. When Doctor *Faustus* had accomplished the Emperours
desire in all things as he was requested, he went foorth into a gallerie,
and leaning ouer a rayle to looke into the priuie garden, he saw many
of the Emperours Courtiers walking and talking together, and casting
his eyes now this way, now that way, he espyed a Knight leaning out
at a window of the great hall; who was fast asleepe (for in those dayes
it was hote) but the person shall bee namelesse that slept, for that he
was a Knight, although it was done to a little disgrace of the Gentleman: it pleased Doctor *Faustus*, through the helpe of his Spirit
Mephostophiles, to firme vpon his head as hee slept, an huge payre of
Harts hornes, and as the Knight awaked thinking to pul in his head,
hee hit his hornes against the glasse that the panes therof flew about
his eares. Think here how this good Gentleman was vexed, for he
could neither get backward nor forward: which when the Emperour
heard al the courtiers laugh, and came forth to see what was hapened,
the Emperour also whē he beheld the Knight with so fayre a head,
laughed heartily thereat, and was therewithall well pleased: at last
Faustus, made him quite of his hornes agayne, but the Knight perceiued how they came, &c.

Faustus, xiii, xiv.

D.L., xxxi. Doctor *Faustus* tooke his leaue of the Emperour and
the rest of the Courtiers, at whose departure they were sory, giuing
him many rewards and gifts: but being a league and a halfe from the
Citie he came into a Wood, where he beheld the Knight that hee had
iested with at the Court with other in harnesse, mounted on fayre
palfrayes, and running with full charge towards *Faustus*, but he seeing their intent, ran towards the bushes, and before he came amongst
the bushes he returned againe, running as it were to meet them that
chased him, wherupon sodainly al the bushes were turned into horsemen, which also ran to incoūter with the Knight & his company, &
comming to thē, they closed the Knight and the rest, & told them
that they must pay their ransome before they departed. Whereupon
the Knight seeing himselfe in such distresse, besought *Faustus* to be

good to them, which he denied not, but let them lose, yet he so charmed them, that euery one, Knight & other for the space of a whole moneth did weare a payre of Goates hornes on their browes, and euery Palfray a payre of Oxe hornes on their head: and this was their penance appoynted by *Faustus*, &c.

D.L., lii. Doctor *Faustus* trauelled towards *Eyszleben*, and when he was nigh halfe the way, he espied seuen horsemen, and the chiefe of them hee knew to be the knight to whome he had plaied a iest in the Emperours Court, for he had set a huge payre of Harts hornes vpon his head: and when the knight now saw that he had fit opportunitie to be reuenged of *Faustus* he ran vpon him himselfe, & those that were with him, to mischiefe him, intending priuily to shoot at him: which when Doctor *Faustus* espied, he vanished away into the wood which was hard by them. But when the Knight perceiued that he was vanished away, he caused his men to stand still, where as they remayned they heard all manner of warlike instruments of musick, as Drummes, Flutes, Trumpets, and such like, and a certaine troupe of horsemen running towards them. Then they turned another way, and there also were assaulted on the same side: then another way, and yet they were freshly assaulted, so that which way soeuer they turned themselues, hee was encountred: in so much that when the Knight perceiued that he could escape no way, but that they his enemies layd on him which way soeuer hee offered to flie, he tooke a good heart and ranne amongst the thickest, and thought with himselfe better to die than to liue with so great an infamie. Therefore being at handy-blowes with them, hee demaunded the cause why they should so vse them: but none of them would giue him answere, vntill Doctor *Faustus* shewed himselfe vnto the Knight, where withall they inclosed him round, and Doctor *Faustus* sayde vnto him, Sir, yeelde your weapon, and yourselfe, otherwise it will goe hardly with you. The Knight that knew none other but that he was inuironed with an hoast of men, (where indeede they were none other than Diuels) yeelded: then *Faustus* tooke away his sworde, his piece, and horse, with all the rest of his companions. And further hee said vnto him; Sir, the chiefe General of our armie hath commaunded to deale with you according to the law of Armes, you shall depart in peace whither you please: and then he gaue the Knight an horse after the maner, and set him theron, so he rode, the rest went on foote vntill they came to their Inne, where being alighted, his Page rode on his horse to the water, and presently the horse vanyshed away, the Page being almost suncke and drowned, but he escaped: and comming home, the Knight perceiued his Page so be myred & on foote, asked where his horse was become? Who answered that he was vanished away: which when the Knight heard, he said, of a truth this is *Faustus*

his doing, for he serueth me now as he did before at the Court, only
to make me a skorne and a laughing stock.

Faustus, xv.

D.L., xxxiv. In like manner hee serued an Horse-courser at a faire
called *Pheiffring*, for Doctor *Faustus* through his cunning had gotten
an excellent fayre Horse, wherevpon hee rid to the Fayre, where hee
had many Chap-men that offered him money: lastly, he sold him for
40. Dollers, willing him that bought him, that in any wise he should
not ride him ouer any water, but the Horsecourser marueiled with
himself that *Faustus* bad him ride him ouer no water, (but quoth he)
I will prooue, and forthwith hee rid him into the riuer, presently the
horse vanished from vnder him, and he sate on a bundell of strawe,
in so much that the man was almost drowned. The horsecourser
knewe well where hee lay that had solde him his horse, wherefore he
went angerly to his Inne, where hee found Doctor *Faustus* fast a
sleepe, and snorting on a bed, but the horsecourser could no longer
forbeare him, tooke him by the leg and began to pull him off the
bed, but he pulled him so, that he pulled his leg from his body, in
so much that the Horse-courser fel down backwardes in the place,
then began Doctor *Faustus* to crie with an open throate, he hath
murdered me. Hereat the Horse-courser was afraide, and gaue the
flight, thinking none other with himselfe, but that hee had pulled
his leg from his bodie; by this meanes Doctor *Faustus* kept his
money.

Faustus, xvi. 18–30.

D.L., xxxv. Doctor *Faustus* being in a Towne of *Germanie* called
Zwickaw, where hee was accompanied with many Doctors and
Masters, and going foorth to walke after supper, they met with a
Clowne that droue a loade of Hay. Good euen good fellowe said
Faustus to the Clowne, what shall I giue thee to let mee eate my bellie
full of Hay ? the Clowne thought with himselfe, what a mad man is
this to eate Hay, thought he with himselfe, thou wilt not eate much,
they agreed for three farthings he should eate as much as he could:
wherefore Doctor *Faustus* began to eat, and that so rauenously, that
all the rest of his company fell a laughing, blinding so the poore
clowne, that he was sory at his heart, for he seemed to haue eaten
more than the halfe of his Hay, wherefore the clowne began to speake
him faire, for feare he should haue eaten the other halfe also. *Faustus*
made as though he had had pitie on the Clowne, and went his way.
When the Clowne came in place where he would be, he had his Hay
againe as he had before, a full loade.

Faustus, xvii. 1–8.

D.L., xl. Doctor *Faustus* desired the Duke of *Anholt* to walke a little forth of the Court with him, wherefore they went both together into the field, where Doctor *Faustus* through his skill had placed a mightie Castel: which when the Duke sawe, hee wondered thereat, so did the Dutchesse, and all the beholders, that on that hill, which was called the *Rohumbuel*, should on the sodaine bee so fayre a Castle . . . but as they were in their Pallace they looked towards the Castle, and behold it was all in a flame of fire . . . and thus the Castle burned and consumed away cleane. Which done, Doctor *Faustus* returned to the Duke, who gaue him great thankes for shewing them of so great courtesie.

Faustus, xvii. 8–35.

D.L., xxxix. Doctor *Faustus* on a time came to the Duke of *Anholt*, the which welcomed him very courteously, this was in the moneth of Ianuary, where sitting at the table, he perceiued the Dutchesse to be with childe, and forbearing himselfe vntill the meate was taken from the table, and that they brought in the banquetting dishes, said Doctor *Faustus* to the Dutchesse, Gracious Ladie, I haue alway heard, that the great bellied women doe alwaies long for some dainties, I beseech therefore your Grace hide not your mind from me, but tell me what you desire to eate, she answered him, Doctor *Faustus* now truely I will not hide from you what my heart dooth most desire, namely, that if it were now Haruest, I would eate my bellie full of ripe Grapes, and other daintie fruite. Doctor *Faustus* answered here-vpon, Gracious Lady, this is a small thing for mee to doe, for I can doo more than this, wherefore he tooke a plate, and made open one of the casements of the windowe, holding it forth, where incontinent hee had his dish full of all maner of fruites, as red and white Grapes, Peares, and Apples, the which came from out of strange Countries, all these he presented the Dutchesse, saying: Madame, I pray you vouchsafe to taste of this daintie fruite, the which came from a farre Countrey, for there the Sommer is not yet ended. The Dutchesse thanked *Faustus* highly, and she fell to her fruite with full appetite. The Duke of *Anholt* notwithstanding could not with-holde to aske *Faustus* with what reason there were such young fruite to be had at that time of the yeare ? Doctor *Faustus* tolde him, may it please your Grace to vnderstand, that the yere is deuided into two circles ouer the whole world, that when with vs it is Winter, in the contrary circle it is notwithstanding Sommer, for in *India* and *Saba* there falleth or setteth the Sunne, so that it is so warme, that they haue twise a yeare fruite: and gracious Lorde, I haue a swift Spirit, the which can in the twinckling of an eye fulfill my desire in any thing, wherefore I sent him into those Countries, who hath brought this fruite as you see: whereat the Duke was in great admiration.

Faustus, xvii. 106–16.

D.L., xxxvii. Doctor *Faustus* went into an Inne, wherein were many tables full of Clownes, the which were tippling kan after kan of excellent wine, and to bee short, they were all dronken, and as they sate, they so sung and hallowed, that one could not heare a man speake for them; this angred Doctor *Faustus*; wherefore hee . . . so coniured them, that their mouthes stoode as wide open as it was possible for them to hold them, and neuer a one of them was able to close his mouth againe.

Faustus, xviii. 1–9.

D.L., lvi. And when the time drewe nigh that *Faustus* should end, hee called vnto him a Notary and certaine masters the which were his friends and often conuersant with him, in whose presence he gaue this *Wagner* his house and Garden. Item, hee gaue him in ready money 1600. gilders. Item, a Farme. Item, a gold chayne, much plate, and other housholde stuffe. This gaue he al to his seruant, and the rest of his time he meant to spend in Innes and Students company, drinking and eating, with other Iollitie: and thus hee finished his Will for that time.

Faustus, xviii. 10–37.

D.L., xlv. The Sunday following came these students home to Doctor *Faustus* his owne house . . . and being merry, they began some of them to talke of the beauty of women, and euery one gaue foorth his verdit what he had seene and what hee had heard. So one among the rest said, I neuer was so desirous of any thing in this world, as to haue a sight (if it were possible) of fayre *Helena* of *Greece,* for whom the worthy towne of *Troie* was destroyed and razed downe to the ground, therefore sayth hee, that in all mens iudgement shee was more than commonly fayre, because that when she was stolne away from her husband, there was for her recouery so great blood-shed.

Doctor *Faustus* answered: For that you are all my friends and are so desirous to see that famous pearle of *Greece,* fayre *Helena,* the wife of King *Menelaus,* and daughter of *Tindalus* and *Læda,* sister to *Castor* and *Pollux,* who was the fayrest Lady in all *Greece:* I will therefore bring her into your presence personally, and in the same forme of attyre as she vsed to goe when she was in her chiefest flowres and pleasauntest prime of youth. . . . I charge you all that vpon your perils you speake not a word . . . And so he went out of the Hall, returning presently agayne, after whome immediatly followed the fayre and beautiful *Helena*, whose beauty was such that the students were all amazed to see her, esteeming her rather to bee a heauenly than an earthly creature.

Faustus, xviii. 38–83.

D.L., xlviii. A good Christian an honest and vertuous olde man, a louer of the holy scriptures, who was neighbour vnto Doctor *Faustus* ... began with these words. ... My good neighbour, you know in the beginning how that you haue defied God, & all the hoast [of] heauen, & giuen your soule to the Diuel, wherewith you haue incurred Gods high displeasure, and are become from a Christian farre worse than a heathen person: oh consider what you haue done, it is not onely the pleasure of the body, but the safety of the soule that you must haue respect vnto: of which if you be carelesse, then are you cast away, and shall remaine in the anger of almighty God. But yet is it time enough Doctor *Faustus*, if you repent and call vnto the Lord for mercy ... Let my words good brother *Faustus*, pearce into your adamant heart, and desire God for his Sonne Christ his sake, to forgiue you. ... All this while Doctor *Faustus* heard him very attentiuely, and replyed. Father, your perswasions like me wonderous well, and I thanke you with all my heart for your good will and counsell, promising you so farre as I may to follow your discipline: whereupon he tooke his leaue. And being come home, he layd him very pensiue on his bed, bethinking himselfe of the wordes of the good olde man, and in a maner began to repent that he had giuen his Soule to the Diuell, intending to denie all that hee had promised vnto *Lucifer*. Continuing in these cogitations, sodainly his Spirit appeared vnto him clapping him vpon the head, and wrung it as though he would haue pulled the head from the shoulders, saying vnto him, Thou knowest *Faustus*, that thou hast giuen thy selfe body and soule vnto my Lord *Lucifer*, and hast vowed thy selfe an enemy vnto God and vnto all men; and now thou beginnest to harken to an olde doting foole which perswadeth thee as it were vnto God, when indeed it is too late, for that thou art the diuels, and hee hath good power presently to fetch thee: wherefore he hath sent me vnto thee, to tell thee, that seeing thou hast sorrowed for that thou hast done, begin againe and write another writing with thine owne blood, if not, then will I teare thee all to peeces. Hereat Doctor *Faustus* was sore afrayde, and sayd: My *Mephostophiles*, I will write agayne what thou wilt; wherefore hee sate him downe, and with his owne blood hee wrote as followeth.

Faustus, xviii. 90–118.

D.L., lv. To the ende that this miserable *Faustus* might fill the lust of his flesh, and liue in all manner of voluptuous pleasures, it came

in his minde after he had slept his first sleepe, & in the 23. yeare past
of his time, that he had a great desire to lie with fayre *Helena* of
Greece, especially her whom he had seene and shewed vnto the students of *Wittenberg*, wherefore he called vnto him his Spirit *Mephostophiles*, cõmanding him to bring him the faire *Helena*, which he also
did. Wherupõ he fel in loue with her, & made her his common Con-
cubine & bedfellow, for she was so beautifull and delightful a peece,
that he could not be one houre from her, if hee should therefore haue
suffered death.

Faustus, xviii. 84–9 and 119–27.

D.L., xlix. And presently . . . he became so great an enemie vnto
the poore olde man, that he sought his life by all meanes possible;
but this godly man was strong in the holy Ghost, that he could not
be vanquished by any meanes . . . And when hee [Mephostophiles]
came home *Faustus* asked him how hee had sped with the olde man:
to whome the Spirit answered, the olde man was harnessed, and that
hee could not once lay holde vpon him.

Faustus, xix. 24–86.

D.L., lxiii. My trusty and welbeloued friends, the cause why I haue
inuited you into this place is this: Forasmuch as you haue knowne me
this many yeares, in what maner of life I haue liued, practising al
maner of coniurations and wicked exercises, the which I haue obtayned through the helpe of the diuel . . . I haue promised vnto him
at the ende and accomplishing of 24. yeares, both body and soule, to
doe therewith at his pleasure: and this day, this dismall day those 24.
yeares are fully expired, for night beginning my houre-glasse is at an
end, the direfull finishing whereof I carefully expect: for out of all
doubt this night hee will fetch mee, to whome I haue giuen my selfe
in recompence of his seruice, both body and soule, and twice confirmed writings with my proper blood . . . and I beseech you let this
my lamentable ende to the residue of your liues bee a sufficient warning, that you haue God alwayes before your eies, praying vnto him
that he would euer defend you from the temptation of the diuell, and
all his false deceipts, not falling altogether from God, as I wretched
and vngodly damned creature haue done, hauing denied and defied
Baptisme, the Sacraments of Christs body, God himselfe, all heauenly powers, and earthly men, yea, I haue denied such a God, that
desireth not to haue one lost. . . . Lastly, to knitte vp my troubled
Oration, this is my friendly request, that you would to rest, & let
nothing trouble you: also if you chance to heare any noise, or rum-
bling about the house, be not therwith afrayd, for there shal no euil
happen vnto you: also I pray you arise not out of your beds.

. . . one of thē sayd vnto him; ah, friend *Faustus*, what haue you done to conceale this matter so long from vs, we would by the help of good Diuines, and the grace of God, haue brought you out of this net, and haue torne you out of the bondage and chaynes of Sathan, whereas nowe we feare it is too late, to the vtter ruine of your body and soule ? Doctor *Faustus* answered, I durst neuer doo it, although I often minded, to settle my selfe vnto godly people, to desire counsell and helpe . . . yet when I was minded to amend . . . then came the Diuell and would haue had me away, as this night he is like to doe, and sayd so soone as I turned againe to God, hee would dispatch mee altogether. . . . But when the Students heard his words, they gaue him counsaile to doo naught else but call vpon God, desiring him for the loue of his sweete Sonne Iesus Christes sake, to haue mercy vpon him.

Faustus, xix. 133–90.

D.L., lix. This sorrowfull time drawing neere so troubled Doctor *Faustus*, that he began to write his minde . . . as followeth.

Ah *Faustus*, thou sorrowful and wofull man, now must thou goe to the damned company in vnquenchable fire, whereas thou mightest haue had the ioyfull immortalitie of the soule, the which thou now hast lost. . . .

D.L., lx. Oh poore, wofull and weary wretch: oh sorrowfull soule of *Faustus*, now art thou in the number of the damned, for now must I waite for vnmeasurable paynes of death, yea far more lamentable than euer yet any creature hath suffered. . . . Ah grieuous paynes that pearce my panting heart, whom is there now that can deliuer me ? Would God that I knew where to hide me, or into what place to creepe or flie. Ah, woe, woe is me, be where I will, yet am I taken.

D.L., lxi. Now thou *Faustus*, damned wretch, howe happy wert thou if as an vnreasonable beast thou mightest die without soule, so shouldest thou not feele any more doubts ? But nowe the diuell will take thee away both body and soule, and set thee in an vnspeakable place of darkenesse . . . Ah that I could carry the heauens on my shoulders, so that there were time at last to quit me of this euerlasting damnation! Oh who can deliuer me out of these fearful tormēting flames, yᵉ which I see prepared for me ? Oh there is no helpe, nor any man that can deliuer me, nor any wayling of sins can help me, neither is there rest to be found for me day nor night.

Faustus, xx.

D.L., lxiii. . . . when the Gentlemen were laid in bed, none of them could sleepe, for that they attended to heare if they might be priuy of his ende. It happened between twelue and one a clock at midnight, there blewe a mighty storme of winde against the house, as though it would haue blowne the foundation therof out of his place. Hereupon the Students began to feare, and got out of their beds, comforting one another, but they would not stirre out of the chamber: and the Host of the house ran out of doores, thinking the house would fall. The Students lay neere vnto that hall wherein Doctor *Faustus* lay, and they heard a mighty noyse and hissing, as if the hall had beene full of Snakes and Adders: with that the hall doore flew open wherein Doctor *Faustus* was, then he began to crie for helpe, saying: murther, murther, but it came foorth with halfe a voyce hollowly: shortly after they heard him no more. But when it was day, the Students that had taken no rest that night, arose and went into the hall in the which they left Doctor *Faustus*, where notwithstanding they found no *Faustus*, but all the hall lay besprinckled with blood, his braines cleauing to the wall: for the Diuel had beaten him from one wall against another, in one corner lay his eyes, in another his teeth, a pitifull and fearefull sight to beholde. Then began the Students to bewayle and weepe for him, and sought for his body in many places: lastly they came into the yarde where they found his bodie lying on the horse dung, most monstrously torne, and fearefull to beholde, for his head and all his ioynts were dasht in peeces.

The forenamed Students and Masters that were at his death, haue obtayned so much, that they buried him in the Village where he was so grieuously tormented.

Glossarial Index to the Annotations

Asterisks draw attention to annotations containing definitions or examples which appreciably supplement those given in the *Oxford English Dictionary*. The insertion of the letter 'A' immediately before a scene-number shows that the reference is to the A-version of the scene in question, as printed in Appendix I.